# Strategic Directions for Human Development in Papua New Guinea

Asian Development Bank
Australian Agency for International Development
World Bank

**THE WORLD BANK**
Washington, D.C.

ISBN-10:        0-8213-6987-3
ISBN-13:        978-0-8213-6987-6
eISBN-10:       0-8213-6988-1
eISBN-13:       978-0-8213-6988-3
DOI:            10.1596/978-0-8213-6987-6

Cover photo: Dominic P. Mellor

**Library of Congress Cataloging-in-Publication Data**

Strategic directions for human development in Papua New Guinea.
    p. cm.—(Directions in development)
    "Asian Development Bank, Australian Agency for International Development, The World Bank."
ISBN-13: 978-0-8213-6987-6
ISBN-10: 0-8213-6987-3
ISBN-10: 0-8213-6988-1 (electronic)
    1. Public investments—Papua New Guinea. 2. Public health—Papua New Guinea—Finance. 3. HIV infections—Papua New Guinea–Prevention. 4. AIDS (Disease)—Papua New Guinea—Prevention. 5. Education—Papua New Guinea—Finance. I. World Bank. II. Asian Development Bank. III. Australian Agency for International Development.

HC683.5.Z9P837 2007
338.9953—dc22                                                        2007022000

# Contents

**Figures**

**Tables**

# Acknowledgments

This report was produced by a team from each of the three contributing agencies—the Asian Development Bank (ADB), the Australian Agency for International Development (AusAID), and the World Bank—led by Ian Morris, Task Team Leader from the World Bank. Peter Heywood, Lead Health Specialist, World Bank, was the co-team leader for the health and HIV chapters of the report. The other members of the team were Denis Davis, Kieran Donaghue, Maryse Dugue, Paul Garner, Robert Harden, Steven Hogg, Susan Hirshberg, John Izard, Carol Jenkins, Romaine Kwesius, Peter Lindenmayer, Tracey Newbury, Ralph Rawlingson, Steven van der Tak, and Elizabeth Wiley. Dorothy Judkins and Juliana Williams assisted with document processing. Muhammad Ali Pate and Reem Hafez provided important comments on the final drafts, and Reem Hafez oversaw final edits of the document.

The World Bank peer reviewers for the report were Regina Bendokat, Deon Filmer, and Christopher Walker. A wide range of institutional comments were received from AusAID and ADB during the reports preparation.

The team gratefully acknowledges the many comments and extensive discussions held with government officials—national and provincial—and with an extensive array of PNG's development partners, church authorities, nongovernmental organizations (NGOs), the business community, and, not least, members of civil society from across many towns and villages visited during the reports' preparation.

# Abbreviations

| | |
|---|---|
| ADB | Asian Development Bank |
| ADRA | Adventist Development Relief Agency |
| AGO | Auditor General's Office |
| AH-IPC | Adult Inpatient Care |
| AH-PHC | Primary Adult Health Care |
| AIDAB | Australian International Development Assistance Bureau |
| AMC | Australian Managing Contractor |
| ANC | Antenatal Clinic |
| ART | Antiretroviral Testing |
| ARV | Antiretroviral |
| AusAID | Australian Agency for International Development |
| BCG | Bacille Camille-Guérin |
| BOM | Board of Management |
| CACC | Central Agencies Coordinating Committee |
| CBO | Community-Based Organization(s) |
| CDU | Curriculum Development Unit |
| CET | Certificate of Elementary Training |
| CH-IPC | Child Inpatient Care |
| CH-PHC | Primary Child Health Care |

| | |
|---|---|
| CHE | Commission of Higher Education |
| CHS | Church Health Services |
| CHW | Community Health Worker |
| CMC | Church Medical Council |
| CRIP | Curriculum Reform Implementation Program |
| DALY | Disability-Adjusted Life Year |
| DCD | Department of Community Development |
| DHS | Demographic and Household Survey |
| DMC | Developing Member Country |
| DNPRD | Department of National Planning and Rural Development |
| DOF | Department of Finance |
| DOF/T | Department of Finance and Treasury |
| DOH | Department of Health |
| DOLIR | Department of Labour and Industrial Relations |
| DOP&RD | Department of Planning and Rural Development |
| DOT | Department of Treasury |
| DOTS | Directly Observed Therapy Short Course (Tuberculosis) |
| DOVET | Diploma in Vocational Education Training |
| DP | Development of Partners |
| DPLL | Department of Local-Level Government |
| DPM | Department of Personnel Management |
| DPT | Diphtheria, Polio, and Tetanus Vaccine |
| DTVE | Diploma in Technical and Vocational Education |
| E1/E2 | Elementary Grades 1/2 |
| ECBP | Education Capacity Building Project |
| EFA | Education for All |
| EHP | Eastern Highlands Province |
| ENB | East New Britain |
| EOSDP | Employment-Oriented Skills Development Project |
| ETESP | Elementary Teacher Education Support Program |
| EU | European Union |
| FER | Functional Expenditure Review of Health |
| FHI | Family Health International |
| FMU | Facilitating and Monitoring Unit |
| FSM | Federated States of Micronesia |
| G1 | Grade 1 |
| GDP | Gross Domestic Product |
| GFATM | Global Fund to Fight AIDS, Tuberculosis, and Malaria |
| GOPNG | Government of Papua New Guinea |

| | |
|---|---|
| GTZ | Deutsche Gesellschaft für Technische Zusammenarbeit |
| HC | Health Center |
| HD | Human Development |
| HEO | Health Extension Officer |
| HIV/AIDS | Human Immunodeficiency Virus/Acquired Immune Deficiency Syndrome |
| HMTEF | Health Medium-Term Expenditure Framework 2004–06 |
| HNSP | (Draft) Health National Strategic Plan 2006–08 |
| HRD | Human Resource Development |
| HSIP | Health Sector Improvement Program |
| HSIPMU | Health Sector Improvement Program Management Unit |
| HSSP | Health Services Support Project |
| HSV-2 | Herpes Simplex Virus Type 2 |
| IES | Impact Evaluation Study |
| ILO | International Labour Organization |
| IMF | International Monetary Fund |
| IMR | Infant Mortality Rate |
| IRC | Internal Revenue Commission |
| IRT | Independent Review Team |
| JCS | Joint Country Strategy |
| JICA | Japan International Cooperation Agency |
| LIC | Low-Income Country |
| LICUS | Low-Income Countries under Stress |
| LLG | Local-Level Government |
| M&E | Measurement and Evaluation |
| MDGs | Millennium Development Goals |
| MHERST | Ministry of Higher Education, Research, Science, and Technology |
| MHS | Minimum Health Standards 2002 |
| MIC | Middle-Income Country |
| MoA | Memorandum of Agreement |
| MOH | Ministry of Health |
| MSM | Men Having Sex with Men |
| MTDS | Medium-Term Development Strategy |
| MTEF | Medium-Term Economic Framework 2002–2007 |
| MTP | Medium-Term Plan 1998–2002 |
| NAC | National AIDS Council |
| NACS | National AIDS Council Secretariat |
| NATTB | National Apprenticeship Trade Testing Board |

| | |
|---|---|
| NCD | National Capital District |
| NDOE | National Department of Education |
| NDOH | National Department of Health |
| NDPRD | National Department of Planning and Rural Development |
| NEB | National Education Board |
| NEFC | National Economic and Fiscal Commission |
| NEP | National Education Plan 2004–2014 |
| NEP 1 | National Education Plan 1995–2004 |
| NEP 2 | National Education Plan 2005–2014 |
| NES | National Education System |
| NGO | Nongovernmental Organization |
| NHAA | National Health Administration Act |
| NHASP | National HIV/AIDS Support Project |
| NHB | National Health Board |
| NHP | National Health Plan |
| NHS | National High School |
| NMA | National Monitoring Authority |
| NOL | New Organic Law on Provincial and Local-Level Government, 1995 |
| NPO | National Planning Office |
| NQF | National Qualifications Framework |
| NRI | National Research Institute |
| NSO | National Statistical Office |
| NSP | National Strategic Plan 2006–10 |
| NSP-HIV/ AIDS | National Strategic Plan for HIV/AIDS |
| NTA | National Training Authority |
| NTC | National Training Council |
| NTP | National Training Policy |
| NTTCP | National Trade Testing and Certification Project |
| OHE | Office of Higher Education |
| OLPLLG | Organic Law on Provincial and Local Level Government |
| PAC | Position Allocation Committee |
| PACS | Provincial AIDS Council Secretariats |
| PASTEP | Primary and Secondary Teacher Education Project |
| PDOE | Provincial Division of Education |
| PEC | Provincial Executive Council |
| PERR | Public Expenditure Review and Rationalization |

| | |
|---|---|
| PESD | Public Expenditure and Service Delivery |
| PHA | Provincial Health Advisor |
| PLWHA | People Living with HIV/AIDS |
| PMGH | Port Moresby General Hospital |
| PMTCT | Prevention of Mother-to-Child Transmission |
| PNG | Papua New Guinea |
| PNGEI | Papua New Guinea Education Institute |
| PNGIF | Papua New Guinea Incentive Fund |
| PNGIMR | Papua New Guinea Institute of Medical Research |
| POM | Port Moresby |
| POSSOP | PNG Occupational Skills and Standards Project |
| PSRMU | Public Sector Reform Management Unit |
| RH-CEOC | Advanced Emergency Obstetric Services |
| RH-EOC | Emergency Obstetric Services |
| RH-PHC | Primary Reproductive Health Care |
| RIGFA | Review of Intergovernmental Financial Relations |
| RMI | Republic of the Marshall Islands |
| SHP | Southern Highlands Province |
| SP | Strategic Plan |
| STD | Sexually Transmitted Disease |
| STI | Sexually Transmitted Infection |
| STR | Student-Teacher Ratio |
| STRU | Skills Training Resource Unit |
| SWAP | Sectorwide Approach |
| TB | Tuberculosis |
| TBA | Traditional Birth Attendant |
| TESAS | Tertiary Education Study Assistance Scheme |
| TFR | Total Fertility Rate |
| TSC | Teaching Service Commission |
| UBE | Universal Basic Education |
| UN | United Nations |
| UNAIDS | Joint United Nations Programme on HIV/AIDS |
| UNDP | United Nations Development Programme |
| UNESCO | United Nations Educational, Scientific, and Cultural Organization |
| UNFPA | United Nations Population Fund |
| UNICEF | United Nations Children's Fund |
| UoG | University of Garoka |
| UPE | Universal Primary Education |
| VAT | Value Added Tax |

| | |
|---|---|
| VCT | Voluntary Counseling and Testing |
| VT | Voluntary Testing |
| WB | World Bank |
| WHO | World Health Organization |
| WHP | Western Highlands Province |
| WNB | West New Britain |

# Overview

There is an emerging consensus in Papua New Guinea (PNG)—both at the governmental level and among civil society more generally—that human development outcomes are far less than satisfactory and that service provision in many parts of the country is collapsing despite the significant level of both government and development partner financing of the human development sectors. In response, the government and the Joint Donors— the Australian Agency for International Development (AusAid), the Asian Development Bank (ADB), and the World Bank—embarked on a Human Development Review to suggest options for improving human development outcomes and government expenditure efficiency.

In this review of strategy options for health, HIV/AIDS, and education, it is argued that human development sectors are at an important crossroad with a large unfinished agenda and a range of critical challenges. Health outcomes have stalled over the last quarter-century and have even been in decline over the last decade, and maternal and infant mortality rates are unacceptably high; HIV/AIDS is an important problem in both urban and rural areas and is fast becoming a fully generalized epidemic; and while efforts to move toward universal basic education have met with some success, some 19 percent of children do not attend school, and as many as 60 percent who start school do not complete the basic cycle.

Notwithstanding the sustained fiscal and debt crisis that emerged over the past decade (as a result of poor growth performance and a lack of fiscal restraint), public expenditures in the three human development sectors have increased from 22.2 percent of government expenditures (6.3 percent of gross domestic product [GDP]) in 1997 to 27.6 percent of expenditures (8.8 percent of GDP) in 2004. This is a considerable achievement and has been a consequence of both considerable social pressures to increase expenditures on human development, particularly education, despite an overriding need for stringent fiscal discipline and a need to re-prioritize and redefine the role of the state in supporting development objectives.

At the same time, major challenges related to the ability of government systems to deliver adequate services have emerged. With provincial governments responsible for implementing the core of health and education programs, problems with intergovernmental relations, particularly in fiscal and accountability matters, constitute a major structural challenge to effective organization and management of the human development sectors. At a systems level, budget, accounting and planning, and personnel management require significant efforts to restore their integrity.

The Medium-Term Development Strategy 2005–2010 (MTDS) reiterates the government's commitment to the Millennium Development Goals (MDGs) and recognizes that health and education outcomes are crucial to meeting PNG's human development objectives. Human development is an essential element of strategies aimed at improving rural welfare, poverty reduction, and export-led development. The government is also becoming increasingly concerned about the health and developmental impacts of the emerging HIV/AIDS epidemic.

Acknowledging that the key sectoral agencies were also in the process of developing new medium- to longer-term plans, the government nevertheless wanted the Human Development Strategy to focus on future strategic options for the development of the health and education sectors and on a response to the HIV/AIDS epidemic. In response to the government's request, the report provides a situational assessment, together with a set of proposed strategies for each of the three areas, namely, health, HIV/AIDS, and education. In addition, it examines a range of cross-cutting issues and proposes a series of next steps. The following briefly summarizes the situational assessments for health, HIV/AIDS, and education; the key issues identified; and suggestions for sectoral strategy priorities and an approach to their implementation, given institutional and governance constraints within PNG. Cross-sectoral issues common to each of the sectors are subsequently discussed and suggestions are made for next steps.

## Health

By the time of independence, a formal government-funded health system provided basic primary care in most parts of the country through frontline workers with minimal amounts of training and limited basic drugs. Various Christian missions supplemented government efforts through government-subsidized health services. The centralized Department of Health managed the whole system, including hospitals, and delegated powers to regional, district, and line staff and facilities. However, since independence there have been successive attempts to decentralize the provision of services to provincial and district governments and to allow provinces to have enhanced control over the resources allocated to the health sector. Since the New Organic Law (NOL) on Provincial and Local-Level Government of 1995 was passed, provinces have been responsible for managing primary health care services (with local-level government [LLG] and communities responsible for maintaining health facilities) managed by a Provincial Health Advisor (PHA), reporting to the provincial administrator. The national government has remained responsible for policy oversight (albeit with very limited capacity to enforce), hospitals (which are managed by autonomous boards), and pharmaceutical purchases. The health system employs about 12,400 staff, and its infrastructure now comprises 614 health facilities, including 19 provincial hospitals, 52 urban clinics, 201 health centers, and 342 subcenters. The Church Mission–managed components of the health system, which is largely government-financed, accounts for 23 percent of all staff and 44 percent of facilities.

Health outcomes in PNG have seen little improvement over the last 30 years. By 2000, infant and maternal mortality had reached 64 per 1,000 live births (72 in 1980) and 370 per 100,000 live births (400 in 1980), respectively. Total fertility rate was high, at 4.6 children per woman, and pneumonia and diarrhea were among the leading causes of death in young children. Among adults, the disease burden is still dominated by infectious diseases, especially tuberculosis (TB), and more recently, HIV. Current estimates indicate that a general HIV epidemic is already under way in PNG. Although life expectancy improved between 1996 and 2000 from 49.6 to 54.2 years nationally, experience from other countries suggests that these gains will be temporary, as HIV infection increases and deaths from TB as a co-infection of HIV rises.

In relation to the population's poor health status, health system performance is also in decline, with decreased coverage and quality of services despite the substantial 35 percent real increase in public funding of the health sector between 1996 and 2004. Nevertheless, major changes in the sources of finance and in the level and composition of health expenditures threaten the quality of health services and their sustainability. As recurrent (government-financed) health expenditure decreased a considerable 9.4 percent in real terms between 1997 and 2004, development expenditures on health increased by 109.7 percent in real terms over the same time period. Government expenditures on goods and services, critical for quality services, fell over 27 percent in real terms while expenditures on capital items fell over 77 percent. At the same time, expenditures on salaries increased by 10 percent in real terms (see Figure 1). Significantly, at least 300 aid posts were closed between 1995 and 2000, antenatal coverage declined from 80 percent in 1991 to 58 percent in 2004, and shortages of basic drugs have been frequent at both rural health posts and hospitals.

Health outcomes are also critically dependent on the size, composition, and deployment of health staff, which, due to the fragmentation of respon-sibilities for staff management, are not monitored systematically—even

**Figure 1. Total Real Recurrent Health Expenditures by Input Category, 1997–2004**
(*kina million*)

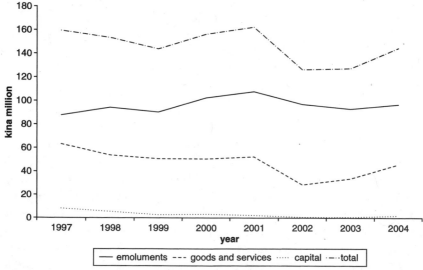

*Source:* Ministry of Health Analysis of Expenditures (various years).

annually. According to data derived from special runs of government major payroll systems for 2004, together with data collected from church health services, the overall size of the health workforce financed by the public sector has grown by 36 percent between 1988 and 2004, from 9,082 to 12,355. In 2004, almost 85 percent of the health staff was accounted for by four cadres: doctors, health extension officers, nurses, and community health workers. The National Health Department, including urban clinics in the National Capital District, accounted for 9 percent of the workforce, while one-third were employed in hospitals. Over 58 percent of staff provided health services in the provinces through government-run provincial services (35 percent of total health staff) and church-run services (23 percent of total health staff) (see Figure 2).

However, the reliability of the 2004 payroll data for establishing the actual number of health staff, particularly qualified staff who are actually working, and their work location, is in question. Considering the number of medical graduates and workforce attrition between 1998 and 2004, the number of medical practitioners listed on the 2004 payroll is indeed a feasible number. However, similar calculations for nurses suggest that there are over 1,000 more nurses on the payroll than is feasible given attrition and the numbers trained over this period. In fact, the calculations suggest there should be fewer people in 2004 than 1998. Similarly, there are about 1,700 more community health workers on the payroll than our analysis indicates is feasible. This suggests potential savings that could be made on payroll costs amounting to approximately K 28.6 million due to duplication of staff and/or extra (unqualified) staff being on the payroll. Moreover, there is considerable evidence that health staff is not optimally allocated. Although church-run health services deliver approximately 50 percent of provincial health services, they have one-third fewer staff than the government-run health services (and are paid about two-thirds the salary). There is also evidence that many government staff allocated to community health centers and the more remote health centers have relocated to urban health centers in towns.

Flaws in decentralization arrangements are clearly connected with the systematic problems of the health sector. First, decentralization has resulted in unclear allocation of responsibilities and inadequate implementation of key system functions. Second, the decentralization process has led to inadequate oversight by the National Department of Health (NDOH). Third, decentralization has been associated with a decline in the integrity of budget institutions and systems. As a result, neither politicians nor public officials, particularly at the provincial and district levels, accepted

**Figure 2. Ministry of Health Workforce by Cadre and Distribution, 2004**
(*percent*)

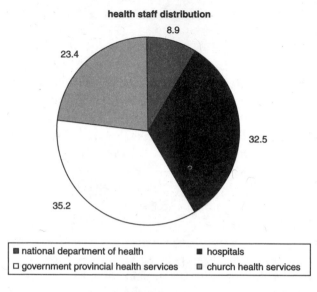

health staff distribution

8.9

23.4

32.5

35.2

■ national department of health        ■ hospitals
□ government provincial health services   ▨ church health services

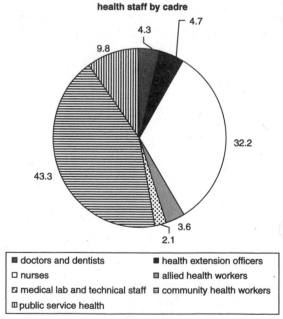

health staff by cadre

4.7

4.3

9.8

32.2

43.3

3.6

2.1

■ doctors and dentists        ■ health extension officers
□ nurses                      ▨ allied health workers
▨ medical lab and technical staff  ▤ community health workers
▥ public service health

*Source:* World Bank estimates—see notes and sources Table 2A.1 in Annex 2A.

responsibility for delivering primary health services and essential public health functions. In fact, these are cross-cutting issues that are not unique to the health sector. The effect of the fragmented structure of the public sector on service delivery is further developed below and is also noted as seriously affecting the HIV/AIDS and education sectors.

Recognizing theses issues, the government responded with the National Health Administration Act (NHAA) of 1998, which defined and described the respective roles and responsibilities of public health administrative structures at all levels of government; the Minimum Health Standards (MHS) in 2002 to inform the planning and budget processes of all standard health facilities; and the Independent Annual Health Sector Review to deal with the problems confronting the health system. The government has also been moving toward a sector-wide approach that has already seen the establishment of an account for pooled donor funds, a biannual summit between the government and its development partners, an independent monitoring and evaluation group for the sector, and, most importantly, the Health Medium-Term Expenditure Framework 2004–2006 (HMTEF) and the Health National Strategic Plan 2006–2008 (HNSP). These latter documents were produced as the basis for a prioritized health expenditure plan for the national level, with emphasis on priority areas of service delivery, such as immunization, malaria prevention, safe motherhood/family planning, and sexually transmitted infection (STI) prevention. While these are critically important steps in the right direction, the need remains to link both resource allocation to priorities—particularly at the provincial level—and implementation capacity to plans. Current health plans lack a central focus on the outcomes to be achieved, consensus on the methods by which to achieve them, and how they are to be financed.

To this end, the proposed strategic directions for the sector will be essential for improvements in health outcomes and health system performance and could be implemented using a dual-track approach that will simultaneously i) address issues within the national and provincial departments of health to improve the quality of health services, and ii) help the central agencies to strengthen their capacity to support the NDOH and the provinces. The proposed strategic directions include the following six elements:

1. Focus scarce management and public finances on high-priority outcomes. This would entail identifying the technical options for achieving these outcomes and the ways in which these might be feasibly packaged

for delivery, setting priorities for public expenditure using public finance criteria, and monitoring and evaluating progress toward the agreed health targets.

2. Reconsider the potential of the whole sector—both public and private. This would entail focusing the public sector on those public goods that it can effectively deliver, promoting the involvement of the private sector in delivery of private goods, and strengthening collaboration between public and private sectors in service delivery.
3. Prepare an expenditure and implementation plan for the public financial contributions to the sector based on the activities identified in and consistent with the medium-term resource envelope.
4. Create fiscal space, where possible, by achieving savings in the sector, making more efficient use of existing funds, and increasing sectoral allocations.
5. Prepare a financing plan covering the resource inputs of national government, provinces, and development partners.
6. Restore and guarantee the integrity of government processes, including that of budget, accounting, planning, procurement, and payroll systems.

## HIV/AIDS

PNG's health sector also faces the added burden of having to deal with one of the most serious HIV epidemics in the Asia-Pacific region. Already, HIV prevalence among sexually active adults exceeds 1 percent in many rural areas, 2 percent in many urban areas, and 3 percent in the capital, Port Moresby. However, these differential prevalence rates must be seen in the context of a population that is still 85 percent rural. As a result, it is estimated that about two-thirds of all infections are in the rural population (despite their lower prevalence rates), whereas 18 percent are in Port Moresby and the remaining 15 percent in other urban areas. All in all, approximately 80,000 adults and children, or 1.5 percent of the population, in PNG are estimated to be now living with HIV/AIDS.

The HIV epidemic in PNG is due primarily to heterosexual transmission, which accounts for 90 percent of all detected cases. The remainder is due to men having sex with men and vertical transmission between mother and child. The pattern of transmission is facilitated by cultural patterns of sexuality and by the high prevalence of STIs. The breakdown of traditional methods of social control in PNG, combined with an emergent cash economy, urbanization, and greater population mobility, has resulted in very significant changes in sexual behavior that result in early sexual debut, multiple partners, commercial and transactional sex, and sexual and intimate partner violence. It is also recognized that there are males who have sex with males, most of whom are bisexually active and are likely to get married. Alcohol is often involved and is also responsible for considerable abuse and violence, including sexual violence against women within communities—both urban and rural. Another disturbing development is the rapidly increasing numbers of reported HIV cases among adolescents (see Figure 3).

While the deterioration in the economy has had a detrimental impact on the HIV/AIDS epidemic, the epidemic will also have significant negative effects on the economy, particularly in the longer run if the epidemic's growth is not reversed. The last decade has seen a period of sustained economic stagnation. All sectors of the economy have experienced decline and stagnation, with real GDP per capita dropping by almost 4 percent per annum between 1997 and 2002. Only modest growth—enough to just sustain real GDP per capita—was achieved through 2005. The more recent upturn in commodity prices will drive some modest export-led growth. The result of the deterioration in the economy has been a dramatic increase in poverty—between 1996 and 2002 the number of Papua New Guineans living on less than US$1 per day is estimated to have increased from 25 percent to 40 percent—mostly in rural areas and highest among female-headed households. One of the few areas in which employment prospects for males remain bright is enclave extractive developments (mining, petroleum, logging, and fishing). For females, however, options for formal employment are

**Figure 3. HIV Cases in Adolescents Aged 15–19, 2001–2004**

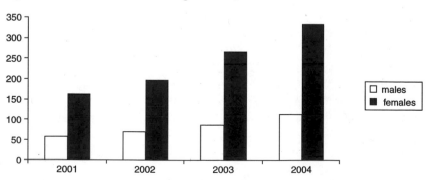

*Source:* National Aids Council and other reports.

far more limited. Less than 5.7 percent of women in the labor force participate in the formal nonagricultural wage-earning labor force, compared with 15.2 percent of men – the lowest rate for the Pacific region. Precisely because of these inequities, enclave economic developments present situations that put both men and women at significant risk of contracting HIV, as increased trade in sex in these industries for cash and/or gifts has been well-documented. Conversely, a report commissioned by AusAID on the economic impact of the epidemic in PNG concluded that HIV has the potential to increase poverty significantly, reduce the labor force, and increase the budget deficit if the current course of the disease is not reversed.

Despite numerous alerts raised in the early 1990s following the identification of PNG's first HIV case in 1987, few people in positions of leadership acknowledged HIV/AIDS as an issue of concern. Government's response to HIV was limited and, by default, relied on donor projects largely implemented outside of the government budget and management systems. While a National AIDS Committee was formed relatively early, it functioned only sporadically between 1988 and 1994. Efforts in the early 1990s to establish a sentinel surveillance system faltered, and by 1995 all that remained was limited passive surveillance in some locations. However, in 1997, a new government response emerged. The National AIDS Council (NAC) was established (using the core of the NDOH surveillance unit as its base) and the Medium-Term Plan 1998–2002 (MTP) drawn up and, more recently, a new multisectoral National Strategic Plan for HIV/AIDS (NSP-HIV/AIDS) for 2006–2010 developed. The multisectoral approach embedded in the new MTP was never costed, prioritized, or implemented. As late as 2004, the government allocated less than $200,000 for domestically financed HIV/AIDS programs (largely for administrative costs of the National AIDS Council Secretariat [NACS]), NACS, the vast majority of the HIV/AIDS response having been financed by donors, especially AusAID. Between 1995 and 2006, AusAID invested $44 million in PNG's HIV/AIDS effort under a number of projects, including, more recently, the National HIV/AIDS Support Project (NHASP). Current domestic financing of HIV/AIDS remains below K 1 million per annum—mainly to expand NACS staffing. A commitment of K 3 million over four years beginning in 2006 as a contribution to the new ADB project has also been made (see below). These projects have supported the implementation of the MTP at both the national level and in 19 provinces. Social mapping exercises have helped familiarize provinces with some of the high-risk settings and then to develop district-level HIV/AIDS programs. A strategy was devised for high-risk settings while also targeting unemployed youth, school children, and sex workers.

The government prepared and submitted its application to the the the Global Fund to Fight AIDS, Tuberculosis, and Malaria (GFATM) in 2004 for US$30 million over five years. The aim of the initial proposal was to bring 7,000 HIV-infected people onto antiretroviral treatment (ART) by 2009. While the proposal indicated a need for focus on prevention for at-risk youth, there was little indication of how this was to be done. Further, the document did not discuss the cost-effectivness of proposed interventions or how it was going to manage adherence to the ART regimen, among other issues. In June 2005, GFATM approved US$8.49 million for the first two years of the program—albeit in a slightly different form. Its prime focus, nevertheless, remains on ARV delivery, voluntary counseling and testing (VCT), and youth. Of the 17 targets/monitoring indicators agreed for the program, only one relates to behavior change—specifically the use of condoms for last sexual intercourse with a nonregular partner is monitored, and the target is to increase this by an extremely modest 5 percent over five years.

Most recently, the ADB, in partnership with AusAID, New Zealand, and the government, has developed an innovative HIV/AIDS prevention and control program in rural development enclaves; community behavior change, social marketing of condoms, and enhanced surveillance is to be implemented over the period 2006–10.

HIV/AIDS became the core responsibility of NACS, and the important role NDOH should and needs to play in any systematic response to HIV/AIDS was not emphasized. NDOH's role remained unclear, with several evaluations arguing that the NDOH should become more involved in both HIV/AIDS control and in surveillance in particular. With the arrival of ART, the medical profession saw a clear role for NDOH and will be involved in treatment and control activities. NDOH established a Health Sector HIV/AIDS Policy document in 2004, and this was incorporated in the new NACS–sponsored MTP.

Subsequently, an updated Australian plan to support the PNG effort to combat HIV/AIDS was released in April 2006. The two key groups of activities emphasized are i) counseling, treatment, and care, emphasizing the role of primary health services and providing greater support to such delivery mechanisms; and ii) education prevention, emphasizing culturally relevant prevention, in particular to high-risk groups and populations in high-risk settings. The strategy also provides support for enhanced measurement and evaluation of proposed activities and includes a social and behavioral research component. Other donors also began to provide significant support to the effort from 2002–03, including the European Union, the government of China, Japan International Cooperation Agency (JICA), U.S. Agency for International Development (USAID), ADB, the British High Commission, New Zealand, various churches, and the UN agencies.

Notwithstanding this considerable external support for HIV/AIDS, the government of PNG still faces serious capacity and financial constraints in implementing an adequate HIV/AIDS response. Critically, the overall national response has not been underpinned by an underlying strategy with clear priorities. Certainly the response has not been consistent with the government's MTDS (or the Millennium Development Goals [MDGs]) objective for HIV—the central focus of which is on programs (prevention) to reduce the transmission of the disease. Based on the situational assessment outlined above and the experience in other countries and of other development partners, several major lessons learned and priorities for further actions can be identified:

- Strengthened surveillance and research are particularly important in PNG given its economic, cultural, and geographic diversity. Notwithstanding efforts to improve and expand surveillance and improve laboratory protocols, considerably more needs to be done. Currently, there are few antenatal sites, their quality is problematic, and their record-keeping poor. As a result, HIV estimates are based on generalization from these few locations. Without adequate information, including an improved understanding of gender relations, it is impossible to undertake evidence-based planning and there is a great risk that programs will be based on erroneous assumptions.

- There is a paramount need for increased emphasis on prevention, particularly in rural areas. Overall, the response to the epidemic has been heavily biased toward Port Moresby and other urban areas. Targeted prevention programs for high-risk groups are lagging behind and are not usually based on international best practice or on adequate understanding of PNG cultures. Data from the World Health Organization (WHO) strongly supports the view that a prevention program combining a high-risk group focus with mass media communication, and a treatment program focused on STIs, are the most cost-effective strategies to reduce transmission of the disease.

- In a country as complex, diverse, and variated as PNG, it is important for prevention strategies to be context-specific. Adequate research is required to know what proportion of HIV infections arises from different populations and, more specifically, what proportion of infections may be attributed to high-risk groups. In short, the most important questions to continually ask are: Where did the last thousand new HIV infections in PNG arise? How do we change behavior in these groups?

- Building implementation capacity to design and implement interventions is critical. The most limiting factor in the delivery of HIV/AIDS control activities at present is implementation capacity, both in government and society more generally. Most of PNG's response to the HIV/AIDS epidemic to date has focused on increased awareness rather than on changing people's behavior. Social mapping of high-risk settings has occurred, and while the results are being used to mobilize a local-level response, these efforts lack the input of international best practice or the necessary in-depth culturally appropriate information to determine what kind of behavior-change programs work. Capacity is needed to systematically estimate the size of the populations at varying degrees of risk, and to reach rural areas.

Monitoring and evaluating programs, and, critically, adjusting programs to improved understanding of and/or changing behavioral patterns, is a hallmark of successful programs internationally. However, internationally proven methods for monitoring risky behavior, measuring change, and applying results to make adjustments in programs are rarely being used in PNG. Without sound evaluation methodologies, trends in behavioural change cannot be tracked and no adjustments can be made to improve the response to the epidemic.

- The coordination of government and donor efforts could be improved if both parties were to commit to unifying their planning, budgetary, expenditure, and accountability requirements. Government also needs to restore the integrity and viability of existing government systems and procedures and to clearly define new roles for the health system and the NACS.

- There is a major risk that accountability at all levels is being compromised in the current system because of the fractured financing and institutional arrangements that govern HIV/AIDS activities. Contractors managing some major projects are primarily account-able to development partners. The Provincial AIDS Council Secre-tariats (PACS) report to the NACS, health staff report to their own department, and so on, with no central coordination or hierarchy of responsibility. Thus, there is no clear system accountability for set-ting national priorities and ensuring funds are allocated to national priorities and spent accordingly.

Taking these lessons into account, the proposed strategic directions for HIV/AIDS involving an intensified HIV/AIDS control effort would need to:

1. Reduce the number of HIV infections by decreasing unprotected sex, reducing the number of sexual partners, and treating and preventing the transmission of STIs.
2. Implement a sound surveillance system that covers the general popula-tion (via antenatal clinics [ANCs] and blood banks) as well as high-risk groups, and make use of this information in program planning.
3. Monitor and evaluate interventions.
4. Coordinate the national response through NACS in the prime minister's office.
5. Prioritize interventions—including treatment and care—according to their cost-effectivenenss in reducing transmission.
6. Build capacity by taking advantage of technical inputs by development partners while ensuring the accountability and integrity of public systems.

## Education

The national education system of PNG includes i) general education, ii) pre-employment education and training, and iii) employment-located training. Within the Ministry of Education, the National Department of Education (NDOE) is responsible for developing and coordinating implementation of national policies and plans; supporting provinces with planning, professional services, and standards; managing pre-service training for basic teachers; control over curriculum; distributing school-fee subsidies; and managing teacher payrolls; while the Teaching Service Commission (TSC) is the employer of teachers in the National Education System (NES) and sets salaries and conditions of employment, approves appointment of teachers, and handles industrial relations. The provinces, through the Divisions of Education, are given overall responsibility for teacher management, including deployment and in-service training, and for capital works and maintenance of secondary schools. LLGs have responsibility for capital works and maintenance at the elementary and primary school levels.

In the decade since the major national education reform of 1993, PNG has seen a dramatic expansion of its educational system. The primary focus of the government's reform was to increase access, equity, and retention at all levels of education and in so doing to support the MDGs and Education for All (EFA) goals of achieving Universal Primary Education (UPE)—which in the case of PNG equates to nine years for universal basic education (three years of elementary and six years of primary). A second focus was revising the curriculum to address concerns about the quality of the teaching and learning in PNG's schools and its relevance to real life. As a consequence of the reform, by 2003, the system provided for 1 million basic and postbasic students (a 100 percent increase), serviced by some 33,000 teachers (a 154 percent increase) in over 7,600 institutions (a 153 percent increase). Consequentially, gross enrollment rates of six- to eight-year-olds in general education rose from 43 to 55 percent between 1997 and 2003. Total resources spent on education increased in real terms from K 185.8 million in 1996 to K 215.4 million (1996 prices)—a real increase of 16 percent—with domestic financing (largely recurrent expenditures) rising about 7 percent in real terms. Since 2003, government-financed education expenditure has further increased to 17 percent of the budget from 16 percent in 2003. This represents a substantial fiscal effort by government.

The ambitious new National Education Plan (NEP 2 2005–2014) was launched in 2005 aiming to expand enrollments in basic education from 957,000 in 2005 to 1,370,000 by 2014 and setting universal enrollment of six-year-olds in the first year of school by 2012. This plan starts with an assesment of the challenges ahead but does not take all issues fully into account. Despite the rapid increase in enrollments, retention in the basic education cycle remains a major problem, with only 53 percent of children who were enrolled in Grade 1 in 1998 completing Grade 6 in 2003 (a decline from 61 percent for those enrolling in 1993) and some 30 percent of children of the basic education age group not attending school and as many as 19 percent of children never attending school. Student absenteeism also remains a serious issue—between 9 and 25 percent in different provinces on any one day. In addition, access to basic and secondary education varies considerably from province to province. Basic education enrolments as a proportion of the population vary from 9 percent in Madang Province, 17 to 18 percent in six provinces, and 26 percent in Bougainville Province.

Notwithstanding this rapid enrollment growth (3.6 percent per annum), the net enrollment rate for the basic cycle would only increase from 71 percent in 2005 to 80 percent by 2014 because of the high population growth rate. Significantly, NEP 2 does not indicate how expansion in access will be managed in a way which will reduce the significant provincial inequality in access discussed above. Neither does it consider how to deal with inequalities in access within provinces in a context where secondary schools (which are small in number) are four hours away from the average primary school—about five hours in poor areas and six hours away from schools in remote areas.

Gender inequalities remain a challenge for PNG. In 2003, girls occupied between 44 and 46 percent of school places across all provinces in the basic education cycle, dropping to an average of 40 percent by Grade 10 and 35 percent by grades 11 and 12—not significantly different from a decade earlier. Capacity to pay is a critical issue. Schools in wealthier communities are better supported by both government subsidies and fees. Significantly increasing poverty levels make payment of increasing school fees a growing problem for many parents. This has implications for quality as, in theory, fees cover critical quality inputs at the school level. Further, government-financed quality inputs, particularly textbooks, are also being underfinanced. Assessment remains weak. School facilities and infrastructure are generally in poor repair. On average, there were 3.3 class rooms per 100 students in 2003, but accounting for those in disrepair (unusable), the proportion drops to 2.3 rooms per 100 students. Only 50 percent of classrooms have a desk and chair for teachers, and 40 percent don't have enough chairs for students.

HIV/AIDS is acknowledged in NEP 2 as an issue that education has a role to play in. However, it does not elaborate a strategy or the areas in which it can play a role and only commits to developing a strategy in the near future. This report argues that HIV/AIDS should be expanded in the curriculum, curriculum materials be developed and distributed, and that the curriculum of all teacher training (pre- and in-service) include appropriate HIV/AIDS content to ensure teachers acquire the relevant skills to impart appropriate knowledge to students.

Many of the government reform initiatives set out in NEP 2 require a coordinated and sustained effort and commitment of the central agencies of government to give effect to the plan. The NDOE and provinces cannot achieve NEP 2 objectives without the proactive support of the central agencies of government. A few key reforms that are appropriate but will stretch implementation capacity are controlling teacher employment and deployment by establishing an annual agreement on teacher allocations, maintaining employment and budgets consistent with national policies, increasing student/teacher ratios and class size in order to effect cost savings, containing secondary school construction and enrollment growth, establishing a mechanism for reviewing the adequacy of national provincial budgets, and reviewing the organizational capacity of the NDOE and Provincial Offices of Education (POEs). There are also serious implementation, cost, and financing challenges threatening the plan's success. NEP 2 assumes that capacity and commitment exist at all levels of governance to implement these strategies, yet the fragmentation of governance has led to i) limited or inhibited mechanisms that effectively support and monitor the decentralized system of public service, including general and vocational education; and ii) the "silo mentality" of different agencies and levels of government involved.

In aggregate terms, NEP 2 estimates that the costs to the government-financed budget of achieving its targets for the general education sector, including vocational schooling, would be K 545 million in 2005, rising to K 726 million by 2014 (2003 prices)—an increase of 3.2 percent per annum. The costs of achieving the proposed basic education goals are expected to rise from K 421 million to K 560 million, taking up the largest share of the education budget (76 percent). It expects that the reforms will result in efficiency gains that result in a significant fall in costs per student, falling from K 435 to K 409 per annum, and a reduction of those in the postbasic system from K 1,051 to K 1,030 (in real 2003 prices)—a fall of 6 percent and 2 percent respectively. It is expected that the basic education system would rise from 15.8 percent of the national recurrent budget in 2005 to 18.3 percent in 2014 (assuming forward budget projections of a real 2.5 percent per annum increase in the total budget).

However, NEP 2 has underestimated the level of resources required for the plan's implementation. It (a) does not adequately cost a minimum package of quality inputs; (b) it does not include school operational costs, which are meant to be covered by schools fees; (c) it does not include the costs of teacher training expansion and other related costs; (d) it does not include most of the development expenditures that are largely financed by development partners, which in recent years have accounted for 11 to 18 percent of total education expenditures; and (e) it assumes that provinces and LLGs will be able to finance the maintenance and infrastructure costs from their finances, which is clearly not the case. These costs are significant—over K 500 million per annum.

Without a change in approach, PNG will not be in a position to move decisively toward universal basic education until 2020 or 2025 at the earliest. This report therefore suggests that the government seriously consider developing a new initiative to enable it to achieve universal completion of basic education consistent with the proposed sector strategy outlined below, and using the suggested public expenditure framework and partnership with development partners also advocated and discussed below. This proposal is consistent with both the government's MTDS priorities and the commitment that expenditure priorities be consistent with the Medium-Term Fiscal Framework. A number of efficiency gains are identified, and it is argued that greater priority could be given to education in total expenditure, and that within education expansion of senior secondary and postsecondary education growth rates can be further constrained—at present, NEP 2 assumes these sectors will grow at the same rate as basic education. If revenues grow, as currently predicted due to new mining and oil projects, the report argues this is entirely feasible.

To this end, the report argues:

a.  The first priority for the education sector over the next 10 to 15 years should be to ensure every child completes the basic education cycle in a system able to provide an education that ensures both literacy and numeracy for all, together with a sound preparation for citizenship;
b.  The second priority should be to provide for a gradually increasing number of students to enter and complete secondary education over the next decade—mindful that the extremely high social demand for secondary education needs to be managed (together with associated costs to the budget) and that basic standards and quality of education need to be maintained;
c.  The third priority should be refom of skills development (including literacy programs) and vocational and technical college programs to ensure they are demand-orientated and have strong links to the world of work; and
d.  The fourth priority should be to reform the tertiary sector, including universities and the array of pre-employment training institutions.

Given the limited capacity of the public sector to deliver services, the central aim of any new strategy will be to reduce the government's direct responsibility for service delivery by diversifying the range of providers—albeit with appropriate subsidies. In identifying these options, policy makers should take into account the need for accountability and transparency and the limited integrity of existing government systems; but despite these problems, they must ensure high-quality education and training is provided.

It is critical that a consensus is developed on the overall priorities for education. The MTDS and governments' commitment to both the MDGs and the EFA initiative all point in a similar direction. An approach to establish a viable strategic direction for education is outlined below. Each of the six elements of the proposed package is necessary for a coherent approach to education development that is implementable with appropriate development partner support. However, none are sufficient on their own. The education and training outcomes prioritized by the government in the MTDS can only improve if the government's expenditure priorities are adjusted accordingly. This means that fiscal space must be created to allow changes in expenditure priorities and must require that funds thus allocated are used in an efficient and transparent manner. Therefore, it is critical that the government and its development partners achieve a consensus on the six elements of the proposed strategy. The strategy should be implemented using a dual-track approach that will simultaneously:

a. Address issues that can be dealt with within the national and provincial departments of education to improve the ability of education to provide quality learning; and
b. Help the central agencies (Treasury, Department of Finance, the Department of Natural Planning and Rural Development [DNPRD], the Department of Personnel Management [DPM], the Auditor General's Office [AGO], and the Department of Intergovernmental Relations) to strengthen their capacity to support the NDOE and the provinces.

The key elements of the proposed strategy directions for education are:

1. Set priorities for each of the education subsectors (as outlined above); identify technical options for achieving the education and learning outcomes and the ways in which the options might be packaged for

delivery; set priorities for public expenditure using public finance criteria; commit to monitoring and evaluating progress toward agreed education and training targets, learning outcomes, and education MDGs.

2. Identify ways to focus the public sector on those public goods that it can effectively deliver; promote involvement of the private sector in the delivery of private goods, such as vocational and technical education for the formal sector, and strengthen the collaboration between the public and private sectors.

3. Prepare an expenditure and implementation plan for the public financial contributions to the sector based on the activities identified in and consistent with the medium-term resource envelope.

4. Create fiscal space, where possible, by achieving savings in the sector, making more efficient use of existing funds and increasing sectoral allocations.

5. Prepare a financing plan covering the resource inputs of national government, provinces, and development partners.

6. Restore and guarantee the integrity of government processes, including budget, accounting, planning, procurement, and payroll systems.

## Common Cross-Cutting Themes

A review of the situational assessments and proposed strategies for health, HIV/AIDS, and education indicates that each of the sectors, while exhibiting features unique to itself, also face a range of common cross-cutting challenges. This should not be surprising, as each of the sectors have to operate within some common parameters, namely: (i) the formal structure of government, which assigns a range of the health and education sector powers and responsibilities to provinces and districts, as well as to the national government; (ii) the general operational structures of government (for example, for budgeting, accounting, planning, and personnel management); (iii) declining growth and rapidly falling per capita incomes; (iv) a significant deterioration in the composition and quality of public spending in the 1990s and the emergence of both unsustainable fiscal policy and significant budget overruns in the early 2000s, resulting in a rapid increase in public debt, which further constrained expenditures; (v) significant political instability and a lack of a consensus on strategic development issues; and (vi) growing uncertainties and concerns between both government and development partners and among development partners on how best to assist and work together in an environment of problematic (fragile) development outcomes. Further, the economy is affecting each sector in critical ways, and government systems are themselves facing critical problems, not the least of which is a crisis of integrity.

The following cross-cutting themes strongly affect each of the sectors:

- Declining growth and falling per capita incomes are an important backdrop to sector performance and directly limit the provision of basic services. While GDP is estimated to have grown by approximately 2.8 percent in the last two years, this followed a six-year period (1997–2002) during which real GDP declined by an average of 1 percent per annum. This, together with the rapid population growth rate, has led to a dramatic increase in the level of poverty in PNG—it almost doubled between 1996 and 2002. The recent improvement in economic performance is welcome but fragile, while medium-term growth prospects remain uncertain.

- The formal structure of the government (especially the revised decentralization arrangements of 1995) is largely dysfunctional. The distribution of sectoral powers and responsibilities across levels of government is unclear, workable oversight arrangements for program delivery at the provincial and local government levels are largely absent, significant inequalities across provinces in their ability to finance sectoral priorities exist, and deployment of resources are ineffective and discordant with sector priorities. As a result, national policies are not articulated in a manner consistent with achieving agreed objectives, nor are they effectively translated at subnational levels into programs and actions with associated budgets. There is considerable evidence that discretionary resources available and earmarked to provinces for the social sectors are not spent on them, in part because of fungibility with development partner financing.

- Government fragmentation has also led to the long-term deterioration of the integrity of budget institutions and systems. A breakdown in accountability has occurred mainly because the government has failed to enforce the rules and regulations of public service. As a result, control of wasteful spending on goods and services, public procurement processes that ensure value for money, transparent management of trust accounts, and budget control and accountability at the provincial levels have all suffered.

- The failure to control the size of the civil service and to ensure that payroll expenditures stay within budget allocations is accentuating public debt and consequently constraining nondebt public expenditures. According to the Public Expenditure Review and Rationalization (PERR) exercise, public sector employment accounts for at least 30 percent of total expenditures. Between 1999 and 2002, the number of staff on the central payroll increased by 11.4 percent and the salaries and wages of national and provincial departments grew by 30 percent. This rapid increase in payroll costs is one of the chief pressures on the budget and a major reason why expenditure on important goods and services needed for health care and education are being displaced (see below).

- Budget allocations and their composition are less than optimal. While PNG accords a relatively high priority to the human development sectors (health, education, and HIV/AIDS accounted for almost one-third of total budget in 2004, and the proportion has been increasing over the past decade), the share of recurrent expenditure in the total has been declining, development expenditures (largely financed by development partners) have been increasing, and nonsalary expenditures, particularly in health and HIV/AIDS essential for quality inputs, has been severely constrained.

These important cross-cutting issues adversely affect sectoral performance and outcomes in the human development sectors, in addition to the sector specific issues identified. Improved outcomes will not be attainable unless there is (a) focus on sectoral outcomes and the inequity of current outcomes, (b) a "whole of government" approach to policy development and implementation arrangements, (c) reduced sectoral fragmentation and isolation, (d) improved oversight and decentralization arrangements, (d) decisive actions to redress the long-term decline in the integrity of the government systems, and (e) improvement in the quality of expenditures in support of sectoral objectives receiving attention as a matter of priority. Given the cross-cutting nature of these issues—across sectors, across level of government, and across line departments and the central agencies of government—national leadership, particularly by the central agencies, is critical. There is need for a new partnership between government and development partners. This will require change in how all do business with one another.

### Next Steps: An Approach to Revised Strategic Directions for Human Development

Given the "crisis" in outcomes in PNG, each of the sectoral chapters proposes a core strategy consistent with the situational assessment as the starting point. These individual sector strategies take account of the core "cross-cutting" issues discussed above as embodied in the "six" elements of each strategy (see each sectoral section). In each of the situational assessments, we have argued that, given the limited capacity of the public sector to deliver services, a central aim of any revised strategy should be to reduce direct government involvement in service delivery by finding alternate, more viable options for doing so. However, the strategy must also take into account the need for accountability and transparency, the limited integrity of government systems as presently constituted, and the need to provide services that will improve high-priority outcomes, particularly for the poor.

It is critical for government and its development partners to reach a consensus on the substance of the six elements of each of the sectoral strategies. It is equally important that government own and manage that consensus. Without agreement on each of the six elements and on a process for the government and its development partners working together, it will be hard to move forward in a systematic manner. Furthermore, carrying out each of the elements of the proposed strategy will require inputs from different agencies of government. This emphasizes that it will be essential to take a cooperative "whole of government" approach that involves the central agencies, the core line departments, and the provinces at every stage of the process.

It is argued that these recommendations are fully consistent with the government's MTDS and the Medium-Term Economic Framework 2002-2007 (MTEF). The MTDS highlights the need for each sector to develop its own detailed sectoral strategies and programs within the medium-term expenditure framework. To this end, it is recommended that government update the MTEF annually as part of the budget preparation process and cover the consolidated budget, including all development-partner financing, which is currently excluded. This is an important omission, given that development partners finance 30 percent of all spending on education and health and 90 percent of HIV/AIDS expenditures. Developing a more comprehensive MTEF will require the cooperation of Treasury (responsible for recurrent expenditures) and DNPRD (responsible for development expenditures).

Within the suggested MTEF framework, which should also provide indicative hard budget constraints for each sector, it is the prime responsibility for line departments to develop strategies that (i) clearly focus on the agreed priority outcomes and the most cost-effective strategies to make progress toward those goals, especially in terms of targeting the poor; (ii) take account of the limited implementation capacity of the government sector; and (iii) actively involve provincial and LLGs in developing programs that are the responsibility of provinces to implement and, at least partially, to finance. Past plans have never been developed within the MTEF framework with province-specific ceilings and envelopes, nor have financing plans been developed. This has often resulted in financially unrealistic plans that could not be financed. It has also resulted in development partners funding their programs outside of the government budget.

This report has also emphasized:

- The importance of developing a realistic implementation plan for strategy and expenditure plans for each sector. As discussed throughout the report, the lack of implementation capacity in each sector at both the national and provincial level has been an important element in the failure so far to design and implement strategies to achieve the desired outcomes. The introduction of decentralization, as discussed, has increased the fragmentation of responsibility for designing and implementing programs. The tensions and frustrations arising from (a) poorly structured fiscal relations between the national government and provinces, and (b) the inability of the national (sectoral) line departments, with the proactive support of the central agencies, to work together in a manner designed to compensate for these structural problems have also contributed to sectoral line agencies (national and provincial) feeling increasingly isolated from each other and unable to effectively communicate with each other. Developing a solid implementation plan requires cooperation between the central agencies, the line departments, and the provinces. The line departments and the provinces need to be able to restructure their budgets and staffing. What will also be crucial is a strong and reliable central information system to which provinces and agencies report information on budgets, staffing, and outcomes on a timely basis. This, notwithstanding considerable investments in this area, is not the case at present.

- The need to create fiscal space and a compact to implement expenditure reforms. Situational assessments for each of the sectors have identified areas where increased fiscal space can be achieved through (i) sectoral savings, (ii) increased efficiency of departmental expenditures, and (iii) increased sectoral allocations from the national fisc. In the current adversarial relationship between central agencies and the line departments (and provinces), there is little incentive for the line departments to propose savings—by and large, savings revert to Treasury. There is a need for a compact or agreement between the line departments, the provinces, and the central agencies (particularly with the Treasury on budgets and the DPM/TSC on staffing) that would create incentives for making fiscal space (savings) within the line departments and provinces. Given the size of the workforce in the education and health sectors, increasing the efficiency of staff deployment and eliminating "ghosts" from the payroll would generate massive savings. To give effect to this, we propose that sectoral task forces should be established comprising representatives of the central agencies, the line departments, and the provinces. The case for allocating additional resources to the key human development sectors (from the government and from its development partners) would be considerably strengthened if such progress were to be made.

- The importance of developing a financing plan for each sector. It is important to make a clear distinction between an *expenditure* plan and a *financing* plan. In PNG there are four main sources of revenue to finance the human development sectors: (i) national government revenues; (ii) provinces' own revenues; (iii) funds from development partners; and (iv) fees and costs collected for services. Developing a financing plan for each sector is complicated in PNG because of the nature of fiscal relations between national and subnational governments. Further, the national government has lacked the resources to finance the provinces to the constitutionally mandated level during much of the period of the NOL, which has been a source of tension between the national and provincial authorities. A second problem is that national government resources for health and education are allocated very inequitably across provinces. Provincially assigned revenues are also very unequally distributed. Thus, it is by no means evident that those provinces that should be expanding their services on access/equity grounds have the capacity to finance their responsibilities under the current decentralization arrangements. Clearly, taking a "whole government" approach is the best way to develop a compact between national and provincial government to finance these programs. Given the large amount of development-partner financing of these sectors, the Treasury and the line departments need to cooperate with their development partners to develop a pipeline of support for the sectors consistent with the agreed expenditure plan. The final section of this report discusses how this might be done (see below).

- The importance of restoring the integrity of government processes has been a central theme of both the PERR and this report. The preceding discussion has emphasized the need for line departments to have the flexibility to restructure the deployment of staff and to reallocate their own budgets—subject to appropriate review by the central agencies. Failing to address these issues would make it extremely difficult for PNG's development partners to increasingly deliver their aid through the government's budget, an objective which the Joint Donors believe is critical because of the shift in accountabilities and the emphasis on accountability for outcomes.

- The critical role development partners play in the human development sector by providing policy advice and by financing a large share of total expenditures (including of critical recurrent expenditures, which should, given public finance principles, be financed by the government). It is critical that development partners do not add to the problems associated with (i) developing national policy coherency in each sector, (ii) undermining efforts to focus on priority sector outcomes, (iii) fragmenting accountability and sector financing arrangements by establishing multiple projects with differing (and even foreign) financing and management accountability frameworks, (iv) inappropriate competition for scarce management time, and (v) operating outside the budget framework and the hard budget constraint established by the rolling MTEF. Achieving these goals is not easy and will require a long-term commitment from key stakeholders and development partners. This will require consistency in policy advice and a strategic focus on outcomes and stakeholder inclusiveness in designing and implementing strategies, strengthening efforts to work through government systems to restore the integrity of government systems and to build systems capacity, identifying options to ensure sustainability of sector financing, and collaborating on economic and sector work with government to underpin sectoral policy dialogue.

Finally, a sectoral compact between government and its devolpment partners is suggested as a way to bring many of the themes together and move forward. The discussion so far has been about how the government can establish clear, coherent sectoral strategies, focused on agreed priority outcomes within a hard budget constraint as embodied in a rolling MTEF process, and the principles by which development partners should cooperate with government to assist this process. In this report, we have tabled a set of recommendations for devising (i) sectoral strategies that focus the capacity of government on the interventions that it is most capable of implementing and ensuring that services are delivered efficiently and equitably and the desired outcomes achieved; (ii) reforms to create fiscal space to fund high-priority sectoral programs accurately; (iii) a feasible and enforceable financing plan that includes the provinces; and (iv) consensual compacts (agreements) between the line departments, the provinces, and the central agencies of government on sector strategies, outcomes to be achieved, and restoring the integrity of core government systems.

The final element of a more coherent, outcome-focused approach is how the government and its development partners can best support such an effort. We recommend that an appropriate way forward be structured along the following lines:

a. An agreement on a strategy and a long-term vision for the outcomes to be achieved for each of the sectors that is developed nationally, but is clearly owned by the provinces, line departments, and the central agencies (in other words, by the "whole government").

b. A set of program/policy reforms (such as an essential health care package, the prevention of the transmission of HIV as the primary sector objective for HIV/AIDS, and universal completion of the basic cycle of education) and a set of organizational policy reforms aimed at implementing the programmatic reforms according to agreed benchmarks and monitoring indicators.

c. A rolling public expenditure and implementation plan covering three to five years consistent with the medium-term resource envelope determined by the government. This should be updated annually and be consistent with a and b above.

d. The planned total expenditures for the current year (both recurrent and development), an associated financing plan (including both government and donor financing), and a procurement plan for each provincial plan and for the central sectoral department.

e. An annual operational plan setting out the detailed reform program designed to be implemented that year (derived from b above) and monitoring indicators and benchmarks for each element of the operational plan (including provincial plans) that can be achieved within the available resources and known capacity constraints.

Elements a–c above represent the medium-term strategy and implementation plan. Elements d and e are annual plans (activity plans) developed by provinces and national departments to implement the agreed program. They should be used as the basis for disbursing resources from PNG's development partners in support of the agreed program. To the extent possible, these resources should be disbursed through the government's own budget. The objective is to include development assistance in the government's budget, accounting, and accountability systems. We suggest that the government and its development partners conduct a midterm review of elements a-c after two years and elements d and e in conjunction with the semiannual budget review exercise to enable it to make any necessary adjustments in policies, reforms, implementation plans, expenditures, and financing. This would allow strategies and programs to remain flexible and to be adjusted over time in response to feedback and outcomes. As part of these agreements, there would be a clear set of baselines and a monitoring and evaluation framework.

This process also reinforces the importance of focusing on the entire resource envelope and management process and not just the recurrent budgeting process or the development budget. Agencies at the national and provincial level need to make and implement regular activity plans to implement agreed policies, to ensure the timely funding of these activities, to manage the flow of financing, and to ensure that accounting and auditing mechanisms and procurement processes are in place.

In a number of areas of this report, there are important questions that cannot be fully or adequately answered based on existing knowledge. Probably the most important area where improved knowledge would help policy making is in better understanding the demand for services—health, HIV, and education—by clients and families. Population-based surveys in each of these areas would add valuable information for planners. There is also quite limited labor market information in PNG since the collapse of the Annual Labor Market Survey. Improved knowledge of trends in the labor market through surveys (including tracer or reverse tracer studies) of graduates of different types of education and training facilities would add extremely valuable insights into education and training performance.

It is now 10 years since a survey directly measured poverty levels in PNG and, without a special effort, it will be a long time before another survey able to do so is done. The decision by government and many development partners not to include a modest income and expenditure module (or a HIV module) to the Demographic Household Survey is a missed opportunity. Given the importance of poverty and HIV to the MDG agenda, it is important that we are able to benchmark status and monitor trends.

As we move forward, government and development partners can jointly address these knowledge gaps as an important part of next steps.

## A Final Word

We hope that this report, with its situational assessments and proposed strategies for health, HIV/AIDS, and education, will enable all parties to enter into a productive partnership and will form the basis of a policy dialogue that will decisively improve sectoral outcomes in PNG. This is an ambitious but feasible objective if consensus on the way forward is built.

# CHAPTER 1

# Introduction

## Rationale for the Report

This report—Strategic Directions for Human Development in Papua New Guinea (PNG)—arose from a dialogue in 2002 and early 2003 between the World Bank, the Asian Development Bank (ADB), and the Australian Agency for International Development (AusAID) with the government of PNG, particularly with senior officials of the National Department of Planning and Rural Development (NDPRD), the Department of Education (NDOE), the Department of Health (NDOH), the National AIDS Council Secretariat (NACS), the Department of Treasury (DOT), and a number of provincial governments. The dialogue focused on:

(a) the centrality of human resource development to the government's medium-term development and poverty reduction objectives;
(b) concerns about both disappointing sectoral performances and the sustainability of current human development programs (particularly in light of recent and prospective resource constraints);
(c) the critical importance of the rapidly emerging human immunodeficiency virus/acquired immune deficiency syndrome (HIV/AIDS)

epidemic to the health of Papua New Guineans and as a threat to growth and development;

(d) problems with intergovernmental relations, particularly on fiscal matters;

(e) the role of core government systems, including budget and planning systems and personnel management systems; and

(f) how PNG's development partners can best assist the government to develop sustainable policies and strategies to deliver services, particularly in rural areas, and support these strategies both by assisting with building capacity and providing financial assistance.

These concerns were reinforced by the Public Expenditure Review and Rationalization (PERR) study, which was undertaken jointly by the government and the World Bank, ADB, and AusAID (the Joint Donors) in 2002–2003. The PERR also reinforced the desirability of proceeding with work on a Human Development Strategy given that:

(a) education, health, and HIV/AIDS expenditures constituted 27 percent of total public expenditures in 2004 (up from 22 percent in 1997), including development activities financed by PNG's development partners, which constituted 27 percent of these expenditures in 2004, up from 14.2 percent in 1997;

(b) there were serious concerns about the effectiveness of current expenditures in improving health and education outcomes; and

(c) there were considerable social pressures to increase expenditures in both of these sectors, particularly education, despite an overriding need for stringent fiscal discipline and a consequent need to re-prioritize expenditures and redefine the role of the state in supporting development objectives.

The PERR also highlighted the need for the government to strengthen the integrity of its core systems, particularly its budget and personal management systems, which were seriously deteriorating, never having been adequately developed to cope with decentralization.

The government's starting point for discussing the Strategic Directions for Human Development report with the Joint Donors was the draft Medium-Term Development Strategy 2003–2007 (MTDS), which was then under development. The MTDS recognized how crucial health and education were to meeting PNG's development objectives, particularly its human development objectives, including the government's rural development and poverty reduction strategies. The government was also becoming increasingly concerned about the health and developmental impacts of the emerging HIV/AIDS epidemic. The MTDS reiterated the government's commitment to the Millennium Development Goals (MDGs).

The government wanted the report to focus on future strategic options and directions for developing the health and education sectors and on a response to the HIV/AIDS epidemic. The key sectoral agencies were also in the process of developing new medium- to longer-term plans. The NDOE was in the process of preparing a new 10-year National Education Plan, the NDOH was preparing a Health Medium-Term Economic Framework (HMTEF) to refocus public expenditures, and the National AIDS Council (NAC) was developing a National Strategic Plan for HIV/AIDS (NSP-HIV/AIDS) for 2006–2010.

## Why Human Development?

PNG has a large unfinished human development agenda. PNG's population of 5.3 million is growing at about 2.7 percent per annum, while the labor force is growing at 2.6 percent per annum and can expect to grow faster in future years.[1] Only 15 percent of the workforce is engaged in formal wage employment, and this figure is probably declining. Gross domestic product (GDP) growth has been negative for much of the 2000s and per capita GDP has declined significantly in real terms in recent years. It is estimated that 40 percent of the population of PNG live on less than $2 per day, and 70 percent live on less than $1 per day.[2] Furthermore, life expectancy remains at only 59 years. The government has estimated the infant mortality rate to be 75 per 1,000 live births, maternal mortality rates are approaching 400 per 100,000 live births, and only 40 percent of the population has access to safe water. Some 19 percent of children do not enter school, and while enrolment growth has increased dramatically over the past decade, over half of those who enter school do not complete the basic cycle of nine years of schooling, and the quality of the schooling remains problematic. PNG is facing a major HIV/AIDS epidemic as well.

Thus, with increasing poverty in PNG and a large unfinished human development agenda, it is an appropriate time to search for options to improve health and education outcomes and prevent the scourge of HIV/AIDS. It is only through significantly improved education levels and with a healthy workforce that all Papua New Guineans will be able to become more productive and create a more dynamic economy. As discussed in Chapter 3, HIV/AIDS has the potential to seriously affect peoples' lives and the productive capacity of the economy, as well as PNG's capacity to improve living standards.

In an institutional context, the major responsibilities for health and education programs (and, to a large extent, HIV prevention programs) are managed and partially financed by provincial governments. Education and health, which constitute over 85 percent of provincial-level staff, have similar management issues and other cross-cutting issues (including the operation of core government systems such as budget and personnel management) and are discussed both as part of individual sector analysis and as part of the common cross-cutting themes analysis. PNG development partners finance almost 20 percent of education expenditures, almost one-third of health expenditures, and over 90 percent of HIV/AIDS expenditures. For human development expenditures, overall development partners account for over one-quarter of total government expenditures. It is thus critical, as very significant financiers of the human development sectors, that development partner expenditures support strategic outcomes in each of the sectors in a sustainable manner.

## Why Produce the Report Jointly?

The Strategic Directions for Human Development Report has been developed in cooperation and partnership with government and the Joint Donors in order to deepen their joint understandings of the situation with respect to health, HIV/AIDS, and education in PNG as a basis for policy dialogue with government. One objective is to provide a consistent voice to PNG stakeholders—government, NGOs and civil society more generally—on policy options and to ensure that programs of financial and technical assistance are consistent and do not add to the pressures of fragmentation in policy development and in implementation already evident in PNG. A number of important principles underlay this approach. First, the work was done in partnership with government, and government leadership was critical. Second, in the spirit of this partnership, the Joint Donors were making a long-term commitment to PNG. Third, policy recommendations should be consistent with the objective of development partners increasingly working through government systems.

## What Questions?

The overarching purpose of the report is to explore various strategic options for reducing poor human development outcomes and poverty in PNG through an analysis of past sector performance and of the underlying constraints that have prevented improved performance in the past. Specifically, the review's aim is to assist the government in setting priorities in each sector and identifying the best way in which to use its oversight capacities and public finances to achieve better outcomes. The review aims to answer two questions:

(1) How can we improve the population's health status and learning outcomes and increase school enrollments in the context of the inter-action between supply and demand, resource constraints, capacity constraints, and other local conditions in PNG, given evidence of what has worked in both PNG and other countries?

(2) How can we (i) increase management capacity in the public sector and (ii) make good use of all potential providers of services—public, non-governmental organizations (NGOs), and private—given the government's current structure and weak capacity and the haphazard state of decentralized governance in PNG in which there are no effective lines of accountability among different agencies and levels of government?

Another important objective of this report is to provide both a basis for sustained policy dialogue and a mechanism to involve key stakeholders, including the churches, NGOs, and development partners, in the process in order to develop a consensus on the best strategies for the health, HIV/AIDS, and education sectors. This also might avoid the situation where developing partners give conflicting policy advice to the government. Suggestions are also made on how development partners and government can best work together in improved ways to sustainably support human development programs in PNG.

## Outline of the Report

Chapter 2 presents a situational assessment of the health sector and proposes the core elements of a revised strategic direction for the health sector designed to address the issues identified by the assessment. This strategic option aims to answer the following fundamental questions regarding the health sector: (1) What services in the short and medium term should be the focus of NDOH given (a) the agreed need to focus on priority health outcomes, especially the MDGs; and (b) public finance criteria that give priority to the financing of health services? (2) What options exist to improve the organization and management of service delivery by (a) making public-sector delivery more efficient; (b) relying on NGOs, local communities, and private providers to broaden service delivery and free up public resources for priority needs; and (c) increasing demand for health services and altering health-related behavior for the better? The chapter concludes with a proposal for strategic directions moving forward.

Chapter 3 presents a situational assessment of HIV/AIDS in PNG and proposes the core elements of a package of strategic options designed to respond to the epidemic, which threatens to undermine not only the health status of the population, but also the strategic development options open to the country. The chapter updates what is known about HIV/AIDS, paying particular attention to the identification of high-risk target groups engaging in behavior conducive to spreading the disease. It also reviews the direction and performance of current HIV/AIDS programs, identifies specific gaps in PNG's response to HIV/AIDS, and makes recommendations on what steps to take to improve this response in the future.

Chapter 4 presents a situational assessment of the education and training system covering both the general education subsector and the postsecondary subsector (which consists of universities, technical and vocational training colleges, and employment-located vocational training). It goes on to propose the core elements of a package of strategic options designed to achieve universal completion of basic education and to make vocational education more applicable to labor market needs and income-earning opportunities in the informal sector. Given that the responsibility for managing the education and training system is fragmented, with overlapping mandates and responsibilities, and that many of the relevant agencies are particularly weak, structural reforms must come high on the agenda to ensure coherence in the policies and management of the education sector in the future.

Chapter 5 deals with cross-sectoral issues and draws out a range of themes common to the health, HIV/AIDS, and education sectors. These themes include (1) the fragility and inequity of current outcomes; (2) the need for a "whole-of-government" approach to policy development, financing, and implementation arrangements; (3) problems associated with the structure of decentralization and devolution arrangements; (4) problems associated with the long-term decline in the integrity of core government systems; (5) the lack of a structural coherence in the relationships between the central agencies and line departments and between the national and provincial governments; and (6) less-than-optimal budget allocations in the sectors, including the large share of development-partner financing in each of the sectors and lack of quality-enhancing nonsalary budgets.

Chapter 6 considers possible next steps to create compacts between (a) line departments and the central agencies, (b) the national government and provinces, and (c) government and development partners in support of a decisive attempt to improve health, HIV, and education outcomes and the lives of Papua New Guineans. Critically, the development of these compacts will require the proactive support of the central agencies to provide the framework within which this can be achieved.

## Notes

1. Assuming HIV/AIDS is controlled and does not dramatically increase the death rate.
2. Compared with 39 percent and 12 percent, respectively, for the East Asia and Pacific Region of the World Bank as a whole.

# CHAPTER 2

# Health in Papua New Guinea: A Situation Assessment and Proposed Strategic Directions

## Introduction

At the start of the colonial era, Papua New Guinea was afflicted with a high burden of infectious diseases and high levels of maternal and child mortality. At the time, the population relied solely on traditional beliefs and medicines. As colonization progressed, the government and missionaries began providing basic Western allopathic health services to the indigenous population, initially for the labor force on plantations and for migrant workers in the limited urban areas, and subsequently for the majority of the population in rural areas.

The health care systems evolved and by the time of independence, there was a formal government-funded health system throughout the country supplemented by the government-subsidized health services provided by various Christian missions. The centralized Department of Health managed the whole system, including hospitals, and delegated powers to the regional, district, and line staff and facilities. The health service provided basic primary care through frontline workers with minimal amounts of training, and with some basic drugs to dispense. The basic health service infrastructure now consists of 614 health facilities (19 provincial hospitals, 52 urban clinics, 201 health centers, and 342 sub-centers). The missions run 44 percent of these facilities, and serve more people in the lowest asset quintile than the government-owned system (Cibulskis 2002).

At the same time, the country witnessed significant improvements in health outcomes. Between 1970 and 1980, the infant mortality rate (IMR) fell from more than 130 per 1,000 live births to only 72 deaths. Health services most likely contributed to these outcomes and, as such, maintaining and strengthening the basic health system became the overriding objective of the managers of the health system after independence. Both the government and its donor partners were also committed to this approach.

The improvements in health outcomes and services were not maintained in the postindependence era. Today, there are few outreach activities, and the peripheral or frontline workers have all but disappeared from the system. In the 30 years since independence, only modest improvements in infant, child, and maternal mortality were maintained, and in some regions, they have actually increased. Control of major infectious diseases, such as tuberculosis (TB) and malaria, remains problematic. At the same time, the health system has had to face new challenges, such as an epidemic of HIV infections.

This paper aims to examine the causes behind the deterioration in health outcomes and system performance and to identify the implications for the health sector strategy for the next decade. The authors have tried to use the rich body of work and earlier studies conducted on various aspects of the topic, where possible, as well as the work done through the PERR process. In fact, this is an important added value of this paper—bringing the two aspects together. Where possible, the authors have also generated new data (e.g., health workforce) and new analysis of data (e.g., public expenditure on health). Hence, the paper takes a unique perspective that brings the cross-sectoral aspects and "whole-of-government" functions together with the sectoral performance. This is important as it relates to PNG, as the analysis will show that it is an essential approach to improve health system performance. This, however, should not take away from the important technical challenges and issues facing PNG.

The paper also acknowledges some important steps taken to help address the health system problems; the paper covers these in the sections on recent government response and recent donor response discussed below. Government has a clear commitment to primary health care and the reduction of the transmission of the HIV virus (discussed more fully in Chapter 3) as core development objectives in the MTDS. The government is committed to the development of the initial health Medium-Term Economic Framework 2002–2007 (MTEF) and the subsequent health NSP-HIV/AIDS as the basis for both setting health priorities and efforts to develop a sectorwide approach (SWAP) for the health sector. The paper then provides some important steps to help move forward on how (i) government's commitment in the MTDS for core sectors to develop prioritized sector plans consistent with the Medium-Term Resources Framework established by Treasury; and (ii) to strengthen and deepen the health NSP-HIV/AIDS process and associated efforts to develop a health sector SWAP.

The report first discusses the current health status of the population and trends in health in recent years. This is followed by an examination of the current performance of the health system. The next sections discuss the trends in infrastructure, labor, funding, and decentralization in the health system. Government response, as well as that of donors, is discussed next, and the chapter concludes by outlining a proposed new strategy for the health sector and the ways in which it might be put into practice.

## Health Outcomes

The burden of disease in PNG is dominated by high maternal and infant death rates and by communicable diseases, which together account for about 60 percent of the disease burden. Pneumonia and diarrhea, together with underlying malnutrition, are the most important causes of post-neonatal death in young children. Among adults, TB is an important cause of morbidity and mortality, and the rapid increase in HIV infections in the last 10 years means that deaths from TB will become the most common co-infection.

Reproductive health has improved very little in the last 30 years, and is at the core of the problem of low maternal health status. The maternal mortality ratio was estimated to be 3.7 per 1,000 live births in 1996, with regional variations that reach as high as 6.25 in the highlands. Recent years have seen no significant improvement. Though there are no recent estimates, the low antenatal coverage, limited supervised deliveries, and declining facility performance all point to the continuation of high maternal mortality. Total fertility rates (TFRs) are high; in 2000, the rate was estimated to be 4.6 births for all women 15–49 years, down from 5.4 births in 1980. But this masks regional differences, as the rate is increasing in the Western, Gulf, and West Sepik provinces.

Although infant mortality declined markedly in the 1970s, only modest additional gains were made between 1980 and 2000 (the latest year for which data are available). In rural areas, the rate in 1980 was

72 deaths per 1,000 live births, and in 2000 it was 64. There were marked differentials between regions (Figure 2.1).

In the Momase region, infant mortality increased between 1980 and 2000, and it did not change in the Southern region. The rates in the Gulf and West Sepik provinces remained over 100 per 1,000 live births. Child mortality improved between the 1980 and 2000 censuses from 45 to 25 per 1,000 live births. Even greater gains were made in urban areas, and in the Momase region, the rate improved from 50 to 39 per 1,000 live births.

Pneumonia causes half of all postneonatal deaths in hospitals. Diarrhea is also a factor in this regard. Malaria contributes to children's poor health status. Sixty percent of the population lives in endemic malaria areas, and the rest in epidemic areas. Malaria mortality is rising, but there is no recent documentation of drug resistance patterns.

Among adults, the disease burden is still dominated by infectious diseases, especially TB and, more recently, HIV. A general HIV epidemic is under way in PNG (see Chapter 3). Current estimates indicate that there are at least 80,000 people in the country who are infected with the virus.[1] Although life expectancy improved between 1996 and 2000 from 49.6 to 54.2 years nationally, experience from other countries suggests that these gains will be temporary as HIV infection increases and deaths from tuberculosis as a co-infection of HIV rises. Hospitals are already reporting that the number of new tuberculosis patients is increasing, and it is now the main cause for admission to their adult inpatient wards. At the national level, inpatient data for pulmonary tuberculosis for 1996 to 2000 show a rise in registration of 21 percent (from 3,916 cases to 4,723), and mortality from TB is also increasing. In one hospital in the highlands, deaths of inpatients from tuberculosis increased from 3.3 percent of all

**Figure 2.1. Infant Mortality Rate by Region**

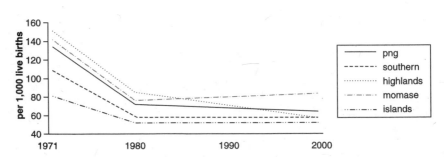

*Source:* National Census Data (various years).

deaths between 2000 and 2002 to 10.4 percent in 2002 and 2003. This is consistent with a high prevalence of HIV infection.

## Health System Infrastructure and Performance

As the early improvements in the population's health status have been faltering, so too has the performance of the health system.

Rural health care infrastructure and staffing management are declining. For example:

(a) The proportion of delivery rooms with running water and a sink decreased from 61 to 51 percent between 2000 and 2002 (the latest year for which there is reasonable data).

(b) Drug supplies have been problematic over the last five years. There have been some recent improvements, probably due to the introduction of aid post and clinic supply kits in response to a crisis in the drug ordering and distribution system.

(c) The proportion of health centers receiving supervisory visits by doctors has declined from 53 percent in 1995 to 41 percent in 2000, although the same proportion for medical officer visits has subsequently stayed static at 33 percent.

(d) Over 300 aid posts were closed between 1995 and 2000, mainly affecting people in lower-asset quintiles and those living in remote areas. Currently, NDOH cannot verify what facilities are operating, but it believes significantly more have closed.

(e) There are fewer doctors and health extension officers (HEOs) atrural health facilities and fewer community health workers (CHWs) working in aid posts—a 25 percent reduction between 1987 and 2000. It is believed further significant reductions of CHWs working at the aid post level have taken place notwithstanding the expansion of the workforce discussed later in this chapter.

Maternal and child health services are inadequate and show little evidence of having improved despite the increase in public funding. Specifically:

(a) Antenatal care coverage declined from 80 percent in 1991 to 58 percent in 2004, with coverage being much lower for those women in the lowest asset quintile (Cibulskis 2002).

(b) Supervised deliveries declined from 52 percent in 1991 to 39 percent in 2004.
(c) Contraceptive use is low, with fewer than 20 percent of women using any method of contraception. Contraceptive use is particularly low among women from the two lowest asset quintiles.

Vaccine coverage in rural areas is low. Specifically:

(a) About 40 percent of children did not receive a third dose of diphtheria, polio, and tetanus vaccine (DPT) in the years leading up to 2002, although this fell to 32 percent in 2003.
(b) Measles vaccinations have stayed static, with a little more than half of children under the age of one covered between 1999 and 2004.[2] As in other countries, official health service data tend to overestimate coverage; 63 percent coverage for third dose of DPT was recorded nationally in 1995, but the Demographic Household Survey (DHS) of that year estimated actual coverage as being 46 percent nationally and only 40 percent in rural areas.

Tuberculosis control is poor. Given that PNG is experiencing a major general HIV epidemic, TB incidence and fatalities are bound to increase:

(a) As few as one-third of new cases of sputum-positive pulmonary TB are detected and treated by the health system.
(b) Only one-third of those enrolled complete their TB treatment.
(c) There are no data on the cure rate. The government, supported by the World Health Organization (WHO), has introduced the Directly Observed Therapy Short Course (DOTS) strategy in 24 districts, which has had variable success, but has raised the detection rate in those areas compared with the rest of the country. TB, as discussed, is the major opportunistic infection associated with HIV.

There is a dearth of appropriate drugs to treat malaria. National guidelines specify that artesunate should be administered to malaria patients whose treatment has failed or who have a severe case of the disease, but there are insufficient stocks to cover all of these patients. The Global Fund to Fight AIDS, Tuberculosis, and Malaria (GFATM) has provided a $20 million grant for malaria control, which aims to ensure that 80 percent of the population will own mosquito bed nets impregnated with insect repellent by 2008, with the procurement and distribution contracted out ($10 million). The project includes the purchase of rapid diagnostic tests for all rural health facilities that do not have diagnostic facilities ($3 million) and the purchase of arte-sunate (US$0.5 million).

Ambulatory care is decreasing, and this will have a negative impact on health outcomes. The number of outpatient visits per person per annum declined from 2.39 in 1988 to 1.49 in 2003. The reduction in access to ambulatory care, combined with declining infrastructure, is likely to con-tribute to poorer health outcomes.

Hospitals represent 30.1 percent of government health expenditure, but are providing fewer services with a lower quality of care across the board. In 2003, the government spent K 90 million on hospitals (K 95.4 million in 2004) and K 12 million on the NDOH for hospital administration, and AusAID provided an additional K 19.2 million for hospital projects. The main characteristics of the hospital sector are as follows:

(a) The 19 public hospitals providing clinical care are most heavily used by the richest quintile of the population, who use hospitals for 50 percent of their children's illness episodes.
(b) Hospitals have some independence from the government, being managed by a CEO and a hospital board, with the expectation that some of their revenues will be generated locally through user fees and community and business fund-raising. This has reportedly improved the management of some of the larger hospitals, but administration remains problematic, as does documentation of service quality.
(c) Inpatient capacity in hospitals has declined, but staff levels have not been reduced. Many hospitals have reported being out of stock of basic drugs, such as antibiotics, paracetamol, and intravenous fluids. Laboratories are providing fewer services. Outpatient numbers have stayed about the same or have increased. Although closures of hos-pitals and increased user charges may have contributed to declining utilization, the overall pattern suggests a decline in service provision.
(d) HIV/AIDS is increasing. In Port Moresby General Hospital, it accounted for a quarter of all hospital deaths in 2004 (one-third if deaths from TB are included).

The performance of the mission health centers is generally consid-ered to be equivalent to or better than the performance of government health centers. Mission health centers and subcenters tend to be in rural areas, and their caseloads are usually higher than those of equivalent government facilities. A costing study conducted in 1989 showed that unit costs at mission subcenters tend to be lower than at equivalent government centers. In addition, other recent studies have shown that their outputs are at least equivalent, but are more cost-effective; however, there has been a decline in some performance indicators over the last five years, including patient visits per capita per annum and the proportion of deliveries supervised, while levels of vaccination and antenatal coverage are the same.

Overall, the capacity of provincial and district governments to deliver quality health services declined and continues to do so. An important factor in this decline has been the successive attempts to decentralize the provision of services—a factor recognized as a key issue in the MTDS. In particular, the aid post system—designed to reach the most remote rural populations—has suffered from a lack of commitment from both provincial and district governments and national government efforts to reduce casual staff (all staff in aid posts were casual employees) in times of fiscal crisis. The closure of more aid posts is continuing. While 75 percent of the original number of aid posts were still open in 1995, only 63 percent were open in 2000. Data for subsequent years are problematic, but the trend is believed to be continuing. As the coverage of basic services shrinks, unmet demand from the more remote populations increases.

## Health Sector Workforce: Size and Deployment

Health outcomes and the cost-effectiveness of those outcomes are critically dependent on the size, composition, and deployment of health staff—particularly as they constitute a very large share of total health care expenditure (as discussed in the section on health expenditure and financing). This includes, however, only limited data on health staff numbers and their deployment.[3]

### Size of the Health Workforce: Possibilities for Increased Fiscal Space

The overall size of the health workforce financed by the public sector has grown by 36 percent (from 9,082 to 12,355) in the 16 years from 1988 to 2004 (see Table 2.1). Over the decade from 1988 to 1998, the workforce grew by 19 percent. The increase in the last six years was 14.5 percent—a growth rate almost twice as fast as in the previous decade.

There are some significant qualifications about the data presented in Table 2.1. It is likely that all cadres are underreported, particularly for

**Table 2.1. Composition and Growth of the Health Workforce, 1988–2004**

| Category | 1988 | 1998 | 2004 | Change 1998–2004 |
|---|---|---|---|---|
| Doctors and Dentists | 384 | 316 | 524 | 65.8% |
| Health Extension Officers (HEOs) | 357 | 233 | 575 | 146.8% |
| Nurses | 2,917 | 2,920 | 3,980 | 36.3% |
| Allied Health Workers | 283 | 372 | 440 | 18.3% |
| Med. Lab. Technical Staff | 159 | 150 | 254 | 69.3% |
| Community Health Workers (CHWs) | 4,982 | 3,926 | 5,358 | 36.5% |
| Public Service—Other Health | n/a | 2,874 | 1,224 | −57.4% |
| Total | 9,082 | 10,791 | 12,355 | 14.5% |

For notes and sources, see Table 2A.1 in Annex 2A.

2004 (see Annex 2A). It is probable that at least 1,000 additional CHWs are on provincial payrolls. There is no evidence to suggest that the Public Service—Other Health category (which includes administrative positions and support staff)—will have fallen between 1998 and 2004. Thus, there may be as many as 15,000 CHWs on the health payroll. The growth in the total health care workforce between 1998 and 2004 may be even larger than 20 percent.

Over the period 1998 to 2004, some cadres of health workers increased significantly faster than the average for all health workers, such as the number of doctors and dentists (a rise of 66 percent), HEOs (150 percent), and technical and medical laboratory staff (70 percent). Most significantly, nurses and CHWs (who account for 75 percent of the health workforce) increased by more than 36 percent over this period.

There is a question about the reliability of the 2004 payroll data for establishing the actual number of staff being paid and whether they are qualified. Considering the number of graduates in the medical field (doctors and dentists) and workforce attrition between 1998 and 2004, the number of medical practitioners listed on the 2004 payroll is indeed a feasible number.[4] However, similar calculations for nurses suggest that there are over 1,000 more nurses on the payroll than is feasible. In fact, the calculations suggest there should be fewer people on the payroll in 2004 than in 1998. Similarly, there are about 1,700 more CHWs on the payroll than our analysis would suggest (see Annex 2A for the basis for these calculations).[5]

While this analysis should be systematically verified, this suggests that there may be potential savings that could be made on payroll costs amounting to around K 28.6 million. These savings would comprise K 15 million on nurses' salaries and K 13.6 million on the salaries of CHWs due to duplications in staff and/or unqualified staff on the payroll and staff receiving more than one paycheck.[6]

An additional problem is that, while the recently introduced Concept payroll system has increased transparency and may improve personnel management, it cannot redress all the payroll anomalies that have evolved over time, including staff who have abandoned their posts, deceased staff whose names remain on the payroll, and staff who change agencies but whose names are not removed from their former payroll.

Furthermore, NDOH officials and PNG's development partners recognize that there is considerable pressure on provincial governments to show that they are spending at least 6 percent of their own revenues on health (a policy agreed to by provincial governors) as a condition of receiving donor funding through the government's Health Sector Improvement Program (HSIP) trust account. This has been known to encourage provincial governments to include nonhealth staff on their provincial health payroll.

A physical census would make it possible to identify all legitimate health staff and to eliminate duplicate records and those of staff who do not exist. The census would also present an opportunity to institute identification cards using technology similar to the system that the Department of Transport currently uses for drivers' licenses.

### Health Workforce Deployment

In 2004, NDOH, including urban clinics in the National Capital District, accounted for about 9 percent of the workforce, while one-third were employed in hospitals. Over 58 percent of staff provided health services in the provinces. Government-run provincial services accounted for 35 percent of total health staff, while church-run services accounted for just over 23 percent (see Table 2.2 below).

Almost 85 percent of the health staff is accounted for by four cadres: doctors and health extension officers (8 percent together), nurses (one-third), and CHWs (43 percent). More than half of all doctors work for NDOH, some 37 percent work in hospitals, and less than 10 percent for provincial health services—the vast majority working for Church Health Services. Health extension officers, originally established as a cadre to manage health centers, are now in significant numbers administered by NDOH (20 percent), while 12 percent are employed by hospitals. Two-thirds are deployed within provincial health services, the

**Table 2.2. Ministry of Health Workforce 2004 by Cadre and Major Health Function**

| | National Dept. of Health (1) | Hospital (2) | Provincial Health Services (3) | Government Provincial Health Services* | Church Health Services* | Total (1+2+3) | Percent of Total Workforce |
|---|---|---|---|---|---|---|---|
| Doctors and Dentists | 287 | 198 | 50 | 11 | 39 | 535 | 4.3 |
| Health Extension Officers | 116 | 73 | 386 | 348 | 38 | 575 | 4.6 |
| Nurses | 165 | 1,475 | 2,339 | 1,206 | 1,133 | 3,979 | 32.2 |
| Allied Health Workers | 87 | 238 | 114 | 80 | 34 | 439 | 3.5 |
| Medical Lab & Technical Staff | 40 | 126 | 88 | 30 | 58 | 254 | 2.1 |
| Community Health Workers | 70 | 1,158 | 4,130 | 2,673 | 1,457 | 5,358 | 43.3 |
| Public Service—Health | 331 | 745 | 139 | 6 | 133 | 1,215 | 9.8 |
| Total | 1,096 | 4,013 | 7,246 | 4,354 | 2,892 | 12,355 | 100 |
| Percent of Total Workforce | 8.9 | 32.4 | 58.6 | 35.2 | 23.4 | | 100 |

For notes and sources: see Table 2A.1 in Annex 2A.
* Government Provincial Health Services and Church Health Services are a breakup of Provincial Health Services (Column 3).

vast majority within the government-managed provincial health service. Church health services are more dependent on doctors and nurses (Table 2.2), while the government's provincial health services are dependent on health extension officers to manage their services.

Of the 3,980 nurses, 58.8 percent are in the provincial service in district health services of which 30.3 percent are in government-managed services and 28.5 percent are in church-managed health services. Hospitals employ 37 percent of all nurses, and fewer than 4 percent are in NDOH. Community health workers are predominately located in provincial health services (77 percent), with 50 percent of the total being employed in government-managed provincial health services.

There is considerable evidence that health staff are not optimally allocated (see Annex 2A). Although church-run health services deliver about 50 percent of provincial health services—as measured by ambulatory care—they have one-third fewer staff than the government-run health services. Furthermore, anecdotal evidence suggests that the quality of services provided by the church health services is better than that provided by the government services. In addition, the salary and allowances provided by the churches are, on average, lower than those provided by the government. There is also evidence of significant overstaffing in government-run health centers relative to workloads, largely due to the reduction in the provision of outreach services. As a result, church services are significantly more cost-effective than government services.

At the same time, the number of outpatient visits to health facilities per capita per annum has been declining, even though staff allocations have increased by about 15 percent over the past six years in the whole system and by 12 percent in the church health system.[7]

The breakdown of management reporting systems since the hospitals became autonomous institutions managed by boards means that only fragmentary data are available on hospital staffing patterns. However, the numbers of hospital wards and beds have been in decline, and bed occupancy rates have stagnated, which may be a sign of reduced staff productivity.

## Health Finances and Expenditures

On the surface, the decline in the health system's performance and its failure to improve health status is at odds with the fact that public funding to the health sector grew in the mid-1990s. However, while the total funding level increased, there were major changes in the sources of finance and in the level and composition of health expenditures between 1997 and 2004,[8] which threatened the quality of health services and their sustainability.

In summary, the share of recurrent expenditures in total health expenditures financed by government fell dramatically over this period while development expenditures—almost entirely financed by development partners—increased to around one-third of total expenditures. In real terms, recurrent expenditures fell by 9.4 percent over the period 1997–2004, and provincial (rural health services) expenditures fell 17 percent in real terms (Table 2.3).[9] Furthermore, input composition of these lower expenditures changed for the worse. Expenditures on goods and services, critical for quality services, fell over 27 percent in real terms while expenditures on capital items fell almost 77 percent. At the same time, expenditure on salaries increased 10 percent in real terms (Table 2.4). The rapid increase in development-partner-financed development expenditures, the majority of which is for goods and services, has in large

**Table 2.3. Total Real Health Expenditures: Recurrent and Development, 1996–2004**

*(year 1996 = 100) (unit: kina million)*

| | 1996 | 1997 | 1998 | 1999 | 2000 | 2001 | 2002 | 2003 | 2004 | % of change '97–'03 | % of change '97–'04 |
|---|---|---|---|---|---|---|---|---|---|---|---|
| NDOH | n/a | 43.9 | 43.9 | 44.1 | 42.3 | 44.1 | 28.4 | 32.3 | 46.9 | -26.4 | 6.9 |
| Hospitals | n/a | 49.2 | 43.4 | 42.7 | 46.4 | 49.9 | 45.3 | 41.0 | 42.5 | -16.6 | -13.6 |
| Church HS | n/a | 0.0 | 0.0 | 0.0 | 13.6 | 13.8 | 17.4 | 18.8 | 18.7 | | |
| Provinces | n/a | 66.6 | 66.7 | 57.4 | 54.4 | 54.6 | 35.4 | 35.5 | 36.5 | -18.4 | -45.1 |
| Total Recurrent | 153.1 | 159.6 | 154.0 | 144.1 | 156.7 | 162.4 | 126.5 | 127.6 | 144.6 | -20.1 | -9.4 |
| Development | 3.4 | 31.9 | 49.0 | 62.5 | 57.9 | 63.7 | 92.6 | 59.7 | 66.9 | 87.0 | 109.5 |
| Total Expenditure | 156.5 | 191.5 | 202.9 | 206.6 | 214.6 | 226.1 | 219.2 | 187.3 | 211.5 | -2.2 | 10.5 |
| Development % | 2.2 | 16.7 | 24.1 | 30.2 | 27.0 | 28.2 | 42.3 | 31.9 | 31.6 | | |
| Recurrent % | 97.8 | 83.3 | 75.9 | 69.8 | 73.0 | 71.8 | 57.7 | 68.1 | 68.4 | | |
| Total % | 100 | 100 | 100 | 100 | 100 | 100 | 100 | 100 | 100 | | |

*Source*: Ministry of Health Analysis of Health Expenditure (various years).

51

**Table 2.4. Total Real Recurrent Health Expenditures by Input Category, 1996–2004**
*(year 1996 = 100) (unit: kina million)*

|  | 1997 | 1998 | 1999 | 2000 | 2001 | 2002 | 2003 | 2004 | % of change '97–'04 |
|---|---|---|---|---|---|---|---|---|---|
| Emoluments | 87.8 | 94.3 | 90.4 | 102.6 | 107.8 | 97.2 | 93.1 | 96.9 | 10.3 |
| Goods & Services | 63.3 | 53.8 | 50.8 | 50.7 | 52.4 | 28.6 | 33.7 | 45.9 | −27.4 |
| Capital | 8.3 | 5.5 | 2.7 | 3.2 | 2.3 | 0.6 | 0.7 | 1.9 | −77.4 |
| Total | 159.4 | 153.5 | 143.9 | 156.4 | 162.5 | 126.5 | 127.5 | 144.7 | −20.0 |

*Source:* Ministry of Health Analysis of Health Expenditure (various years).

**Table 2.5. Real Health Development Expenditures by Input Category, 1997–2004**
*(year 1996 = 100) (unit: kina million)*

|  | 1996 | 1997 | 1998 | 1999 | 2000 | 2001 | 2002 | 2003 | 2004 |
|---|---|---|---|---|---|---|---|---|---|
| Emoluments | n/a | 0.1 | 0.1 | 0.1 | 0.6 | 0 | 0.1 | 0.01 | 0 |
| Goods & Services | n/a | 26.7 | 37.0 | 36.8 | 38.4 | 43.9 | 74.2 | 46.0 | 52.8 |
| Capital | n/a | 5.1 | 11.9 | 25.6 | 19.6 | 19.8 | 18.4 | 13.2 | 14.1 |
| Total | 3.4 | 31.9 | 49.0 | 62.5 | 58.6 | 63.7 | 92.8 | 59.3 | 66.9 |

*Source:* Ministry of Health Analysis of Health Expenditure (various years).

part compensated for the declining recurrent expenditures on these items (Table 2.5). Development expenditures are also particularly important for augmenting family services, disease control, and health promotion, all of which have strong public good characteristics and should be financed by the government (Table 2.6). This section considers these points in more detail.

Total health expenditure—both recurrent and development—increased from K 156.5 million in 1996 to K 475.2 million in 2004. In real terms, health expenditure increased from K 156.5 million in 1996 to K 226.1 million in 2001—an increase of almost 30 percent in five years (Table 2.3). Real expenditures subsequently fell significantly, so that in 2003 it was K 187.3 million—marginally below the 1997 level. Subsequently, in 2004 real health expenditures increased almost 13 percent to K 211.5 million because of significant increases in both domestically financed recurrent expenditure and in development expenditures, to be 10.5 percent above real expenditure in 1997. The share of total health expenditure accounted for by the recurrent budget decreased from 97.8 percent to 68.4 percent between 1996 and 2004, while the development budget's share (97 to 99 percent of which is financed by development partners) increased from 2.2 percent in 1996 to 31.6 percent in 2004.[10]

**Table 2.6. Health Recurrent and Development Expenditures by Health Program, 2004**
*(unit: kina million)*

| Program | Recurrent | | Development | | Total | |
|---|---|---|---|---|---|---|
| | Kina (M) | Share (%) | Kina (M) | Share (%) | Kina (M) | Share (%) |
| General Administration | 34 | 11 | 18 | 12 | 52 | 11 |
| Urban Facilities | 113 | 35 | 10 | 7 | 123 | 26 |
| Rural Facilities | 106 | 33 | 20 | 13 | 126 | 27 |
| Family Facilities | 2 | 1 | 28 | 18 | 30 | 6 |
| Disease Control | 2 | 0 | 21 | 14 | 23 | 5 |
| Environment & Water | 2 | 1 | 1 | 0 | 3 | 1 |
| Promotion & Education | 1 | 0 | 2 | 1 | 3 | 1 |
| Supplies & Equipment | 43 | 13 | 39 | 26 | 82 | 17 |
| HRD | 13 | 4 | 5 | 4 | 19 | 4 |
| Support Services | 8 | 2 | 7 | 5 | 15 | 3 |
| Total | 325 | 100 | 150 | 100 | 475 | 100 |

*Source:* Ministry of Health Analysis of health expenditures (various years).

Recurrent health expenditure decreased by 20.1 percent in real terms between 1997 and 2003, but a large increase in 2004 meant that the 2004 value was only 9.4 percent lower than 1997 (Table 2.3). NDOH expenditures fell more than a quarter in real terms between 1997 and 2003, largely in 2002 when AusAID financed a very large share of pharmaceuticals and medical supplies under the development budget. In 2004, the national department took over financing pharmaceuticals once again, and real recurrent expenditures exceeded the 1997 levels by 6.9 percent. However, given the rate of population increase of 2.7 percent per annum, real recurrent expenditures per capita on health have declined significantly over this period.

Trends in the input composition of recurrent (government-financed) health expenditure are a cause for concern (Table 2.4). For instance, expenditure on goods and services that are essential for a quality health care system, decreased by 46 percent in real terms between 1997 and 2003. However, in 2004 pharmaceutical purchases previously supported by development partners were added back into the budget.

As a result, real expenditure on goods and services increased 36 percent in 2004 compared to 2003. Notwithstanding this, expenditures were still over 27 percent lower in 2004 compared to 1997. Real expenditures on recurrent capital items—crucial for maintaining equipment and capital stocks—fell almost 77 percent, while real expenditures on staff salaries and benefits have increased by 10.3 percent in real terms from 1997 to 2004.

Health development expenditures increased almost 250 percent in real terms between 1996 and 2004. The largest single increase was in 1997, when real expenditures increased from K 3.4 million to K 31.9 million (1996 prices) as a consequence of a new program of AusAID-financed projects coming on-stream (Table 2.5). Development expenditures on goods and services increased by over 100 percent in real terms, while expenditures on capital items increased by 176 percent. Because the input items used in the recurrent budget do not report development expenditures by bilateral donors, it is difficult to say if development budget expenditures are directly substituting for recurrent budget expenditures. However, a substantial number of PNG staff are financed under the goods and services category, as are pharmaceuticals and medical supplies and operational expenses at both the national and provincial level. Consultant services are typically allocated to this category, but not exclusively.

Under the decentralizing NOL, the provinces were to have much more control over the resources allocated to the health sector. Despite poor documentation of the provinces' expenditures on health, these are recorded to have declined by 45 percent in real terms between 1997 and 2004 (Table 2.3). This decline is exacerbated by the national department taking over responsibility for the financing of church health services (CHS) in 2000; however, total provincial health expenditures, the backbone of the rural health system (the sum of church system and provincial expenditures), still declined 17 percent in real terms over this period. Real recurrent hospital expenditures have also declined 13.6 percent over this period.

Health expenditures by program—recurrent and development—are presented in Table 2.6. Some 11 percent of the budget is spent on general administration. Over one-third each of recurrent expenditures was spent on urban facilities (which includes hospitals) and on rural facilities, but only 13 percent were spent on supplies and equipment. In many countries, this would represent 25–40 percent of the budget. Interestingly, over one-quarter of development expenditures (i.e., development-partner-financed) is for supplies and equipment—in some part to augment the recurrent budget in this area. Similarly, development expenditures significantly augment total expenditures on family facilities (93 percent), disease control (91 percent), promotion and education (66 percent), Human resource development (HRD) (26 percent), and support services (47 percent). Total expenditures (by either government or development partners) on environment and water (given the mandate of rural water supplies and sanitation to the health sector) of only 1 percent of total expenditures seems very low, given its importance to some of the major underlying health problems in the country.

Thus, government health spending has actually decreased 9.4 percent between 1997 and 2004, and an increasing proportion is spent on wages and salaries and less is spent on goods and services. The government relies almost totally on donors to fund the development budget, which is increasingly used for items that are recurrent in nature. Overall, the financing, expenditure, accounting flows, and accountability for health have all become increasingly diverse, fragmented, and fragile, as all the institutional changes have taken place. Intergovernmental financial relations have become increasingly unsustainable, particularly as the national government has faced periodic fiscal problems that are getting deeper (see Chapter 5). The rapid growth of development partner financing of health projects during this period—largely off-budget and outside of government systems—has further complicated the picture.

The steady decline of the government's budget institutions and systems during the last 30 years of decentralization efforts has had a negative effect on the level of government resources available for the health sector and the efficiency with which those resources contribute to the delivery and quality of health care services. In an attempt to circumvent weakening central agencies and systems, PNG's principal development partner, Australia, shifted its bilateral assistance from budgetary support to project-based assistance with targeted objectives and activities managed by private contractors.

## Decentralization, Accountability, and Integrity of Government Systems

Flaws in decentralization are connected with the systemic problems of the health sector. First, decentralization has resulted in unclear allocation of responsibilities and inadequate implementation of key functions. The enactment in 1995 of the NOL did not adequately address implementation issues, leaving various levels of government to negotiate their responsibilities with respect to each other. This lack of guidance resulted in incomplete and open-ended arrangements with responsibilities poorly matched to authority and the lack of uniformity across government (also see the detailed discussion of decentralization in Chapter 5).

Second, the decentralization process has led to inadequate oversight by the NDOH. From 1997, provincial governments have had the capacity to set local priorities within the national policy framework developed by the NDOH; however, the ability of the NDOH to influence provincial operations and priorities has waned significantly given its limited oversight capacity and as additional functions having been devolved to the provinces.

Third, decentralization has been associated with a decline in the integrity of budget institutions and systems.[11] In the early 1990s, the introduction by line agencies and provinces of trust accounts outside of the budget framework to accommodate development partner financing underscored the lack of trust held by development partners in the government's core systems. Eventually, the government itself recognized trust accounts, providing for them under the Public Finances Management Act of 1995. Because of poor financial control mechanisms, some trust accounts later became a vehicle for the widespread dissimulation of government funds, for purposes unrelated to their initial intent, especially in the provinces.

Problems with the financing of key health system components have led the government to restructure administration and to ask for increased donor funding in the health sector:

(a) The government recentralized control over provincial hospitals in order to prevent them from collapsing, since many provinces had failed to provide them with adequate resources on the assumption that the NDOH would intervene. The result is a split public health system with a decentralized primary health system and a centralized hospital system whose respective functions contradict one another. This tension is well recognized and a range of options to improve hospital and health service coordination has been proposed. The Western Highlands Province is experimenting with the integration of all services in the province under the hospital administration.

(b) Before the NOL, the NDOH administered the grants given to church health services. After the NOL was passed, these grants were sent to the provinces as constitutional grants, and the provinces were supposed to pass them along to their respective CHS; however, many provinces neglected to do this, and the very existence of CHS was threatened. As an emergency measure, the government reassigned the administration of the wages grant to CHS to the NDOH in mid-1999. The churches' operational grant was recentralized to NDOH in 2003 for the same reasons. See Annex 2B for a comparison across various services of the arrangements for channeling funds to provinces.

The result of these problems with decentralization over time is that neither politicians nor public officials (particularly at the provincial and district levels) accepted responsibility for delivering primary health services and essential public health functions. The haphazard structure of government processes that resulted from the flawed process of decentralization facilitated a crisis in accountability, and, in the process, also impaired the integrity of government. This impairment is both a consequence and a cause of the decline in health services and outcomes. With a view to these problems the government, through the National Economic and Fiscal Commission (NEFC), has commissioned a review of the NOL, which is being supported by key development partners. This work may well be pivotal. The MTDS, as already noted, also emphasizes the importance of dealing with national-provincial relations—including fiscal relations—in order to redress the dysfunction of service delivery systems in the country.

## Recent Government Response

Government, at the sectoral, provincial, and central agency level, have increasingly recognized that (a) health outcomes have been at best stagnating over the past decade or more, (b) health system performance has been variable at best, and (c) aggregate health staff payroll numbers have increased relatively rapidly since 1998. At the same time, public expenditures on health have increased substantially since the mid-1990s—with the increases entirely financed by development partners.

There has also been an emerging consensus, reflected in official documents, including the 2005–2010 MTDS, the earlier National Health Plan (NHP) 2001–2010 and, more recently, the HMTEF and the (health) Strategic Plan (SP) 2006–2008 that (a) decentralization arrangements are a major cause of the current dysfunctionality of service delivery, (b) oversight and stewardship mechanisms have been inadequate, (c) provincial expenditures on health (including for church agencies) have been both unreliable and inadequate, (d) there has been a decline in the integrity of both budget and payroll institutions and systems, and (e) fragmentation of resourcing mechanisms are problematic (see Chapter 5).[12] On the other hand, there has been little consensus on how to deal with these problems and how to sequence reforms—most of which require a "whole-of-government" approach.

The National Health Administration Act (NHAA) of 1998 defines and describes the respective roles and responsibilities of public health administrative structures at all levels of government. It sought to reestablish vertical integration in the public health system through the creation of provincial health boards and district health-management committees. While some benefits accrued from the Act and there was improved clarity on some roles and responsibilities, the structures proposed under the NHAA performed poorly and the public health system remains fractured.

The NDOH also developed Minimum Health Standards (MHS) in 2002 to inform the planning and budget processes of all standard health facilities; i.e., to guide provincial authorities in preparing health budgets; however, the standards established under the MHS are too ambitious and expensive given current financing capacities and arrangements.

More recently, the NDOH, launched another initiative: an Independent Annual Health Sector Review, with the support of AusAID and, more latterly, with other major development partners, to deal with the problems confronting the health system. The first review (October 2002), pointed out that (a) the sector and organizations within the health sector are unstable—the patterns of inputs, processes, and outputs are inconsistent and performance seems not to be system-based, but rather person- (manager-) dependent; and (b) there was a need for strategic change—not just fine tuning. The report also argued the need to: (i) prioritize activities and tasks that have the highest health status improvement, (ii) increase supportive supervision between national and provincial levels and from provinces to districts and facilities, and (iii) use a prioritized strategic health plan as a basis to move toward development of a sectorwide approach to development partner assistance.

The NDOH responded to this report by producing the HMTEF as the basis for (a) a prioritized health strategic expenditure plan for the national level (the NDOH portion of the budget represents only one-third of the recurrent budget)[13]; and (b) a basis for working with development partners on a sectorwide approach (see next section). The HMTEF focused on priority areas of service delivery, mainly: immunization, malaria prevention, safe motherhood/family planning, and prevention of STIs; however, most of the funding for these programs remained at the provincial level and below.

As for additional support for health, at the instigation of NDOH at a provincial governors' conference, an agreement was reached that provinces would allocate at least 6 percent of provincial revenues to health. This was an initial pragmatic step to ensure provincial governments were making some contribution to health and as a crude mechanism to reduce the level of substitution of provincial government money for development partner resources. While this became a "condition" for some donor funding in provinces, it was not enforceable by NDOH and Treasury did not feel able to enforce it at the time of provincial budget approval or involve NDOH in the provincial health-budget review process until preparations for the current 2006 budget.

Two other important points related to the HMTEF: (a) the process could not address issues related to staffing (both cost and mix) because of the constraints of the budgeting process; and (b) budgets for hospitals were not addressed, although there is recognition that they are constrained and expenditure overruns became practice.

NDOH has started the process of establishing a SWAP capitalizing on the building blocks initiated under the ADB's HSIP; however, progress has been slower than planned. Progress includes establishing: an account for pooled donor funds, a biannual summit between the government and its development partners, a partnership agreement between some development partners and the government in support of the SWAP, and an independent monitoring and review group with development partner support.

While these are important steps, much has yet to be put in place, and what is in place remains very fragile. There is a need to link resource allocation to priorities—particularly at the provincial level—currently, no mechanism exists for provinces to be signaled for what medium-term domestic and/or donor financing may be available to them as a basis for program planning. Current health plans lack a central focus on outcomes (more than priority basic services) to be achieved or explore how best selected outcomes might be achieved. A medium-term expenditure plan costing activities to be done to achieve agreed outcomes or an associated implementation and financing plan have yet to be developed. Evidence of further improved coordination between the budget and the health SP/SWAP processes with the active involvement of central agencies, the NDOH, and provinces would help to improve the current situation.

The MTDS is a central tool for sectoral planning and provides important building blocks for addressing the unfinished agenda. The MTDS requires each sector to develop detailed and prioritized sectoral strategies within a rolling public expenditure framework consistent with the Treasury's MTEF. Importantly, the health SP and NDOH efforts to establish a SWAP provide a start to the development of a more comprehensive plan. Specific suggestions of how an appropriate health strategy might be developed are discussed below. Chapter 5 discusses in some detail a range of specific cross-cutting issues that need to be redressed and Chapter 6 sets out some suggested next steps on how a "whole of government" development partner approach to sector planning and program implementation might proceed.

It is also noteworthy that in preparing for the 2006 National Budget, the Treasury and Department of National Planning and Rural Development (DNPRD) made a concerted effort to ensure that the budget would reflect national development priorities—including primary health care—and to increase the efficiency of the government in delivering health care services. In doing so, attempts were made to ensure that sector priorities were consistent with the MTDS and the MTEF, both of which include fiscal stabilization initiatives to reduce the fiscal deficit over the medium term. This was achieved by setting budget ceilings within which agencies can produce budget requirements consistent with MTDS priorities and implementation plans. It is not clear yet whether the quality and level of expenditures on health at the provincial level improved as a consequence of this effort.

## Recent Donor Response

The response of PNG's development partners to the health problems was initially poorly coordinated, and following a diagnostic phase, is now seeking a new integrated approach.

AusAID and ADB have been, and will continue to be, the major partners providing assistance. Some important past AusAID-funded initiatives were under a project that concentrated on strengthening hospitals, the Women and Children's Health Project, the Pharmaceuticals Upgrade Project, and the Health Services Support Project. The ADB has collaborated with the government on four projects over the last decade—the Rural Health Services Project, the Health Sector Development Program, HSIP, and technical assistance and drugs for the pilot HIV care center.

Nevertheless, progress in the sector has been slow, and in response, the government and donors have carried out several reviews,[14] all of which have helped to identify flaws in the system and have made recommendations. The reviews have also examined issues surrounding the way in which development partners fund projects within PNG.

All of these reviews have recognized the realities facing the PNG government—the declining government recurrent health budget and the increasing development budget funded by foreign assistance at a time when health performance indicators have been stagnant at best. There was also serious concern about the transaction costs of so many stand-alone projects. As a result, donors, led by AusAID, are moving away from project-based funding and toward capacity building. The main element of AusAID's next program will be the Capacity Building Service Center, which will build capacity in the health sector at the individual, agency, and system level through technical assistance and other mechanisms. The intention of this aid is to complement the government's HSIP, a developing SWAP endorsed by the National Executive Council.[15] Built upon systems established in the Health Sector Development Program (funded by the ADB), the HSIP will succeed if the integrity of the systems are maintained and if the central agencies live up to their responsibilities.

Two administrative structures were required for the HSIP to function well enough to convince the development partners of the viability of the government's public sector reforms and the SWAP in the health sector. These structures are the Health Sector Improvement Program Management Unit (HSIPMU) and the HSIP Secretariat. The HSIPMU, which is now operational, is situated within NDOH as a project management unit to coordinate inputs to the program (instead of through mainline departmental units). The HSIP Secretariat, which was located in the Treasury and is now also within NDOH, has responsibility to oversee accounting arrangements—particularly at the provincial level; however, the HSIP Secretariat has recently had its functions contracted out to an accounting firm. This may be viewed alternatively as a move toward greater integrity in bookkeeping, or a loss of support from the central government—or both. It is reported that some additional support has been provided by the central government through a new HSIPMU and Secretariat structure.[16]

Any development that could enhance the HSIP Secretariat's capacity to perform will come at a time when the work to be performed by the Secretariat has increased. Funds from GFATM are supposed to be managed by the HSIPMU, with oversight and accounting provided by the HSIP Secretariat. Also, the NDOH plans to extend access to the HSIP Trust Account funds to other agencies, which is likely to stress the current capacity of these bodies in terms of volume of transactions, supervision, accounting, verification processes, and reporting.

## Where to from Here?

The key government support agencies in PNG—the NDOH, DNPRD, Treasury, Department of Personal Management (DPM), the Department of Finance, and provincial and district governments—have been unable to ensure that the health system functions at a level that yields continued improvements in health outcomes. Therefore, new arrangements are necessary. The NDOH is working within the framework established by the MTDS, but the pace of reform needs to quicken and will require stronger partnerships between the NDOH, the provinces, and the central agencies.

Given the limited capacity of the public sector to deliver services, the central aim of any new strategy should be to prioritize delivery of services, particularly at the provincial and district level, and, to reduce the government's direct responsibility for service delivery and put in place more viable options. In identifying these options, policy makers must take into account the need for accountability and transparency and the limited integrity of existing government systems, but despite these problems, they must ensure that high-quality health services are provided that will be effective in improving health outcomes, particularly among the poor.

Key service indicators show that the performance of the health sector is declining or, at best, stagnating. This is despite increases in public expenditures on the health sector of about 35 percent in real terms between 1996 and 2004. This decline in performance has been accompanied by overextended responsibilities of an inadequately trained, poorly supervised, and excessively decentralized workforce. This double problem constitutes a serious threat to improving general health outcomes, to organizing an adequate response to the HIV/AIDS epidemic, and to PNG's development aspirations.

There is also a need to improve health outcomes in order to achieve the MDGs for health in PNG; however, this will not be accomplished without also improving the performance and integrity of the health system. Within this context, the Joint Donors have proposed strategic directions to improve health sector performance as outlined below.

Each of the six elements of the proposed strategic directions are key for the health status improvements in PNG; however, none of them is sufficient in itself. The health outcomes prioritized by the government in the health SP can only improve if the government's expenditure priorities—at both the national and provincial level—are adjusted accordingly. This means that fiscal space must be created to allow the changes in expenditure priorities and requires that the funds thus allocated are used in an efficient and transparent manner. Therefore, it is critical that the government and its development partners achieve a consensus on the six elements. The proposed strategic directions could be implemented using a dual-track approach that will simultaneously:

(a) Address issues that can be dealt with within the national and provincial departments of health to improve the ability of public health systems to provide quality health services, and

(b) Help the central agencies (Treasury, Department of Finance [DOF], the DNPRD, the DPM, the Auditor General's Office [AGO], and the Department of Intergovernmental Relations) to strengthen their capacity to support the NDOH and the provinces.

The proposed strategic directions for the sector include the following six elements:

1. **Focus on high-priority health outcomes using the most cost-effective strategies, with particular emphasis on targeting the poor.** There is a consensus in PNG that the high-priority health outcomes are those set out in the MDGs and the MTDS—reducing infant, child, and maternal mortality and controlling the major infectious diseases (TB, HIV, malaria, and the vaccine-preventable diseases). Improvements in these health outcomes will be achieved by (a) improved implementation of cross-sectoral priorities (water supply and sanitation, transport and communications, and education, particularly of girls), (b) efforts to en-hance the demand for health services, and (c) improving the supply of health services to meet demand.

   Therefore, the health strategy should sharpen the focus on achiev-ing these. There are three ways to put this approach into practice. The government should:

   (a) **Identify technical options for achieving these outcomes and ways in which the options might be packaged for delivery.** These might include village-based treatment for pneumonia in children to reduce child mortality, programs to extended vaccination coverage or targeted health promotion, condom distribution, and sexually transmitted disease (STD) treatment for groups at high risk of HIV (Annex 2C and its Table 2C.1 set out one approach to the technical options for interventions to achieve the MDGs by level of service).

   (b) **Set priorities for public expenditure using public finance criteria** (equity and alleviation of market failures) within the context of the health SP (see Annex 2C).

(c) **Commit to monitoring and evaluating progress toward the agreed health targets, including the MDGs.** This will involve ensuring that the Health Information System (including disease surveillance) is revitalized and sustained and that appropriately structured population-based surveys (such as demographic household surveys) are conducted on a timely basis.

2. **Public and Private Sector Interfaces.** There is a need to explicitly consider the potential of the whole sector—both public and private—to contribute to health outcomes. To this end, it is important to identify ways to:

    (a) **Focus the public sector on those public goods that it can effectively deliver;**

    (b) **Promote appropriate involvement of the private sector in the delivery of private goods, such as ambulatory care;** and

    (c) **Strengthen collaboration between the public and private sectors in service delivery.** The inability to supervise and manage the aid post workforce and to retain functioning health workers in the public system (particularly in rural and remote areas) is perhaps best remedied by concentrating the public sector on achieving high-priority health outcomes and on providing core functions that require public funding and provision. The same process can be used to identify those services best provided by private practitioners at the village level.

3. **Prepare an expenditure and implementation plan** for the whole publicly funded part of the health sector (covering all government- and donor-financed programs) based on the priorities and activities identified in the preceding steps and consistent with available resources and with the requirements of the MTDS.

4. **Create fiscal space.** This can be achieved in three ways—achieving savings in the sector, making more efficient use of existing funds, and increasing sectoral allocations.

    (a) **Savings** can be sought in a number of different areas. The most important is cleaning up the payroll. Improved procurement procedures, particularly for drugs, housing rentals, office supplies, travel, civil works, and the hiring of casual staff would also achieve important savings, as would prevention of theft.

(b) **Increased efficiency in the use of existing departmental funds** can also create fiscal space. This approach is particularly emphasized in the health SP process and underpins the proposed reallocation of funds within the sector to reflect the new emphasis on priority health outcomes. This is at the core of the government's overall Public Sector Reform program and its efforts to implement the recommendations of the PERR. Critically, a capacity to reduce and redeploy staff is essential. Establishing mechanisms that enable Treasury and health agencies to share savings could assist in this process.

(c) **Increasing sectoral allocations is also important in creating fiscal space,** particularly once the reforms to improve efficiency have already been made. This could be very important in the emerging scenario of increased medium-term revenues from mining and oil/gas.

5. **Prepare a financing plan.** Having decided on what programs to emphasize and implement and having prepared an expenditure and implementation plan, the NDOH will have to secure the resources to make this happen. This will require ensuring that the national government, the provincial governments, and the major donors indicate what resources they can make available for the health sector over the next specified number of years. This will then allow the NDOH to make realistic plans. It has not been possible to do this before, as the resource flows have never been clear. This financing plan would be a necessary complement and elaboration of the current health SP. Present ongoing reforms to the budget process are a significant move in the right direction, but they also need to cover all public expenditures at both the national and provincial levels. The work of the NEFC is beginning to show the great differences between provinces in their financing capacity (discussed in Chapter 5). The Treasury and the DNPRD are working to ensure expenditure plans are consistent with the development objectives of the MTDS and in this process will need to look at capacities for NDOH and provinces to finance programs.

6. **Restore and guarantee the integrity of government processes.** The progressive erosion of the integrity of government processes, especially as decentralization was implemented, was a major factor influencing donors to move their funds off-budget in an effort to ensure adequate transparency. This move has itself created other problems in the sector.

It is important to bring these funds back on-budget in due course so that the NDOH can take into account the full level of resources available to the health sector from all sources. Restoring and maintaining the integrity of government processes is the first step in this effort. The government established the HSIP as a vehicle for restoring donors' confidence in the integrity of government budgeting and accountability arrangements, and to create a new paradigm. It is vital to maintain the independence of this agency; however, by virtue of this very independence, it is not at all clear who will back the secretariat in times of conflict and assault on the integrity of government processes. The main way to ensure its independence and also to provide it with effective backup is to appoint an independent third party to oversee the work of the HSIP Secretariat and to report directly to the NDOH and to donors. The key is for the government to ensure "budget integrity" (budgeting, accounting, monitoring, and transparency) both in transitional arrangements, such as the HSIP, and in the core budget processes.

## Annex 2A: Health Sector Workforce

As noted in the chapter text, it is important to note significant qualifications to the data—particularly for 2004, as it is likely that it is underreported. The sources for 1988 and 1998 data are special surveys conducted by the Ministry of Health (MOH), with 1998 data being used as a base for the NHP. All subsequent survey data is very unreliable with very significant and patchy gaps—hence it is not possible to present annual data. The 2004 data derives from the national payroll (Concept) managed by the DPM, and that payroll data also has important gaps and problems. Most importantly, it does not include those parts of the provincial payroll system not yet incorporated in the national payroll system. It is likely therefore that all categories of staff in 2004 are underreported in Table 2A.1. It is known that there will be significant underreporting of both the Community Health Worker category and the Public Service—Other Health category. In this regard, there is little evidence that the Public Service—Other Health category, which includes some administrative positions, support staff, and others, diminished during the period from 1998 to 2004.

### Conclusions

If these assessments, based on available payroll data and informed discussions in the field, are correct, total health sector employment in 2004

**Table 2A.1. Composition and Growth of the PNG Health Workforce, 1998–2004**

| Category | 1988 | 1998 | 2004 | Change 1998–2004 |
|---|---|---|---|---|
| Doctors & Dentists | 384 | 316 | 535 | 69.3% |
| Health Extension Officers | 357 | 233 | 575 | 146.8% |
| Nurses | 2,917 | 2,920 | 3,979 | 36.3% |
| Allied Health Workers | 283 | 372 | 439 | .18.0% |
| Med. Lab. Technical Staff | 159 | 150 | 254 | 69.3% |
| Community Health Workers | 4,982 | 3,926 | 5,358 | 36.5% |
| Public Service—Health | n/a | 2,874 | 1,215 | −57.2% |
| Total | 9,082 | 10,791 | 12,355 | 14.5% |

*Sources:*
1988: Papua New Guinea—Management, Manpower, Money: A Select Review of Health and Population in Papua New Guinea; World Bank Report No. 8959-PNG, 1991.
1998: Papua New Guinea—National Health Plan 2001–2010; National Health Profile, Vol. III, Part One, 2001.
2004: DPM, Concept Payroll System, December 16, 2004.
*Notes:*
1988, 1998, and 2004: figures include Public Health Services, CHS, and expats.
1988: Allied Health Workers include health inspectors, dental therapists & technicians, dispensers, and radiographers.
1988: Medical Lab. Technical Staff include medical lab. assistants & technicians and medical technologists.
1988: CHWs comprise nurse aides, hospital orderlies, and aid post orderlies.
1988: Public Service—Health normally includes some administrative positions, support staff, and others.
1998: Allied Health Workers include dental technicians and radiologist assistants.
1998: Medical Lab. Technical Staff include environmental health officers and malaria officers.
2004: Public Service—Health (support staff, some admin. staff, and others) are understated, especially in the provinces. Aid post staff are included in 1988 (aid post orderlies—2,821) under CHW; in 1998, there were 1,816 employed as casuals and are not included here. In 2004 the number is not known—see text.

may have been as high as 15,000. This would imply a growth of the total workforce over the period 1998–2004 of 19 percent[17]—an extremely high growth rate, much of which will have occurred in government-managed provincial health services.

Some cadres have increased significantly faster than the average over the period 1998–2004. Doctors and dentists have increased 66 percent, health extension officers 150 percent, and technical and medical laboratory staff 70 percent. Most significantly, the two largest cadres, nurses and CHWs, which account for 75 percent of the non-casual health workforce, also increased by more than 36 percent over this period.

A key question, as discussed, is: How reliable is the 2004 payroll data for establishing the actual number of staff working in health as distinct from the number on the payrolls? Drawing on information contained in two health human resource studies[18] and checking graduate output numbers since 1998[19] for medical practitioners, nurses, and CHWs by the various health training schools/programs provides the following significant insights:

(a) *Medical Practitioners*. Over the period 1998–2004, about 300 medical graduates were produced at about 50 per year to add to the 1998 workforce of 316. Assuming an attrition rate of 5 percent per annum, a total of 90 (about 15 per year) will have ceased working in the public sector. These numbers suggest that the medical officer workforce on the payroll for 2004 is of the correct magnitude—524 (i.e., 316 – 90 + 300 = 526).

(b) *Nurses*. Over the period 1998–2004, about 800 graduates were produced by all nursing schools at an average of 135 graduates per year to add to the 1998 workforce of 2,920. Assuming a conservative attrition rate of 5 percent per annum,[20] a total of about 875 workers will have left the workforce over this period at an average of about 146 workers per year. These numbers suggest the nurse workforce in 2004 was less than the 1998 workforce at about 2,846 (i.e. 2,920 + 800 – 875).[21] However, the number of nurses employed in 2004— 3,980—is some 1,060 more than employed in 1998.

*Community Health Workers*. Over the period 1998–2004, about 1,300 CHWs were produced by all of the CHW schools in the country at an average of 220 graduates per year to add to the 1998 workforce of 3,926. Assuming a conservative attrition rate of 5 percent,[22] a total of 1,600 workers will have left the service over this period at an average of about 265 per year. These numbers suggest that the total number of CHWs on the payroll in 2004 should be less than the 1998 workforce at about 3,625 (i.e., 3,926 + 1,300 – 1,600).[23] However, the CHWs employed in 2004 (5,358) is some 1,733 more than were employed in 1998. It may be that a significant number of CHWs have been made public servants over this period and that the number of casuals has fallen. The current systems have no way of documenting this.

While there does not appear to be a discrepancy in the number of doctors on the payroll compared to the new supply and likely attrition rates over the past six years, this is not true for the two cadres that constitute 75 percent of the health workforce: nurses and CHWs. The above analysis indicates as many as 1,000 nurses and up to 1,700 CHWs currently on the payroll cannot be accounted for. Further, as discussed, it is believed that as many as an additional 1,000 additional CHWs may remain on the provincial payroll system. Without clear data on the number of CHWs that moved from the casual workforce to Concept over this period, it is hard to determine what the true picture is.

This analysis has still to be verified; but it suggests that there are potential savings of upwards of K 28.6 million, comprising K 15 million of nurses salaries (1,000 * K 15,000 average salary and allowance per year) and K 13.6 million for CHWs (1,700 * K 8,000 average salary and allowances per year). This takes no account of the unknown number of CHWs who may have been moved from the casual payroll to Concept over this period, or for the additional 1,000 (or more) workers who may exist on the provincial payroll.

The government is to be commended for working to improve the payroll so it can be used as a source of management information; however, it is critical that every effort is made to unify the payroll systems and reconcile all on the payroll to specific positions. It is entirely possible—even probable—that many staff remain on both payrolls receiving duplicate salaries. While the Concept payroll system has improved transparency and the potential to contribute to improved personnel management, it cannot of itself redress all the anomalies that have evolved over time in the government payroll systems prior to the recent introduction of Concept. Cases in point include staff who have abandoned their post, deceased staff who go unreported, staff who change agencies and who are not removed from the former while being added to the latter.

Furthermore, it is also recognized within MOH and within the development partner community that there is pressure on provincial governments to show a spending of at least 6 percent of their own revenues on health as a basis for triggering donor funding through the HSIP trust account. This is known to encourage provincial government budgeting of staff on the provincial health payroll—whether or not they are working on health.

A physical census would permit verification of legitimate health staff and allow for eliminating duplicate records and staff who do not exist. The census would also be an opportunity to institute identification cards.

The breakdown of management reporting systems since the establishment of hospitals as autonomous institutions under the management of a board means that there is only fragmentary data available on hospital staffing patterns; however, as discussed above, hospital wards and bed numbers have been in decline and bed occupancy rates have stagnated and in some cases fallen. This is suggestive of reduced productivity of staff.

**Annex 2B. Comparison of Health-Related Revenue Streams to Provinces (Mission Documentation)**

| Characteristics | Govt. Primary Health Services | Church Health Services | Provincial Hospitals | Health Sector Improvement Program (HSIP) | Health Services Support Project (HSSP) | National HIV/AIDS Support Project (NHASP) |
|---|---|---|---|---|---|---|
| Funding—Primary | Nat'l—Grants | Nat'l—through NDOH | Nat'l—through NDOH | ADB, AusAID, New Zealand Agency for International Development—Development of Partners (DP) | AusAID | AusAID |
| Funding—Secondary | Prov. revenues | User fees | User fees | | | |
| Budget Approval | Provincial Executive Council/NDOH/ National Department of Health DOF/ Department of Finance/Treasury | Church Medical Council/ NDOH/ DOF/T | Hosp. Board/ NDOH/ DOF/T | DPs/Provincial Health Advisor (PHA)/NDOH/ DOP & RD National Planning and Rural Development now called Department of National Planning and Monitoring /DOF/T | AusAID/HSSP NDOH consultation | AusAID/AMC NDOH consultation |
| Budget Format | Std.10 programs 9–19 provinces | CMC format | Gov't chart of accounts (item categories) | Std. 10 programs | Internal to HSSP/AusAID | Internal to AMCAustralian Managing Contractor/ AusAID |

| | | | | | | |
|---|---|---|---|---|---|---|
| Legal Framework | Public Finances Management Act | | Public Finances Management Act | Public Finances Management Act, bilateral Memorandum of Agreement | Internal to HSSP/AusAID | Internal to AMC/AusAID |
| Accounting Responsibility | Prov. Treasuries | NDOH > transfers CMC/Churches | NDOH > transfers Prov. hospitals | Prov. health offices Prov. treasuries HSIP Secretariat | HSSP | AMC |
| Supervision/Quality Control | No formal mechanism | No formal mechanism | Hospital boards No formal mechanism from NDOH | Supervision by HSIP Secretariat in place since 1998 | Internal to HSSP/AusAID | Internal to AMC/AusAID |
| Financial Reporting | Nat'l grants—annual (Qtr. reviews not done) Prov. rev.—none | Nat'l funding—none User fees—none | Nat'l funding—annual, some hospitals only User fees—none | Monthly to gov't and DPs | Internal to HSSP/AusAID | Internal to AMC/AusAID |
| Expenditure Format | Mixed/std.10 programs Some provinces | CMC format | Gov't chart of accounts (item categories) | Std. 10 programs | AusAID item categories | AusAID item categories |
| Audits | Nat'l grants—none Prov. rev.—none | No formal arrangement Nat'l funding—none User fees—none | AGO responsible; in recent years; Nat'l funding—none User fees—none | AGO responsible; Internal audits (NDOH) and external audits (private sector) | Internal to HSSP/AusAID | Internal to AMC/AusAID |
| Unused Funds beyond end of fiscal year | Remain with provinces; Not accounted for | Remain with CMC; Not accounted for | Remain with hospitals; Partial accounting | Remain with HSIP; Balance rolled-over and accounted for | Not applicable | Not applicable |

## Annex 2C: Technical Options and Delivering Health Priorities

The NHP commits NDOH to the minimum health standards, which are consistent with the MTDS 2005–2010 commitment to the MDGs and primary health care; however, the minimum health standards are unlikely to be feasible given the current decay of the aid posts and health centers. They also do not take into account the MTDS priority for prevention of HIV/AIDS. The current Strategic Plan for the Health Sector 2006–2008 has focused targets that go some way toward recognizing the current problems with implementation, but contains no implementation strategy yet.

In order to achieve the MDGs as set out in the MTDS, there is a need to develop a strategy that takes into account the current limited implementation capacity in the government sector. To do this, we outline a method that identifies priorities and alternative mechanisms for care delivery. The method has four steps: a) review the technical options that will contribute to achieving the MDGs; b) package these options; c) identify how the private sector could deliver some of these packages, and d) use public financing criteria to identify where public subsidies are appropriate. The aim is to focus both priorities and to reduce the volume of direct government service provision and management responsibilities to a private sector (embedded already in indigenous health systems) and the NGO/church sector so that the efficiency and effectiveness of the remaining government system can be improved.

**Reviewing technical options:** Table 2C.1 (developed by mission) lists, by MDG, where the health sector can intervene and the technical options that are known to be effective. For example, most maternal deaths are caused by hemorrhage, sepsis, eclampsia, and labor complications; each of these problems has a series of technical options to prevent or treat them.

**Packages:** Each technical option is mapped onto a package. Thus, the technical option for preventing hemorrhage at delivery with oxytocic drugs fits into a reproductive health primary health care package, while removing a retained placenta requires an emergency obstetric services package. Each package is then listed in Table 2C.2. Eight packages are identified in the health sector, plus one package for social marketing delivery (condoms and impregnated mosquito nets), and one package to be tackled by other sectors (water supply and sanitation; housing construction, and household smoke exposure).

**Options for private sector delivery:** In Table 2C.2, current provision of the package is assessed and options to enhance provision are proposed.

**Table 2C.1. MDGs—Technical Options for Interventions by Level of Service**

| MDG | Problem | How to intervene | Technical options | Lowest level to implement package |
|---|---|---|---|---|
| Maternal mortality | Hemorrhage | Prevent at delivery | Drugs at delivery | RH-PHC |
| | | Prevent severe antenatal | Iron and folic supplements | RH-PHC |
| | | Anemia | Detection and treatment | RH-PHC |
| | | | Drugs to prevent | RH-PHC |
| | | | Impregnated nets | DC-Soc market |
| | | Reduce risk with high parity | Tubal ligation | RH-Hospital |
| | | | Access to temporary methods | RH-PHC |
| | | | | RH-Soc market |
| | | Treat postpartum hemorrhage | Drugs and resuscitation | RH-PHC |
| | | | | RH-EOC |
| | | Manage retained placenta | General anaesthetic & remove | RH-EOC |
| | Sepsis | Ensure clean delivery | Kits for attendants | RH-PHC |
| | | | Supervised births | RH-PHC |
| | | Treat | Antibiotics | RH-PHC |
| | Eclampsia | Treat | Magnesium sulphate | RH-EOC |
| | | Treat pre-eclampsia | Antenatal care | RH-PHC |
| | Obstructed lab | Manage promptly | Vacuum extraction | RH-EOC |
| | | | Cesarean section | RH-CEOC |
| | | Anticipate | Antenatal care | RH-PHC |
| | | Reduce risk | Contraception for teenagers | RH-PHC |
| | Labor compl. | Treat | Anaesthetic, blood, theatre | RH-CEOC |

*(continued)*

**Table 2C.1. MDGs—Technical Options for Interventions by Level of Service** (continued)

| MDG | Problem | How to intervene | Technical options | Lowest level to implement package |
|---|---|---|---|---|
| Neonatal mortality | Sepsis | Prevent (clean delivery) | Supervised delivery | RH–PHC |
| | | | Supervised birth attendants | RH–PHC |
| | Asphyxia | Resuscitate at birth | Supervised delivery | RH–EOC |
| | HIV | Prevent congenital infection | Antiretrovirals (ARVs) to prevent transmission | RH–CEOC |
| 1 month –5 yr mortality | Pneumonia | Treat early | Antibiotics | CH–PHC |
| | | Prevent measles | Vaccination | CH–PHC |
| | Diarrhea | Reduce smoke exposure | House construction; stoves | DC–public health |
| | | Improved water and sanitation | Wells, water supply, latrines | DC–Public health |
| | | Improved hygiene at home | Health education | DC–Public health |
| | | Oral rehydration solution | Dispense sachets | CH–PHC |
| | Malaria | Reduce transmission | Impregnated mosquito nets | DC–Soc market |
| | | Treat | Promptly treat with Artemesinine Combined Theorpy (short course) | CH–PHC |
| | Meningitis | Treat | Promptly treat with antibiotics | CH–PHC |
| | | | | CH–IPC |
| Infectious diseases | Malaria | Vector control | Impregnated nets | DC–Social marketing |
| | | Treatment | Effective drugs | CC–PHC |
| | | | Treat severe disease | CC–IPC |
| | | | | AH–IPC |
| | Tuberculosis | Prevent | BCG vaccine | CH–PHC |
| | | | Contact tracing | CH–PHC |
| | | | | AH–PHC |
| | | Treat | Short course | CH–PHC |
| | | | | AH–PHC |

| HIV/AIDS | Change behavior in at-risk groups | Safe sex with condoms + peer education | HIV—prevention |
| | | Supply of condoms at high-risk sites (bars, hotels, clubs) | HIV—prevention |
| | Reduce risk of infection | Prompt treatment of STDs + condom promotion | HIV—prevention |
| | | Counseling with VT + condom promotion | HIV—clinical |
| | Awareness raising | Mass media condom promotion & partner reduction | HIV—prevention |
| | Reduce morbidity and delay death | Treat common infections | AH-PHC |
| | | TB outpatient treatment | AH-PHC |
| | | ARV drugs for life | HIV—clinical |

**Table 2C.2. Options for Private Involvement and Use of Government Subsidies in the Delivery of the Basic Package**

| Service packages | Technical options in the package | Current provision | Options for enhanced provision | Expected impact | Externalities? | Pro-poor? | Options for public sector contribution |
|---|---|---|---|---|---|---|---|
| 1. Primary reproductive health care (RH-PHC) | Contraception | Declining, poor coverage | Private midwife & CHW | Improved rural coverage | Y | Y | Subsidize supplies |
| | Sterilization | Limited | Contract private provision | Increased availability | Y | N | Contract |
| | ANC | <45% | Private midwife & CHW | Improved rural coverage | N | Y | Subsidize supplies |
| | Supervised delivery | <45% coverage | Private midwife & CHW | Improved rural coverage | N | Y | Subsidize supplies |
| | Support to Traditional Birth Attendants | Only special projects | Midwife contracted to support TBAs | Improved rural coverage | N | Y | Provide kits |
| 2. Emergency obstetric services (RH-EOC) | Obstetric emergencies: vacuum, retained placenta; transfuse | Limited to hospitals and major health centers | Strengthen health centers; increase units functioning at this level | Improved coverage in rural areas | N | Y | (remains same) |
| 3. Advanced emergency obstetric services (RH-CEOC) | Emergency obstetric, inc. Cesarean section and blood | Limited to hospitals | Strengthen hospitals | Improved quality and availability | N | Y | (remains same) |
| | VCT; ARVs during labor | Nonexistent | Strengthen health centers | Fewer child deaths from HIV | N | N | (remains same) |

| Service | Intervention | Current status | Provider | Outcome | Y/N | Stance | Government role |
|---|---|---|---|---|---|---|---|
| 4. Primary child health care (CH-PHC) | Treat pneumonia, diarrhea, malaria | Low (aid posts closed) | Private CHW | Increased coverage & quality | N | | Subsidize drugs |
| | Vaccination | <32% | Private CHW | Increased coverage and quality | Y | | Provide vaccines |
| | Treat tuberculosis | <33% | Private CHW | Increase coverage | Y | | Diagnosis, drugs, monitor (remains same) |
| 5. Child inpatient care (CH-IPC) | Severe acute infections | Patchy | Improve health-centers quality | Increased quality and impact | N | | Contract to NGO |
| 6. HIV prevention program (HIV-public health) | Safe sex in high-risk groups with condoms + peer education | Not established | Specialist NGOs condom use | Increased | Y | | Contract to NGO |
| | Supply condoms at high-risk sites (bars, hotels, clubs) | Not established | Specialist NGOs | Increased condom use | Y | | Contract to NGO |
| | Mass media condom promotion & partner reduction | Commenced | Specialist NGOs | Increased condom awareness | Y | | Contract to NGO |
| | Treat STDs | Patchy | Private CHW, midwife | Increased coverage | Y | Neutral | Drugs |

*(continued)*

**Table 2C.2. Options for Private Involvement and Use of Government Subsidies in the Delivery of the Basic Package** (continued)

| Service packages | Technical options in the package | Current provision | Options for enhanced provision | Expected impact | Externalities? | Pro-poor? | Options for public sector contribution |
|---|---|---|---|---|---|---|---|
| 7. Adult primary care | Treat TB | Low (aid posts closed) | Private CHW (HCs for diagnosis) | Increased completion rates | Y | Y | Diagnosis, drugs, monitoring |
| | Treat TB in HIV+ | Low (aid posts closed) | Private CHW | Increased completion | Y | Y | Diagnosis, drugs, monitoring |
| | Treat intercurrent infections in HIV+ve | Low (aid posts closed) | Private CHW | Alleviate morbidity | Y | Y | Drugs |
| | Treat malaria | Low (aid posts closed) | Private CHW (strengthen HCs for severe) | Increase coverage; reduce severe disease | Y* | Y | Drugs |
| 8. Clinical HIV service | Voluntary counseling and testing | Limited | Increase church capacity | Increase coverage | Y | N | Kits |
| | ARV delivery | None | Hospitals and special mission facilities | None | N | N | International subsidies |
| 9. Social marketing | Condoms; impregnated nets | Limited | Involve private contractors | Increased coverage | Y | Y | Contracts |
| 10. Disease control—public health | Wells, water supply, latrines; smoke exposure | Unclear | Advocate action with relevant sector | Not known | Y | Y | Through sector |

*Assuming treatment with artemisinin derivatives, which have gametocydal effect.

**Table 2C.3. Summary of Options for Private Sector Involvement and Use of Government Subsidies in Delivering the Basic Package**

| Service packages | Strategy | Externalities? | Pro-poor? | Options for public sector contribution |
|---|---|---|---|---|
| 1. Primary reproductive health care | Develop private practitioners | Some | Y | Subsidize supplies |
| 2. Emergency obstetric services | Strengthen health centers | None | Y | Provide |
| 3. Advanced emergency obstetric services | Strengthen hospitals | None | Neutral | Provide |
| 4. Primary child health care | Develop private practitioners | Some | Y | Subsidize supplies |
| 5. Child inpatient care | Strengthen health centers | None | Y | Provide |
| 6. HIV prevention program | Contract specialist NGOs | High | Y | Fund through contracts |
| 7. Adult primary care | Develop private practitioners | None | Neutral | Supplies |
| 8. HIV treatment at hospitals | Government hospitals, mission facilities, external funding | None | N | Should be determined by financial planning |
| 9. Social marketing | Mosquito nets and condoms | High | Y | Contracts |
| 10. Disease control—public health | NDOH advocacy with relevant gov. sector or other agency | High | Y | Through relevant sector |

These changes identify options for private sector involvement. The anticipated impact of the enhanced provision is outlined.

**Apply public financing criteria to identify subsidies:** In Table 2C.2 where increased private provision is envisaged, the package is assessed in relation to externalities or whether the change is pro-poor (in that services are extended to the rural areas) to determine whether public sector subsidies should be given. Table 2C.3 summarizes Table 2C.2. The NDOH might use this approach in developing the technical options needed to achieve the priority outcomes set by the MDGs, and then learn how to improve delivery by developing the private sector, determining appropriate subsidies for those with important externalities, and setting priorities for strengthening the remaining government health system.

## Notes

1. See Chapter 3 for a fuller discussion of the HIV/AIDS epidemic.

2. DPT 3 and measles vaccination rates are the best indicators of the overall performance of the vaccination program.

3. The health workforce data for 2004 were derived from special runs of the major payroll systems—national and provincial—operating within the government by Ministry of Finance staff for the report.

4. The attrition rates used by the mission are a conservative 5 percent per annum compared to the 7.7 percent per annum used in the two major human resource reports prepared by the Ministry of Health—the Report on the Future of Nurse and Community Health Worker Education (Ministry of Health Task Force Report 2001) and Papua New Guinea Human Resource Development Study: Realigning and Enriching the Skills of a Workforce that Cannot Be Enlarged (Aitken et al. 2002). The mission has used the output estimates used in these reports. There is some evidence, however, that this overstates outputs, given the disruptions to training programs during this period. Furthermore, some graduates will have chosen other careers.

5. The mission could only assemble data for these three cadres, but they cover the bulk of the workforce.

6. The average salary and allowances for nurses is K 15,000, and K 8,00 for CHWs. Treasury officials, after reviewing these findings, agreed that the orders of magnitude were in fact probable.

7. Data on Church Health System growth derived from church health budgets.

8. Aggregate data is available for 1996 and is used where relevant, but because of the transition to new decentralization arrangements, detailed breakdowns of expenditure for 1996 and earlier years is not available.

9. Over the period 2000–2004, Provincial Health Services comprise both Church Health Services and Provinces, as presented in Table 3. i

10. Actual development partner financing for 1996 was probably higher than that recorded in the budget because of underreporting; however, it is known 1997 levels of development partner funding were much higher than in 1996.

11. The documentation of the collapse of the integrity of budget institutions and systems is a central theme of the Public Expenditure Review and Rationalization Study (World Bank 2003).

12. The PERR undertaken jointly by government and the Joint Donors and the subsequent plan of action being undertaken by government with support of many development partners recognizes that significant governance challenges have undermined institutions and systems. Redressing these challenges, it is recognized, will require (i) strong leadership and political support, (ii) reduced institutional isolation and improved interagency and intergovernmental

relations, (iii) improved transparency in financial reporting and audit processes, and (iv) improved accountability and personnel management.

13. Hospitals and provincial health programs (primary health care delivery) each account for approximately one-third of the recurrent budget.

14. The 2001 Functional Expenditure Review of Health Services, the 2002 Annual Sector Review prepared by the Independent Review Team, and the 2003 PERR.

15. The National Executive Council is the executive body of government, chaired by the prime minister.

16. According to the Independent Monitoring and Review Group Report, November 2005. (Ministry of Health 2005).

17. This was calculated using the base in 1998 of 3,926 CHWs plus those employed as casuals in 1998 (see note for 2004 data to Table 1) of 1,816 (total 5,742) and data for 2004 of 5,358, plus the 1,000 CHWs estimated to be on casual payrolls in the provinces. It also assumed that there were at least an additional 1,650 casuals elsewhere in the system under the "Public Service-Other Health" category.

18. The Report on the Future of Nurse and Community Health Worker Education (Ministry of Health Task Force Report 2001) and Papua New Guinea Human Resource Development Study: Realigning and Enriching Skills of a Workforce that Cannot Be Enlarged (Aitken et al. 2002).

19. There is some evidence that this in fact overstates outputs, given the disruptions to training programs over this period. Furthermore, some graduates will have chosen other careers.

20. Previous MOH human resource strategy documents have used a much higher attrition rate of 6.7 percent per year.

21. During this period, there was no pool of unemployed nurses that could have been a major source of additional supply.

22. Previous MOH human resource studies have used a much higher attrition rate of 6.7 percent per year.

23. During this period, it is possible that there was some reemployment from a pool of unemployed CHWs, but the pool is thought to have been relatively small. Furthermore, many had been retrenched and should not have been eligible for reemployment.

# CHAPTER 3

# Control of HIV/AIDS in Papua New Guinea: A Situation Assessment and Proposed Strategic Directions

*"My husband looks after the children when I go to work. I help my family, brothers, and parents with the money I earn. My parents pretend that they don't know what I do. . . . Sometimes I think I should not have married at all and when I look at my children, I forget this way of thinking and just get on with it. I really don't have any other way of making money except to sell myself.*
*I want to ask one thing: Can you ask the bar and hotel management to help you sell condoms or give them out for free?" Port Moresby sex worker, 1997*

*". . . communities, like individuals, cannot respond to the challenges of HIV unless they can express the basic right to be involved in decisions that affect them."*

—*Jonathan Mann*

## The Current Status of the HIV/AIDS Epidemic in PNG

HIV was first reported in Papua New Guinea (PNG) in 1987. From the mid-1990s onwards, the epidemic started to grow quickly. Although the epidemic at first seems to have been confined to Port Moresby, it soon spread to other urban areas such as Lae, a major port and the origin of the Highlands Highway that terminates at the Porgera gold mine. By the mid-1990s, cases were being reported in nearly every province, and transmission rates quickly increased. The number of new HIV infections detected in 2004 was 2,497, compared with 2,300 in 2003 and 1,718 in 2002 (NACS 2005).

At the end of 2004, a National Consensus Workshop was held to review available data on HIV/AIDS in PNG (NAC and NDOH 2005). The workshop came up with consensus estimates that the number of people ages 15 to 49 years old with HIV in 2004 ranged from 24,528 to 68,966 (depending on which scenario was used). The estimated prevalence ranged from 0.9 percent to 2.5 percent of the 15-to-49 age population, with a median estimate of 1.7 percent. If people below and above that age range are included, then the medium estimate of infected people rises to 80,000, with a prevalence of about 1.5 percent of the total population (NAC and NDOH 2005).

These estimates indicate very clearly that a general HIV epidemic is under way in PNG. The virus is firmly established in the general population, with prevalence rates in the population ages 15 to 49 years old of between 3 and 4 percent in Port Moresby, well over 2 percent in other urban areas, and over 1 percent in rural areas. The country's sentinel surveillance has recently been expanded to include 18 sites in 12 provinces, including three in rural district-level centers, but results are available from only a few sites at this time (see Table 3.1). Serology for syphilis is also performed in these sites, but these data have not yet been published. As of midyear 2005, the antenatal clinic (ANC) at Port Moresby General Hospital (PMGH) was reporting a HIV prevalence rate of 1.5 percent. Most disturbing is the fact that teenage mothers (ages 15 to 19 years old) at the PMGH ANC had an HIV prevalence of 10 percent in 2003 and 8 percent in 2004.[1]

**Table 3.1. HIV Prevalence at Sentinel Surveillance Sites in PNG**
(percent)

| Year | 2001 | 2002 | 2003 | 2004 |
|---|---|---|---|---|
| PMGH Antenatal | 0.5 | 1.0 | 1.4 | 1.2 |
| PMGH STI | 9.0 | 9.6 | 10.8 | 19.9 |
| PMGH TB | | | 19.0 | |
| Mt Hagen STI | | | 6.3 | |
| Goroka STI | <1 | 1.6 | 4.0 | |
| Goroka Antenatal | | 0.9 | 2.0 | |
| Goroka TB | | | 10.0 | |
| Lae Antenatal | | | 2.5 | |
| Lae TB | | | 15.0 | |
| Daru Antenatal | | | 0.6 | |

Source: National AIDS Council Secretariat and Department of Health HIV/AIDS Quarterly Report, 9/04.

However, these differential prevalence rates must be seen in the context of a population that is still 85 percent rural. As a result, it is estimated that about 66 percent of all infections are in the rural population (despite their lower prevalence rates), whereas 18 percent are in Port Moresby and the remaining 15 percent are in the other urban areas. In contrast to the urban-rural distribution of cases that is apparent from our indirect estimates, around 60 percent of known cases have been detected in Port Moresby, where the most frequent testing has been done at PMGH, as HIV testing in rural areas is still very limited. However, other information on HIV prevalence, which has so far not been included in the sentinel surveillance system, also indicates that a serious epidemic is under way. Recent data from Western Highlands and East New Britain illustrate this:

(a) In the Western Highlands Province, a combined total of more than 500 patients tested positive for HIV in the 12 months between June 2003 and June 2004 at Mount Hagen and Kudjip hospitals.
(b) A recent study of about 165 sexually transmitted infection (STI) patients at Mt. Hagen's Tiniga Clinic found 9 percent of them also had HIV (Kovacs 2005).
(c) In East New Britain Province, 1 percent and 3 percent of blood donors at Vunapope Catholic Hospital and Nonga Base Hospital respectively were found to be HIV positive.[2]

As problems in sampling and testing still exist at some sentinel sites, perhaps the most reliable continuously collected data representative of the general population are those from the transfusion blood banks. Figure 3.1 presents the screening results found at blood banks outside of Port Moresby. In Madang, officers-in-charge stated that a high proportion of donors came from rural areas.

This information, now available from a number of provinces, has been taken into account in the calculations made by the National Consensus Workshop, and is compelling evidence that a major epidemic is under way in PNG, with a high proportion of cases in rural areas.

Despite the limitations of current surveillance arrangements, the broad characteristics of the epidemic can now be identified. It is also possible to identify other cultural, economic, and epidemiological factors that have contributed to the evolution of the epidemic in PNG.

The HIV epidemic in PNG is due primarily to heterosexual transmission, amounting to about 90 percent of all detected cases.[3] The remainder

**Figure 3.1. HIV Prevalence at Blood Banks Throughout PNG**
*(percent)*

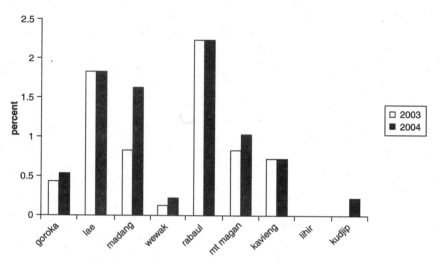

*Source:* Data collected from blood banks by World Bank mission.

is due to men having sex with men (MSM) and vertical transmission between mother and child. This pattern of transmission is facilitated by cultural patterns of sexuality and by the high prevalence of STIs. Another disturbing development is the rapidly increasing numbers of reported cases among children and adolescents. Figures 3.2 and 3.3 illustrate the increasing proportions of cases in the 2-to-9 age group and the 15-to-19 age group between September 2001 and September 2004. In each case, females are overtaking males. While better data and more research is required to explain what caused these infections, the increasing availability of data on child sexual abuse suggests that coercive sex may be responsible for at least some of these cases. The next section goes into the details of these sets of factors that facilitate transmission in PNG.

## HIV/AIDS, Sex, and Culture

The breakdown of traditional methods of social control within both villages and urban areas in PNG, combined with an emergent cash economy, urbanization, and greater population mobility, has resulted in very significant changes in sexual behavior. Among young boys and girls, first sexual intercourse occurs at 15 or 16 years of age in both urban and rural

**Figure 3.2. Increasing Numbers of HIV Cases in 2- to 9-Year Age Group, PNG**

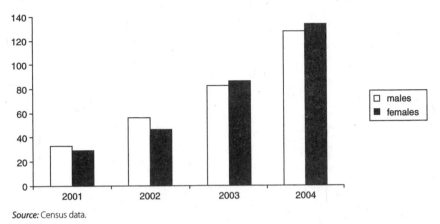

*Source:* Census data.

**Figure 3.3. Increasing Numbers of HIV Cases in 15- to 19-Year Age Group, PNG**

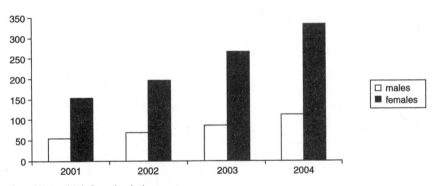

*Source:* National Aids Council and other reports.

areas. Numerous beliefs and practices encourage young people to take a plurality of sexual partners, both in and out of marriage. Most importantly, the use of sex as a means of making money or acquiring other goods or services is widespread and increasing as the number of people living in poverty grows. In addition, there appears to be little difference in the nature of sexual behavior between urban and rural areas. Furthermore, antagonism and violence in sexual relationships appears to be exacerbated by poverty and declining traditional support systems. This section discusses the confluence of social, cultural, and economic factors that have an impact on the rate of transmission of the disease.

The continuum of risk associated with sexual behavior can be illustrated with survey results. Among 15- to 24-year-old women interviewed in 1994 for a study of rural, urban, and periurban youth, those who never took cash for sex had a median number of partners in the previous year of one (although 32 percent had more than one). For those who only accepted noncash gifts for sex, the median number of partners in the previous year was 5.5 (with 23 percent having 15 or more). Among the young women who accepted cash for sex, the median number of partners in the previous year was 16 (46 percent had 30 partners or more). However, the similar number of partners for self-defined, full-time commercial sex workers was 150 to 300 or more (Jenkins 1994b, 1995a, 2000; Mgone et al. 2002b).

Apart from the overall numbers of sexual partners, age patterns in sexual partnerships are critically important. Age-discordant sexual partnerships, in which younger women form cross-generational sexual partnerships with older men, are common in PNG. Such partnerships expose young and often biological immature and thus HIV-susceptible young women to the cumulative HIV exposure of older, often highly sexually experienced men.

### Commercial and Transactional Sex

While the appropriateness of the term "sex worker" in PNG is debated, few deny that the selling of sex is common. Wardlow (2004) points out the motivation for selling sex among the Huli is often anger, revenge, and the expression of personal agency. Others emphasize poverty and the lack of income-earning opportunities. Still others note that family members often push a woman into selling sex, and there have been reports of parents selling their daughters to men or to brothels (Bradley 2001; Hammar 1998; UNICEF 2005a, 2005b). The major differences in PNG between self-identified sex workers and women who engage in opportunistic transactional sex is the number of partners and the degree to which the behavioral response to personal risk relates to a self-recognized identity.

In rural areas, commercial sex is available at markets, clubs, discos, bingo games, and even at government stations where male wage workers gather. One study that mapped risk zones along the Highlands Highway in 1995 found that women also exchanged sex for betel nuts at markets, for beer at small clubs, and for rides on trucks and buses (Jenkins 1995) In many areas, some people claimed that the bride-price had become a commercial transaction ("*Meri em i samting bilong bisnis*"), which led to some young women wishing to be paid for sex when they grew up, as they wanted the money for themselves. These practices, which certainly can contribute to the wider spread of HIV, have been cited in several studies (NSRRT and Jenkins 1994a, Decock 1997, NHASP 2003). More research is needed to understand how widespread they are and how many partners these women actually have, in order to design future interventions. Also, as Annex A attests, there is longstanding evidence of women being attracted to logging camps, mines, fish factories, and numerous other economic enclaves in rural areas, particularly on paydays, to sell sex to the men (Hughes 1991; Jenkins and Passey 1998).

Sex workers in urban areas range from expensive escorts to the proverbial "two kina" *meri*. While most are freelance sex workers operating from public, opportunistic locations, others operate out of residences. Cell phones are likely to play a major role in coordinating the sex trade in the near future. Clients of sex workers in Port Moresby and Lae are most often office workers, businessmen, foreigners, policemen, loggers, soldiers, truck/bus drivers, security guards, and students, in that order (Mgone et al. 2002b). A nationwide study of rural and periurban men found that 36 percent had paid for sex with cash at some point in their lives, most of whom were married. In addition, another third usually paid in gifts (NSRRT and Jenkins 1994a). Studies of specific occupational groups done in 1998 found varying proportions of men who had accessed commercial and casual sex in the previous week. For example, 15 percent of truckers, 30 percent of dockworkers, 54 percent of sailors, 49 percent of policemen, and 52 percent of security guards (Jenkins 2000).

### Multiple Partners

Based on a survey (Table 3.2), there are high levels of multiple partners among both young (ages 15 to 25) male (n = 111) and female (n = 123) Eastern Highlanders. Though not a random sample, the results are consistent with another study where 48 percent of unemployed young urban women surveyed claimed partial income support from sex work (Levantis 2000). Studies indicate that most married men have extramarital sexual partners at some time during their married life and that most wives recognize this (Jenkins and Pataki-Schweizer 1993a; NSRRT and Jenkins 1994a). Among rural and periurban men, 71 percent reported having extramarital sex, 19 percent having had more than five extramarital partners. Many men justified such affairs by their belief that they should not have sex with their wives while they were pregnant or lactating. Far fewer married women (21 percent) reported having extramarital sex. More than half of the men married to a single wife reported having had additional partners during the previous year (an average of two), and widowers, divorced, or separated men reported having an average of 4.2

**Table 3.2. Results of 1998 Eastern Highlands Youth Survey**

| Risk factor | Married men | Single men | Married women | Single women |
|---|---|---|---|---|
| No. of partners last year (median) | 5 | 5 | 2 | 4.5 |
| % with 10 partners or more last year | 29 | 22 | 11 | 20 |
| % Accepted cash for sex | 28 | 8 | 36 | 20 |
| % Paid cash for sex | 28 | 12 | 7 | 20 |
| % Paid gifts for sex | 40 | 30 | 7 | 24 |
| % Paid both cash/gifts for sex | 20 | 7 | 2 | 15 |

*Source:* Eastern Highlands Youth Survey, PNGIMR, 1998.

partners the previous year. A significant minority of rural men and women, approximately 15 percent, had had five or more sexual partners the previous year.

### Sexual and Intimate Partner Violence

Sexual violence against women and girls, particularly rape, is common. Most reported rapes in PNG are perpetrated by groups of men. In the national study, most of these rapes (known as "line-ups") involved an average of 10 men having sex with a single woman. In the national rural/periurban sample, 60 percent of men of all ages who discussed the issue (n=70) reported having been involved in a "line-up" at least once in their lives. Only 3 percent of women reported having been victims of a "line-up" explicitly in that study, but 55 percent of 130 said they had been forced into sex against their will at some point. Among these women, 61 percent stated that this had happened to them more than twice.

In a youth study (Jenkins 1995a), in a sample of 66 women and 82 men who discussed "line-ups," 11 percent of women (as a victim) and 31 percent of men (as a perpetrator) reported having personal involvement in a "line-up." Of the men, the majority had been involved on numerous occasions. Nearly all considered that they had forced the woman and that she had no choice. Among the women who had been involved, over half considered it rape; the rest were sex workers who had participated willingly. An additional 9 percent of young men who claimed no involvement in "line-ups" said that they had forced women into sex acting alone. Thus, the total proportion of male respondents who admitted to forcing a woman to have sex was 40 percent. While only 5 percent of young women admitted to having been raped, nearly 30 percent went on to describe, often in extraordinary detail, the rape experiences of their girlfriends. It is likely that some of these women were discussing their own experiences. Another study of young people (Goroka 1997a) revealed that 24 percent of males and 3 percent of females admitted to being in "line-ups." "Line-ups" can also involve homoeroticism. In PNG, about one-quarter of the young men who discussed having sex with other men explained that they had done so within the context of a line-up (Jenkins 1996).

Young girls, and sometimes boys, are very vulnerable to sexual abuse, particularly from adults near to them such as family members, neighbors, teachers, and church officials. The WHO reports statistics showing that 47 percent of PNG rape victims were 15 years old or younger, and 13 percent were under 7 years old (WHO 1997). While more recent studies of child sexual abuse seem to indicate that there has been an increase in the rape of younger children, this may simply be due to increased reporting (Help Resources/UNICEF 2005). Recent efforts to design legislation have suffered from a lack of analysis, which points to the need for more research (Luluaki 2003). Nonetheless, the frequency of rape in PNG and other forms of sexual abuse is clearly sufficient to warrant special interventions, both to reduce their frequency and to prevent HIV among survivors of all ages.

Domestic or intimate partner violence is very common in PNG and has been estimated to affect 70 percent of women (Brouwer et al. 1998). Partner violence, including domestic violence between spouses, has now been shown to be a marker of increased STI and HIV risk (Dunkle et al. 2004, Van der Staten et al. 1998, Maman et al. 2002, Martin et al. 1999). Furthermore, data from Africa shows that up to 14 percent of women have suffered from serious violence when seeking voluntary counseling and testing (VCT) or after disclosing their serostatus (USAID/Synergy 2004).

The following graph (Figure 3.4) from Rakai, Uganda, powerfully illustrates the relationship between sexual coercion and HIV incidence.

### Men Who Have Sex with Men
The fact of men (or boys) having sex with men is recognized and, while not socially acceptable, appears to be widespread in PNG, especially among young people, but with no implications for sexual identity. Rarely does anyone label themselves as "heterosexual" or "homosexual," let alone "MSM," and the terms do not exist in most local languages (Jenkins 1993a). The term "gay" has emerged as an identity term among some men who have sex with men under the influence of foreign patterns. Most men who have sex with men in PNG, as elsewhere, are

**Figure 3.4. Sexual Coercion and HIV Incidence Among Women Under 25 Years in Rakai, Uganda, 2004**

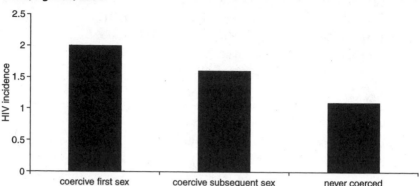

*Source:* Cassell (2005). Could Preventing Optimism Be an Antidote for Preventing HIV Prevention Pessimism? P. 37.

bisexually active and are likely to get married. The male sex trade occurs in a number of urban areas, along wharfs and on boats, with some men selling sex to both men and women (Jenkins 1995a) as well as buying sex for themselves.

In the national sample, 12 percent of 89 men questioned stated that they had engaged in homosexual intercourse and/or mutual masturbation to the point of climax. The equivalent percentage in the youth study was 22 percent (out of 78). Men often report having male-to-male sex for payment, when drunk, and in enforced all-male residential scenes, such as jail, mining camps, or on oil rigs. Nearly all of these men also engage in sex with women, most are or will be married, and may, at any time they choose, engage in same-sex activities again. Although the frequency of male-to-male sex remains unknown, HIV risks in unprotected anal intercourse are high, and prevention programs must ensure that they reach men who have sex with other men. Because their behavior is so stigmatized and most men who have sex with men do not admit to it, they can typically only be reached or identified by their sexual partners, and these interventions must be community-led, designed, and implemented.

Thus, many Papua New Guineans today have a diverse sex life with potentially wide networks of sexual partners. Sexual activity commences early for both sexes, and premarital and extramarital sex is common, as are multiple partners. Sex is increasingly viewed as a commodity to be exchanged for gifts and/or cash with a resulting risk of exposure to sexually transmitted diseases.

**Figure 3.5. HIV Prevalence Among People Consuming Alcohol and Among Nondrinkers, Carletonville (Mine), South Africa**

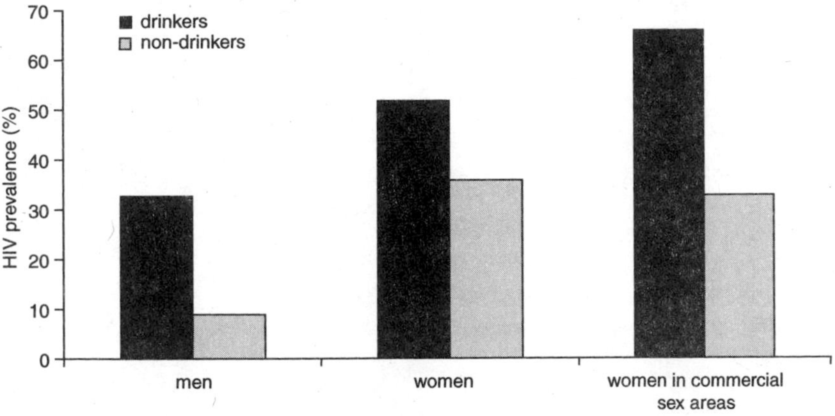

*Sources:* UNAIDS Epidemiology Slides (2001); Campbell et al. (2004).

## Alcohol Abuse

Numerous studies indicated exceptionally high rates of alcohol abuse in PNG. Studies from South Africa's mining communities (Figure 3.5), which bear some resemblances to PNG's mines, show that alcohol abuse is a major predictor of HIV infection, as the graph below from Carletonville mine demonstrates.

## Sexually Transmitted Infections (STIs)

The prevalence of STIs is high in both males and females. One 1997 survey of sex workers in Port Moresby and Lae found high levels of chlamydia (31 percent), syphilis (32 percent), and gonorrhea (36 percent). In a sample survey of village women living on secondary roads in the Eastern Highlands, prevalence levels were similar for chlamydia—26.5 percent, but lower for syphilis—4 percent, and gonorrhea—18.2 percent. A recent study by the Papua New Guinea Institute of Medical Research (PNGIMR), a statutory body under the MOH, at Porgera (a voluntary sample) showed high levels of syphilis both among men (6.9 percent) and women (9.5 percent) (NAC and NDOH 2005). Another recent study in remote areas of Western Province showed 27.4 percent of 351 adults were infected with the herpes simplex virus type 2 (HSV-2), known as a potent facilitator of HIV infection (Suligoi et al. 2005). Evidence from Africa suggests that HSV-2 may play a powerful and tenacious role in

HIV transmission. Unlike bacterial STIs, which fall steeply in mature generalized HIV epidemics, HSV-2 levels remain persistently high.

In 2000, WHO estimated that more than 1 million new cases of STI occur every year in PNG, two-thirds of them being chlamydial infections (WHO 2000). However, viral STIs were not considered in the WHO study. Trichomoniasis was found in 43 to 50 percent of not only the high-risk population but also of the low-risk population. To date, only limited drug resistance has been found in isolates of the organisms causing gonorrhea and chlamydia. The recent adoption of azithromycin in PNG is reportedly bringing about improvements in treatment.

## HIV/AIDS and the Economy

As of 2004, the population of PNG was projected to be 5.7 million (GOPNG and UN 2005). Approximately 17 percent of the population is employed in the formal economy, in enclave extractive industries (mining, petroleum, logging, and fishing), government, limited manufacturing activity, and a small services sector. The informal sector, primarily domestic food production, supports 83 percent of the population. Despite having many sources of economic growth, the PNG economy has been in deep recession for the past decade. All sectors of the economy have experienced decline, and GDP contracted steadily between 1997 and 2002 (real GDP per capita declined almost 4 percent). Real GDP in 2002 was below its 1996 level, and foreign investment had fallen sharply. Only modest growth—enough to just sustain real GDP per capita—was achieved through 2005. The more recent upturn in commodity prices will drive some modest growth. Nevertheless, largely as a consequence of this slow growth, only one in 10 school-leavers are likely to find a job in the formal sector. This, together with a public sector facing fiscal challenges, and a need to increase the quality of expenditures by increasing nonsalary budgets, means that there are likely to be very limited formal-sector employment opportunities over the next decade.

One of the few areas in which employment prospects for males remain bright are enclave extractive developments, which have improved the employment prospects of a limited number of highly skilled staff and of unskilled staff drawn from the adjacent populations. For females, however, options for formal employment are far more limited. Less than 5.7 percent of women in the labor force participate in the formal nonagricultural wage-earning economy compared with 15.2 percent of men in the labor force—the lowest rate for the Pacific region (GOPNG and UN 2005).[4]

Precisely because of these inequities, enclave economic developments present situations that put both men and women at significant risk of contracting HIV, as the increased trade in sex in these industries for cash and/or gifts has been well-documented. Annex A shows selected existing enclave developments and estimates of the size of these affected populations. As many as 200,000 to 250,000 rural people are likely to be directly affected by these enclave developments.

The result of the deterioration in the economy has been a dramatic increase in poverty—between 1996 and 2002 the number of Papua New Guineans living on less than US$1 per day is estimated to have increased from 25 percent to 40 percent. Most of the poverty is in rural areas and is highest in female-headed households. This is reflected in the Gini coefficient for PNG, a measure of disparities in income and consumption, of approximately .50, the highest in the South Pacific region (GOPNG and UN 2005).[5]

The serious economic situation in the country has resulted in a rising fiscal deficit that exceeded 5 percent of GDP in 2002. There has been a serious deterioration in the integrity of budget institutions and of mechanisms for ensuring accountability for public expenditure. The end result has been reduced public expenditure, deteriorating infrastructure, and a very marked deterioration in public service delivery.

While the economic situation has a detrimental impact on the HIV/AIDS epidemic, the epidemic will have negative effects on the economy as well. A report commissioned by AusAID on the economic impact of the epidemic on PNG concluded that HIV has the potential to increase poverty significantly, reduce the labor force, and increase the budget deficit (Center for International Economics 2002).

In summary, the HIV/AIDS situation in PNG is already a major general epidemic as the result of high levels of transmission in the last decade. The potential for further rapid spread of the virus is high due to a set of conditions that favor transmission, including:

(a) A demographic profile in which a high proportion of the population is of reproductive age and sexually active.
(b) Cultural and economic conditions that foster a wide continuum of risk, from professional full-time sex workers in urban centers and their clients, to men and women practicing opportunistic transactional sex in many urban and rural settings, to those with many noncommercial casual partners, all of which delineates different patterns of extensive sexual networking.

(c) The extent of male sexual privilege in PNG has not been adequately acknowledged in simple messages encouraging changes in behavior. Promoting fidelity to women is not enough when there are few more risky situations than a faithful woman married to an HIV-positive man who does not know or disclose his status.

(d) Current patterns of sexual relations, including early initiation of sexual intercourse, multiple partners (both premarital and extramarital), and the exchange of sex, often for cash and gifts, by a large proportion of the population.

(e) High levels of domestic violence and rape, particularly gang rape, and suspected high levels of sexual abuse of children.

(f) High levels of STIs in the general community, including both viral and bacterial ulcerative pathogens.

(g) The absence of male circumcision as defined by complete exision of the foreskin.

(h) Depressed economic conditions, associated increases in poverty, and low formal employment rates, especially for women and young people.

(i) Widespread alcohol abuse.

(j) A pattern of economic development that is heavily reliant on enclave extractive developments that can provide formal and informal employment and a setting for the local population to provide services for cash (including sex) in and around centers of economic activity, making the populations in these areas highly vulnerable to the HIV epidemic.

## The Response of the Government of PNG to HIV/AIDS

The response by government to the HIV/AIDS epidemic since the identification of the first HIV case in 1987 has been inadequate compared to the threat posed by the disease—especially as the potential impact of the disease became more fully understood in the 1990s. As late as 2004, the government allocated less than $200,000 for domestically financed HIV/AIDS programs. Nevertheless, the government's response has gradually improved in important ways since 1987 as discussed below.

### Early Response (1987–1997)

Despite numerous alerts raised in the early 1990s, few people in positions of leadership acknowledged HIV/AIDS as an issue of concern. With encouragement and funds from the Global Program on AIDS, the National AIDS Program was formed, under the aegis of the NDOH, and enlisted membership from a wide variety of stakeholders into a National

AIDS Committee. The National AIDS Committee functioned sporadically between 1988 and 1994. Efforts in the early 1990s to establish a sentinel surveillance system faltered, and by 1995, all that remained was limited passive surveillance in some locations. Between 1995 and 1999, AusAID funded the Foundation Project, which improved STI services, condom distribution, and a targeted intervention for sex workers and their major clients in the transport industry, the Transex Project, among other activities.

### The Establishment of the National AIDS Council and the Medium-Term Plan (1997–2003)

In 1997, a new government response emerged with the establishment of the National AIDS Council (NAC) as a statutory body and the National AIDS Council Secretariat (NACS) to service the council. A Medium-Term Plan (MTP) was drawn up covering the years 1998 to 2002. The next AusAID-funded project, the National HIV/AIDS Support Project (NHASP), which began in 2000, supported the MTP. The multisectoral approach and objectives of the MTP, however, were never costed, prioritized, or implemented.

In the 2003 and 2004 budgets, the NACS received an allocation of approximately US$180,000, a substantial part of which was used to provide salaries for the staff of the NACS. Only about 80 percent of the budget was made available. Much of NACS activity has been concentrated in Port Moresby, and initiatives at the provincial level have been more limited. Provincial AIDS Committee Secretariats (PACS), established under NAC, have been slow to mobilize provincial resources. Funds for these PACS have been largely provided through the NHASP and NACS. With the exception of programs in Milne Bay, Madang, and a few others, implementation has been very limited and with little strategic direction. In most cases, awareness campaigns appear to be the principal activity. Condoms are distributed through the PACS, largely when local people or groups come to collect them. Free condom distribution is seen by many to conflict with the socially marketed condom campaign, which recommends abstinence as first choice of prevention. In some cases, authorities object when free condoms are sold; in other cases (as in Enga Province), the selling of free condoms is permitted, even encouraged, in order for them to reach small rural trade stores. No culturally appropriate face-to-face promotion is carried out on a widespread scale, as in other nations, and no discussion of sex and sexuality accompanies the advertising. These inconsistencies are likely to be causing confusion about the value of condom use (Jenkins, 1994c). Condom social marketing campaigns have increased knowledge and use of condoms in mostly urban populations. However, these levels are still low, with only 36 percent of males and 17 percent of females reporting having used a condom during their last sexual encounter (National HIV/AIDS Social Marketing Campaign 2003). More recently, a social marketing campaign was conducted to reduce the stigma of HIV/AIDS (without promoting condoms), and a new campaign to promote condom use is being carried out now. In 2006, the government led a HIV Prevention Summit, where an attempt was made to reorient the national response effort toward prevention.

### Global Fund Application (2004) and Approval (June 2005)

The Government of PNG submitted an application for $30 million funding over five years from the fourth round of the GFATM. The aim of the initial proposal was to bring 7,000 HIV-infected people onto anti-retroviral treatment (ART) by 2009. In year one, 80 percent of funds were to be allocated to churches, the government, the private sector, people living with HIV/AIDS (PLWHA), NACS, and educational institutions. The program proposal stated it would emphasize prevention among at-risk youth, although there is little indication of how this was to occur. No evidence-based approach was cited as part of the proposal. It seems that all young people were to be targeted. The document did not address the issue of the relative cost-effectiveness of the various proposed interventions for prevention,[6] nor did it discuss how to manage adherence to the ART regimen or how to collaborate with NGOs to support patients, or the role of men in care-giving, or the very poor status of health care delivery overall, including shortages of staff and inadequate management of the drug supply. In June 2005, GFATM approved $8.49 million for the first two years of the program—albeit in slightly modified form—with the NDOH as the principal recipient and to be managed through the government's HSIP. Its prime focus, nevertheless, remains on antiretroviral (ARV) delivery, VCT, and youth.

### Health Policy on HIV/AIDS (2004)

The role of the NDOH with respect to the national response to HIV/AIDS has been unclear in the five years since the government transferred the responsibility for surveillance activities to the NACS. Other than in providing clinical services, the NDOH has had little input into the national program; however, several evaluations have recommended that the NDOH should become more involved in HIV/AIDS control and in surveillance in particular. As a result, the NDOH will now play a larger role, although it will need additional human resources and skills to be fully effective.

With the arrival of ART, the medical profession has a new role to play and will be more widely involved in treatment and control activities. A revised NSP-HIV/AIDS (discussed below) was developed that combined the NACS plan and an early health-sector HIV/AIDS policy document from 2004. Most of the plan's goals relate to the treatment, care, and support of infected people by clinical services, civil society, the private sector, and communities. The new strategy calls for evidence-based interventions aimed at changing behavior and proposes that appropriate research will be conducted.

### Adjusting the NAC and New National Strategic Plan (2006–2010)

A proposal to move the NACS into the prime minister's department with the aim of positioning it to lead a "whole-of-government" response was approved by the cabinet in November 2003 and awaits implementation. The National HIV/AIDS Management and Prevention Act, which was passed in parliament and gazetted in 2004, established the legal context for HIV prevention and care. A new multisectoral National Strategic Plan (NSP) for 2006 to 2010 was developed with wide consultation, although many of those participating (for example, young people and MSM) were disappointed that their issues were not mentioned. The document does not consider the serious capacity constraints that face implementation of an adequate response to HIV/AIDS. The activities proposed in the NSP have also not been costed, and it has no financing plan; however, it has been endorsed by the National Executive Council as the basis for government's program. The capacity and expertise of NACS to coordinate an increasingly complex response to the HIV/AIDS epidemic needs to be strengthened. To this end, NACS is currently drawing up a corporate plan that sets out its intended roles and requirements.

The PNGIMR has begun a series of HIV, STI, and behavioral surveys with funding from AusAID. There is a need to strengthen the capacity for conducting HIV-related sexuality studies. Most studies to date do not make use of internationally recognized methodologies that would make it possible to compare data over time and thus analyze trends. Recently, three small surveys using respondent-driven sampling have been completed by PNGIMR and Family Health International.

An adequate monitoring and evaluation plan is required that emphasizes analysis of outcomes and adequate second-generation surveillance (combining both sero and behavioral surveillance). The NHASP will engage consultants to design behavioral surveillance surveys, which may begin to create much-needed, well-sampled baseline data. To date, quantitative behavioral surveys have been carried out at four STI clinics and among the defense force.

A monitoring and evaluation framework was designed for the GFATM-financed program. Out of the 17 monitoring indicators, only one dealt with behavior change. This indicator—the percentage of young people ages 15–24 who report the use of a condom during last sexual intercourse with a nonregular partner—increases by at least 5 percent between baseline and end-of-strategy (2009) surveys. This anticipated extremely little increase in condom use. Such an increase (presumably from low levels) would have no impact on the epidemic in that age group and would require an enormous sample size to measure accurately. In addition, as most females acquire HIV from older men, large proportions of the male partners will not be captured by the proposed monitoring. It is clear that slowing the spread of HIV in PNG would need indicators based on more contextualized and in-depth knowledge, a commitment to improving condom distribution, destigmatizing condom use for both genders, and providing explicit sex education for young men and women (Jenkins and Alpers 1996).

Furthermore, the new strategy documents, as available at the time of this review (2004–2006), do not discuss the links between prevention and treatment. They imply that VCT, treatment, and support will bring about secondary prevention (with no attempt to quantify the relationship), but they do not address the very real possibilities of disinhibition with treatment (disregarding the risks of unprotected sex because of the availability of treatment), the development of ART resistance, continuing transmissibility, and probable high dropout rates or interrupted drug supplies arising from either logistics problems or changes in the availability of donor financing of ART. While the new NSP is a far better document than anything produced earlier, it still emphasizes treatment and care over prevention. In the observations under Remaining Challenges, we question this approach. With both the NDOH and NACS (and the international community through their support of the proposed GFATM program) advocating for improved treatment and care, there does not seem to be any room for high-quality prevention services.

## The Response of Key Development Partners

### (a) AusAID

AusAID has been the leading player in the initial response to the epidemic, having invested $44 million in PNG's HIV/AIDS effort over the years 1995 to 2006 under a number of projects, including the Trans Sex Project, the Foundation Project (1995–1999), and, more recently, the significant NHASP. These projects—particularly NHASP—have supported the implementation of the initial HIV/AIDS MTP at both the national level and in the 19 provinces. The project objective was to be a comprehensive response to the epidemic and aimed to strengthen government responses at many levels in STI treatment, legal issues and policy, peer education, multisectoral planning, surveillance, counseling, education and information, the social marketing of condoms, and the funding of PACS. Considerable funding was also available for both medical and sociological research, developing improved clinical services, and supporting community-based organizations (CBOs) and NGOs. In its early years, it was hampered by weak capacity in government and lack of a clear implementation strategy. Considerable effort in 2003 and 2004 resulted in key revisions to the project, and new project leaders intensified the response. Many counselors have been trained, and VCT policy and accreditation processes are in action. Nearly 60 VCT centers and community-based care facilities in 20 locations have been opened.

Social mapping exercises were carried out in 19 provinces with the local PACS to familiarize them with some of the high-risk settings and then to develop district-level HIV/AIDS programs. A strategy was devised for dealing with high-risk settings while targeting unemployed youth, young people in schools, sex workers, and MSM. The overall management is to be carried out by the Behavior Change Advisory Committee within NACS. After being given some training, local NGOs, PACS, and various occupational groups are responsible for formulating and carrying out their own behavior-change programs. More recently, AusAID is planning a project focused on establishing STI treatment in view of the high levels of STIs within the country.

An updated Australian plan to support the PNG effort to combat HIV/AIDS was released in April 2006. This ambitious strategy aims to strengthen government responses for all seven focus areas of the NSP 2006–2010. The two key groups of activities are discussed below.

*Counseling Treatment and Care:* The Australian plan document emphasizes the role of primary health services in VCT and as such provides for greater support to such delivery mechanisms. The program supports using clinical needs rather than gender to determine access to health care, while ensuring gender equality in HIV/AIDS treatment access in more general terms.

*Education Prevention:* The strategy emphasizes culturally relevant prevention messages, in particular to high-risk groups and populations in high-risk settings. The role of gender inequity is recognized, as is the importance of reducing stigma and discrimination against PLWHA. The strategy supports providing grants to community- and church-based prevention activities. There is a holistic set of activities planned for high-risk settings, such as peer education, STI services, VCT, condoms, and treatment and care.

In addition, the strategy provides support for enhanced measurement and evaluation (M&E) of proposed activities, as well as surveillance; however, the strategy does not provide details on what indicators will be developed in support of M&E. As discussed above, the indicators used in the past for the Global Fund program activities were problematic; however, given the great diversity in settings and situations and the lack of technical and management capacity among many NGOs/CBOs working on HIV in PNG, the Australian behavioral change strategy will face challenges in reducing transmission rates. The international literature on prevention in mining communities indicates that a great deal of financial and human resource investment was required to deal with both the unique situations of miners and the complex gender-power relationships of local committees, NGOs, clinical providers, and stigmatized sex workers (Steen et al. 2000, Campbell and Mzaidume 2001). Successful sex worker interventions require an entirely different approach than do prisons. Women in prisons require different interventions than men in prisons. The majority of MSM are generally unidentifiable, except to the men with whom they have sex, and they also have sex with women. The present strategy does not require any measurement of the size, changes, or categorization of at-risk people. Inasmuch as HIV risk is distributed along a continuum and those who do not call themselves sex workers are far less likely to use condoms, other strategies than those used for professional sex workers will be needed. Married women are often in denial about their own risk of contracting HIV, and every opportunity must be taken to reach them.

The new Australian strategy has a social and behavioral research component, along with a dissemination focus. This component should commission formative research to identify the continuum, size, and characteristics of at-risk groups, with adequate samples, technical assistance, and continued supervision by managers of the HIV/AIDS response. It is essential to take into account the well-documented international experience on this topic, as the wide range of actions and interventions have made an impact on the epidemic, at least at the local levels.

### (b) Other Donors

Other donors began to provide significant support to the HIV/AIDS effort in 2002–2003. These include the European Union (EU), the Government of China, Japan International Cooperation Agency (JICA), U.S. Agency for International Development (USAID), ADB, the British High Commission, New Zealand, various churches, and the United Nations (UN) agencies, especially United Nations Children's Fund (UNICEF), United Nations Population Fund (UNFPA), WHO, United Nations Development Program (UNDP), the Global Fund, and the Joint United Nations Program on HIV/AIDS (UNAIDS). The main recipient of USAID funds has been Family Health International, which is partially funding Save the Children's program working with sex workers and MSM. The EU Sexual Health Project is developing peer education programs in 13 provinces and has begun working with the police. The extent of this support and the activities that are being planned or implemented is shown in Annex B.

As discussed, the Global Fund initiated a two-year project begun in June 2005 aimed at scaling up HIV/AIDS treatment, care, and prevention and giving little focus to designing or implementing prevention programs.

The ADB, now the second-most important player in terms of financing the response to the epidemic, has funded a pilot project on ART (in collaboration with WHO), and has allotted about US$1 million for HIV components of fisheries projects (for an HIV prevention activity in the fisheries industry) over a five-year period from 2003. In 2006, ADB approved the Papua New Guinea: HIV/AIDS Prevention and Control in Rural Development Enclaves Project, which is jointly financed with AusAID, New Zealand, and government for a total of $25 million. The project involves an innovative HIV/AIDS prevention and control program to be implemented from 2006–2010 in rural development enclaves (22 percent); community behavior change and social marketing of condoms (45 percent), and enhanced surveillance (14 percent), with the remaining 19 percent including project management, taxes, and contingencies.

Most recently, the Clinton Foundation has agreed to finance a modest program of support for the supply of ARVs for the ARV program at

PMGH. Plans are under way to significantly expand the support from the Clinton Foundation.

## The Response of Nongovernmental Organizations and Churches

Few international NGOs with HIV/AIDS expertise can be found in PNG, though some agencies that have never done HIV work are said to be moving into the field. Recently, with support from USAID, Family Health International has established an office and is developing a program. World Vision and Save the Children PNG (formally affiliated with New Zealand STC [Save the Children]) also have a presence in the country and have begun to work in the field. Faith-based NGOs, such as Hope Worldwide, Adventist Development Relief Agency (ADRA), the Salvation Army, and the Red Cross of PNG, conduct HIV awareness training and plan to implement programs. Churches, subsidized by the government, run nearly 50 percent of the country's health facilities and potentially have a very important role to play in HIV care, treatment, and prevention; however, accounts from the field suggest that many faith-based programs will not promote condoms on principle. As yet, there are not many indigenous NGOs ready and able to work on HIV, although local community groups frequently request funds from both government and development partners to do so. There is a severe shortage of trained people available to work in such NGOs/CBOs. Fostering and training such organizations to do HIV/AIDS work will require considerably more investment in training, mentoring, and supervision than is currently the case. Frequent monitoring surveys with rapid feedback would be useful to help these agencies understand the impact of what they are doing.

To date, the NHASP project has held several workshops at which NGO/CBO representatives have received training, but there is no capacity to meet their technical needs once they return to their own environments. As leadership and understanding are less developed in other towns and rural areas than in Port Moresby, it is likely that international agencies will be needed to enable local NGO/CBOs to work on HIV/AIDS on a long-term basis.

Several churches, such as the Catholics and the Anglicans, have responded by providing VCT, setting up support groups for people living with the virus, promoting prevention of mother-to-child transmission (PMTCT), and teaching youth life-skills education in schools and to out-of-school youth. Anglicare received external funds to build one

HIV counseling and care center in Port Moresby that opened in 2003. There are other such centers associated with several churches in the Highlands. The number of AIDS orphans has risen to detectable levels in Port Moresby, and one Catholic organization provides them with some services. The Baptist Union has plans to develop a program of detection, care, and support.

## The Response of the Private Sector

It has long been recognized that mines, logging camps, fisheries, and other enclaves of economic production have high potential for spreading HIV. Some of the mines have begun to respond by developing awareness and prevention programs, though much more work is required. Enga Province, the location of the Porgera Gold Mine, with the help of PNGIMR, has conducted surveys that show high levels of HIV among miners and members of the surrounding villages. A peer-based education and prevention response is planned. The Ok Tedi mine in the Western Province is now developing a comprehensive plan to manage HIV among its workers. Oil palm plantations are also considered to be at risk. All industries will need additional technical support to respond to this problem in their midst. Logging companies, shipping and trucking companies, maritime industries, and possibly others collectively represent a great opportunity for instituting effective preventive interventions. The NHASP high-risk-setting strategy aims to target these groups, as well as the police and correctional institutions. The new ADB project, discussed above, will be an important attempt to respond to some of these challenges.

## Financing the Response

The total amount of resources available for the response to HIV/AIDS is high—well in excess of $20 million, or more than US$3.5 per person per capita in 2005; however, less than 10 percent of current funding came from the government of PNG in 2005. For the first half of the 1990s, government only financed the core salaries and minimal operational expenditures at a cost of less than $200,000 per annum. Budgets have been increased modestly since, but in its financing proposal to the Global Fund (which was approved), the government anticipated a decline in government funding over the next five years. More recently, the Government has agreed to joint financing for the new ADB HIV project, with its contribution to be $3 million. A number of provincial governments are beginning to allocate modest funds in support of HIV programs, mainly for coordination and modest operational costs.

A complete documentation of individual projects is not available (see Annex 3B for a list of agencies operating in PNG and their focus on HIV). Expenditure on HIV/AIDS is evolving. Historically, AusAID has been the major development partner financing HIV/AIDS activities. In 2002, AusAID financed about 90 percent of a $13 million total expenditure on HIV. More recently, AusAID allocated $22 million for 2005–2006 to support implementation of the NSP 2004–2008 through NASP (National AIDS Support Program). Plans are under way to design significant new interventions—including a focus on STDs more generally—to support the new NSP.

The ADB contributed a $450,000 grant in 2003 to fund a pilot project on treatment and care (implemented in partnership with WHO) and about $1 million in credit for HIV activities under its Coastal Management and Development Project, approved in 2002. Earlier this year, ADB approved the Papua New Guinea: HIV/AIDS Prevention and Control in Rural Development Enclaves Project, which is jointly financed as follows: ADB, $15 million; AusAID, $3.5 million; and New Zealand, $3.5 million, for a total of $25 million (including $3 million from the government).

The Global Fund approved a grant of $8.49 million in June 2005 to cover a two-year period for scaling up HIV/AIDS treatment, care, and prevention. USAID makes grants of $1 million per annum to HIV/AIDS and infectious diseases in PNG through its sponsored NGO, Family Health International. The Clinton Foundation has began a modest program of supplying ARV drugs for HIV patients at PMGH, and plans are being developed to expand this assistance to a national program.

## Major Lessons Learned and Priorities for Further Action

Based on the above analysis and the experience of other development partners, several major lessons of experience and priorities for further action are identified.

### Melanesian Epidemics Are Poorly Understood

Melanesian countries comprise a tiny fraction of the Asia-Pacific region's population, but a significantly higher proportion of the region's most fragile states and its most intractable health, development, economic, institutional, and development challenges. HIV in Melanesia, as a relatively recent health challenge in a subregion beset with development challenges, is poorly understood, and there is a danger it may be subsumed within a wider but inappropriate Asian lens or superficially and perhaps mislead-ingly compared with Africa. There may be immense value in a rigorous comparison with Africa and many important lessons to be learned from such an analysis, but superficial comparisons are undesirable. Above all, Melanesia's HIV epidemics call for their own analysis and understanding. This requires intensified country analysis and more regional comparisons. It is noteworthy that Melanesia's HIV epidemic is largely still confined to the island that Papua and Papua New Guinea share. Rates in the Solomons, the Timors, and Fiji remain far lower.

### Strengthen Surveillance and Research

In a related vein, while it is clear that HIV in PNG is primarily hetero-sexual in character and generalized in its transmission patterns, and that the epidemic is already extremely advanced in many areas, both HIV surveillance and research remain limited. Strengthened HIV surveil-lance and research is urgently needed. In particular, there is a dearth of population-based surveillance and research and of high-quality, inte-grated biobehavioral surveillance.

While new sentinel sites have been added and laboratory protocols are being improved, record keeping remains particularly poor, with as many as 30 percent of standard reporting forms being completed without any age recorded for the patient. Surveillance activities, while improving, do not make use of the additional information that is already available in some provincial and district hospitals, nor the syphilis data collected during HIV sero-surveillance. The effort to date has been hampered by a lack of funds and staff, no systematic standardization of procedures, insufficient supervision and quality control, and the failure to use avail-able information for planning purposes. The new Australian plan supports building the capacity of service deliverers to undertake surveillance, and to ensure that sex-disaggregated data is collected. However, behavioral surveillance of the whole population, or more importantly, key high-risk groups, has not yet been implemented systematically.

Antenatal surveys, particularly in PNG, where antenatal participation rates in the highlands are among the lowest in the world, do not ade-quately sample women of all ages, rural communities, and men. We now have new data emerging from population-based HIV prevalence surveys. To date, approximately 20 countries in Africa and Latin America (including Botswana, Burkina Faso, Burundi, Cameroon, Dominican

Republic, Ethiopia, Ghana, Guinea, Kenya, Lesotho, Mali, Senegal, Sierra Leone, South Africa, Tanzania, and Zambia in Africa and the Dominican Republic and Peru in Latin America) have undertaken population-based HIV surveys, largely using the DHS plus methodology, (which includes a test of HIV Status and undertakes a behavioral survey). These population-based surveys have helped to improve the accuracy of HIV prevalence estimates, locally and nationally. More recently they are planned for Papua Province in Indonesia and in other Asian settings.

Strengthened surveillance and research are particularly important in PNG. It is an exceptionally disparate and fragmented country. It currently has few antenatal sites and as a result, HIV estimates are based on extreme generalizations, initially largely from urban sites. The distribution of antenatal sites nationally is highly uneven and antenatal coverage is among the lowest in the Pacific and is far lower than many African countries. PNG is also a highly distinctive country; culturally and economically quite different than many of its neighbors. This makes it harder to understand prevalence trends and transmission patterns by analyzing data from several similar countries, as has proved useful in Africa and other regions. To date, we have very broad estimates of HIV infection levels and inadequate rigorous evidence of the ultimate HIV epidemic potential in PNG.

We also have a limited understanding of the age and geographic distribution of HIV in PNG. More seriously still, we have limited understanding of the transmission dynamics in this country. Without this data, it is impossible to undertake evidence-informed planning. There is a great danger that programs will be based on erroneous HIV estimates and assumptions about transmission patterns, perhaps imported from other regions with different epidemics and transmission drivers.

Evidence from Africa and elsewhere shows how HIV surveillance and research can provide a comprehensive overview of an epidemic and invaluable insights into factors amplifying or inhibiting HIV transmission.

### Increase Emphasis on Prevention, Particularly in Rural Areas
Overall, the response to the epidemic has been heavily biased toward Port Moresby and other urban areas. Targeted prevention programs for high-risk groups are lagging behind and are not usually based on international best practice or an understanding of PNG cultures. A recent stakeholder document (UNAIDS/AusAID/NAC 2004) listed only four agencies (Salvation Army, World Vision, Anglicare, and SCiPNG) capable of dealing with the very large number of sex workers in the country. While

communities as a whole are being engaged, there has been little effort to develop self-help groups of at-risk people capable of leading the implementation of targeted prevention activities. Data from the WHO (in Table 3.3 below) supports the view that a prevention program combining a high-risk group focus with mass media communications, and a treatment program focused on STIs, are the most cost-effective strategies.

Cost-effectiveness analysis is an essential component of informed debate about priority setting for HIV/AIDS. Table 3.3 below was based on WHO's CHOICE databases (calculated by the GOALS Model, Futures Group), and demonstrated the relative cost-effectiveness of various combinations of interventions at several levels of coverage. Expressed in dollars adjusted to the purchasing power in a variety of countries, disability-adjusted life years (DALYs) saved were calculated for different types of investment. While the exact costs vary somewhat by country (and those for ART have seen some downward adjustment thanks to international efforts on drug costs), the differences would still exhibit an order of magnitude that is universal.

Despite the international evidence of the success of such approaches there is no significant attempt in PNG to engage the most at-risk people and involve them in policy-making decisions. There are no grassroots groups of the people most in need of prevention to call for improved prevention services, as these people are socially and legally marginalized. Targeted interventions for the men (and women) who purchase sex are rarely discussed among policy makers, other than the policy of educating the police and the military. Though the new Australian strategy mentions tackling gender inequity and violence, most policy makers have not in the past addressed some of the major sociocultural factors that are driving the epidemic, including male sexual privilege, intimate partner violence, and male control of female sexuality. Most projects rely almost exclusively on unpaid peer educators to spread awareness. It is unclear if they are supervised or if this approach is effective.

The receipt of the Global Fund grant may further skew the response in favor of Port Moresby and the larger urban areas. This is despite the fact that at most only 15 percent of people with HIV live in the capital and perhaps 30 percent in urban areas overall, whereas more than half and possibly as many as three-quarters of infected people are in rural areas. The ADB project focus on prevention and control in enclave development sites is important in its effort to focus on high-risk rural (nonurban) settings. More generally, policy makers seem to be expecting churches and

**Table 3.3. The Cost Effectiveness of Different Types of HIV Interventions**

*(international dollars)*

| Intervention | Average year cost (in international dollars) | | | Effectiveness DALYs averted: | Cost-Effectiveness | |
|---|---|---|---|---|---|---|
| | Program | Patient | Total | Avg 1 year | Avg | Incremental* |
| ARV, standard monitoring | 43,562,499 | 720,413,069 | 755,643,050 | 1,057,857 | 714 | Dominated** |
| ARV, standard monitoring & 2nd-line drugs | 42,258,474 | 2074,253,082 | 2,109,483,063 | 1,337,873 | 1,577 | Dominated |
| ARV, intensive monitoring & 2nd-line drugs | 42,258,474 | 3494,436,024 | 3,529,666,004 | 2,124,198 | 1,662 | Dominated |
| Educating sex workers & STI treatment (50%) | | | 15,481,107 | 5,801,143 | 3 | Dominated |
| Mass media (100%) | 13,749,271 | | 13,749,271 | 10,293,139 | 1 | Dominated |
| School-based education (50%) | 62,785,700 | | 62,785,700 | 3,908,581 | 16 | Dominated |
| School-based education (80%) | 116,902,231 | | 116,902,231 | 5,132,671 | 23 | Dominated |
| STI treatment (95%) | 22,911,002 | 25,775,065 | 48,686,068 | 29,709,759 | 2 | 1.80 |
| VCT (95%) | 72,758,958 | 278,777,581 | 351,536,539 | 3,667,363 | 96 | Dominated |
| PMTCT | 24,511,461 | 223,960,034 | 248,471,495 | 1,267,477 | 196 | Dominated |
| Educating sex workers (50%) & mass media (100%) | | | 13,749,271 | 10,293,139 | 1 | 1.34 |

*Source:* WHO Web site (2006).

* Incremental Cost-Effectiveness Ratio: the change in cost divided by change in effectiveness (DALYs averted).

** Dominated: An intervention that is more costly and/or less effective than other, more efficient interventions.

PACS to handle the rural workload. Overall implementation of existing policies and programs in these areas has been weak and hampered by both a severe lack of human resources and a feasible strategy to drive the response. In addition, some churches and NGOs are apparently unwilling to promote condom use, which further hampers these critical prevention efforts.

A summary of the responses to date by type of activity and agency is shown in Annex 3C. From this summary, it is evident that the total response to the epidemic needs to be better coordinated, to be based on evidence-based approaches to prevention, and to be buttressed by better research and training. The government and donors have yet to develop a coordinated strategy and to set priority activities to deal with the epidemic, despite the fact that reducing the number of new cases of HIV is an explicit key aim in the MTDS, the HMTEF, and the SP for the PNG Health Sector (2006–2008).

### Context-Specific Strategies

To understand the *specific* transmission dynamics in each context, it is important to first ask, what proportion of HIV infections arises from different populations and, more specifically, what proportion of infections may be attributed to high-risk groups? In short, the most important question to continually ask is, where did the last thousand new HIV infections in PNG arise? A key issue in a country as complex, diverse, and variegated as PNG is how best to reach high-risk populations and areas, in different contexts. For example, in PNG, as the above review notes, most sex workers do not work in establishments or clearly identified red-light districts, where they would be relatively easy to identify and target on a large scale. Government-led programs to promote 100-percent condom use in sex establishments, which helped to check HIV infection in Thailand and, to a lesser extent, in Cambodia, are harder to introduce in PNG or anywhere sex work is largely informal and widely dispersed. One way to reach widely dispersed informal and part-time sex workers, as well as highly sexually active men and most of the MSM who do not identify themselves as gay, is by prevention campaigns that target high-transmission areas in which it is not necessary for members of vulnerable groups to self-identify. Given the importance that high-risk behaviors play in driving the epidemic, it is essential to reach as many people as possible who engage in them.

**Figure 3.6. HIV Infection by Risk Group and WHO Region**

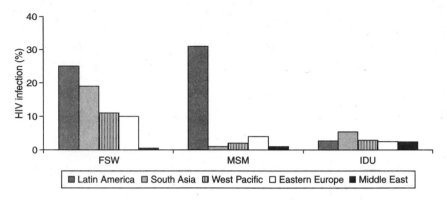

*Source:* Policy project (2004). Coverage of selected services for HIV/AIDS prevention, care, and support in low- and middle-income countries in 2003.
*Notes:* FSW = Female sex workers; IDU = Injecting drug users.

## Increase Coverage of Priority Interventions

Expanding coverage of priority interventions is the major challenge in the global HIV response, and this challenge is particularly important in PNG, which is a nucleated and, in many areas, geographically inaccessible country. The following UNAIDS graph (Figure 3.6) shows how low HIV rates are, including in the West Pacific region, which includes PNG.

Throughout the Western Pacific, coverage of sex workers is estimated to be approximately 10 percent while coverage of MSM is acknowledged to be around 1 percent at best. The sex-worker coverage estimate may be optimistic, particularly in PNG, where there are few targeted interventions outside Port Moresby and some urban areas. Expanded coverage will require a far greater emphasis on improved planning and management of the national response.

## Build Implementation Capacity

The most limiting factor in the delivery of HIV/AIDS control activities is implementation capacity. Most of PNG's response to the HIV/AIDS epidemic has consisted of efforts to increase awareness rather than to change people's behavior. Social mapping of high-risk settings has occurred and the results are being used to mobilize a local-level response, but this effort lacks the input of international best practice or the necessary in-depth information about what kind of behavior change program will be most culturally appropriate for PNG. Also, size estimation of the population at various levels of risk of contracting the virus has not been done anywhere on a systematic basis, and there are even fewer estimates of the coverage and the level of effort or funding needed to provide an adequate response to the scale of the epidemic. As discussed, there are very few activities to date designed to reach rural areas, particularly those populations that are at higher risk by virtue of their location in the vicinity of enclave development projects (such as logging, mining, and fishing). There is little access to condoms, as socially marketed distribution by and large has not been reaching these high-risk settings or rural areas, and a planned intersectoral response is lagging far behind what is needed.

In addition to the many medical and laboratory skills needed, if ART were to be made available equitably throughout the PNG health system, a large number of health care workers would need additional training in delivering prevention counseling. To date, the most effective counseling carried out as part of the VCT process has been couple counseling, a useful prevention tool in generalized epidemics. Because of time pressures in clinical care, a more practical approach would be to incorporate nonhealth workers into the team. Adherence counselors, peer treatment educators, and other persons would be needed to help an ART program function. At the present time, given the poor performance of the DOTS TB program, there is little evidence that the health services will be able to deliver a program of expanded access to ART, with the possible exception of some church-affiliated services, for a long time to come. But even if the goal is reached of bringing 7,000 PLWHAs under treatment and each of these people adhered strictly to safer sex behavior, transmitting no new infections to others, the epidemic would not be diminished.

### Base Program Design on International Best Practice, Adapted to PNG

It is vital that PNG takes into account experiences in other countries, as these can provide a useful base of evidence and information to inform the design and implementation of programs. In Thailand, for example, the key to the relative success of addressing HIV/AIDS was effective prevention among high-risk groups (particularly, in the Thai context, commercial sex workers and their clients). The Thai response was also grounded in a comprehensive and technically sound surveillance system. Surveillance identified some of the key sources of the

**Figure 3.7. Thailand's HIV Estimates With and Without Prevention Interventions, 1985–2010**

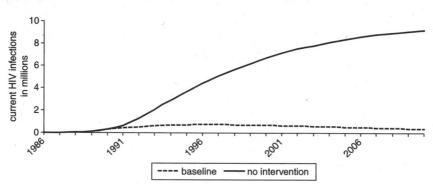

*Source:* Brown, T. (2003). HIV/AIDS in Asia. East West Centro Mimeo No. 68.

disease and monitored the effectiveness of public health interventions. The public health system was able to respond adequately to the needs of the population at risk. Condom use increased significantly toward 100 percent usage among sex workers and their clients, and HIV and other sexually transmitted disease incidence decreased dramatically. It is estimated that there would have been 6.7 million additional infections in Thailand by 2000 without the prevention program initiated in 1989 (Figure 3.7).

### Monitor and Evaluate Programs and Adjust Them to Changing Behavioral Patterns

Internationally proven methods for monitoring risky behavior, measuring change, and applying results to make adjustments in programs are rarely being used in PNG. The monitoring and evaluating of HIV/AIDS epidemics has made great progress around the world, but these lessons are generally not being applied in PNG. The introduction of ART will also require considerable monitoring, including behavioral monitoring. Ultimately, without replicable evaluation methodologies, trends cannot be tracked and no adjustments can be made to improve the response to the epidemic through improved planning, activities, funding, or training designed to achieve reduced transmission of the disease.

### Improve Donor and Government Collaboration

The coordination of the efforts of the government and donors could be improved if both parties were to commit to unifying their planning, budgetary, expenditure, and accountability requirements. What is also needed is for the government to restore the integrity and viability of existing government systems and procedures and to clearly define and implement new roles and responsibilities for the health system (the NDOH, provincial health services, and church-run health services) and the NACS.

### Strengthen Financial Accountability at All Levels

There is a major risk that accountability at all levels is being compromised in the current system because of the fractured financing and institutional arrangements that govern HIV/AIDS activities. Contractors managing some major projects have their primary accountability to donors, the PACS report to the NACS, health staff report to their own department, and so on with no central coordination or hierarchy of responsibility. As a result, there is no clear system accountability for setting national priorities and ensuring that funds are allocated to national priorities and spent accordingly. Even in the cases where there are clear priorities, the system often inadequately accounts for the resources that it uses.

### Centrality of Gender

Gender inequity and the low status of women in PNG strongly influences gender relations, sexual behavior, and the capacity of women to protect themselves from gender violence and HIV infection. HIV responses must reflect and address gender determinants of behavior and HIV vulnerability.

### Overcoming Stigma and Discrimination and the Role of a Supportive Environment

Numerous studies and reports confirm that stigma, discrimination, and denial are widespread in PNG. Evidence from Africa suggests that overcoming stigma and denial and building openness and a willingness to confront HIV openly are central to effective HIV prevention. The case of Uganda is particularly noteworthy. In Uganda, social communication at the community level helped to pierce denial, promote personal risk perception, instill personal proximity to the epidemic, and thus change community norms and reduce HIV transmission. Activities were locally led by political, religious, and community leaders who promoted changes in community norms, not just individual actions, and created enabling and protective environments long before the concept gained currency. The involvement of faith-based communities is especially noteworthy: The founding leaders of Uganda's AIDS Commission were Catholic and Anglican bishops. All of this was accomplished without large-scale involvement by specialist agencies, and most of the country's gains preceded the growth in formal HIV services. As a result, even today, surveys reveal far more openness about AIDS in Uganda than in neighboring countries, where people are just as likely to personally know someone who has died as a result of AIDS. The cumulative effect of this cultural shift ultimately had a far greater direct impact on the epidemic than did any specific activities.

In addition to formal interventions, communities have a unique function in the mosaic of the national HIV response. Most of the determinants of sexual behavior, particularly in PNG, are deeply rooted in cultural norms, beliefs, roles and practices that are established, maintained, enforced, and amended at the local level. They cannot be influenced by national interventions alone. Stigma and silence, in particular, can be overcome only where community organizations and communities contribute to a participatory process of social empowerment and social diffusion. In this realm of social change, knowing "what's best" is not a matter of technical expertise, but of local knowledge and local involvement. By definition, this can be supported—but not directed—from the outside. As Catherine Campbell notes:

"The best-designed technical interventions cannot succeed if the social environment is unsupportive. In treatment programs in Africa, for instance, it is common for a significant share of people diagnosed with HIV to decline ARV treatment, even when it is free of charge. Quite literally, they would rather die than face the stigma or social isolation of admitting their HIV status. The most influential theories of behavior change recognize the centrality of community influence. For example, social diffusion theory (an outgrowth of diffusion of innovation theory in agriculture) notes that individuals are more likely to be positively influenced by the testimonies and examples of close, trusted neighbors and friends than external experts." Thus, it is vital to work with and through communities, particularly in PNG.

## Proposed Strategic Directions for HIV/AIDS

In order to deal with these real and, in some cases, severe constraints, the government of PNG needs to adopt new strategic directions that have the overall goal of reducing the number of new HIV infections. This will require the following order of priorities.

1. **Reduce the Number of New HIV Infections.** This should be accorded the highest priority and should include interventions targeted to high-risk groups that are designed to induce behavior changes in a culturally appropriate way. These high-risk groups include sex workers, their clients, those involved in transactional sex, MSM, those employed in enclave developments and the surrounding population, and the population congregating at marketing centers throughout the country. The most immediate interventions to be implemented should be those that aim to:

   (a) Decrease unprotected sex;
   (b) Decrease the number of sexual partners, particularly concurrent sexual partners;
   (c) Treat and prevent the transmission of STIs.

   This will require a much clearer definition of the roles of the various agencies responsible for leading the response (in particular, the DPM, the NEC National Executive Council, the NDOH, the NACS, and provincial governments) and of well-articulated (and widely publicized) performance expectations. This will also require the government to demonstrate the political and administrative will to hold these agencies and their leaders publicly accountable for their performance. In particular, the NDOH and provincial health offices should be required to and assisted in taking a more active role in leading HIV prevention activities within the health sector. The NACS, on the other hand, needs to take a much stronger role in advocating, coordinating, and seeking resources for those HIV prevention activities that are better handled by civil society organizations, including the private sector.

2. **Establish a Sound Surveillance System.** The surveillance system should concentrate on:

   (a) The general population (through surveillance of the ANC population and blood donors);
   (b) High-risk groups, including those in and affected by enclave development sites;
   (c) Behavioral surveillance, particularly of the most at-risk groups, executed according to international standards;

(d) Using the surveillance information, including the syphilis data, in program planning; and

(e) Accomplishing these functions through clearly delineated roles and responsibilities.

3. **Develop Monitoring and Evaluating of Interventions and Their Effectiveness.** This should include developing indicators that reflect the importance of prevention and reduced transmission of the disease and conducting operational research, including of the potential impact of ART in promoting safer sexual behavior and reduced transmission (if any).

4. **Coordinate a Comprehensive National Response Through NACS from the Prime Minister's Office.** Coordinating the HIV/AIDS response at the highest possible level of government—the prime minister's office—can ensure that:

   • Prevention of the disease is the most important measure of success;
   • The surveillance provides timely data for program planning;
   • Clear coherent messages are delivered to the public;
   • Both social and financial sustainability is attained;
   • The response remains adaptable to changing conditions as necessary; and
   • The work of all agencies active in the HIV response (the government, churches, NGOs/CBOs, the private sector, and donors) is well coordinated.

5. **Prioritize Other Interventions.** Make sure that all interventions, including care and treatment and VCT, are prioritized according to their contribution to preventing the spread of HIV/AIDS and on their overall cost-effectiveness.

6. **Build Capacity.** Building capacity involves pooling international and national talents, learning from worldwide experiences, and taking advantage of the technical input offered by such agencies as the Global Development Learning Network of the World Bank. As discussed in Chapter 5, improved policy coherency, improved integrity of core government systems, and clear accountabilities for program design and implementation within a clear national strategy that taps all the capacities in the country (NGOs, private sector, schools, and churches) will also enhance the capacity of government to mount an adequate response to this devastating disease.

**Annex 3A. The Estimated Size of At-Risk Groups in and Near Selected Existing Enclave Developments**

| Highly vulnerable enclaves | Provinces | No. of sites | Number | Total | Comments |
|---|---|---|---|---|---|
| **MINES** | | | | | |
| (Ok Tedi; Porgera, Lihir, Tolukuma oil fields, Hides Gas)[a] | Enga, Western, N. Ireland, Central, S. Highlands | | | | HIV, Porgera: 4.5%; Ok Tedi 1.1% (2003) |
| Employees[a] | | 6 | 6,250 | 6,250 | |
| Contractors[a] | | 6 | 4,540 | 4,540 | |
| Squatters[a] | | 6 | 12,100 | 12,100 | Combined with villagers |
| Villagers[a] | | 6 | 69,200 | 69,200 | Porgera: 1.5–3.7%, Ok Tedi : 0.9% (2003) |
| Mt Kare Gold Prospect[b] | S. Highlands | 1 | 8,076 | 8,076 | 2000 census- <15 km |
| Kutubu (Moro) Gas Field[b] | S. Highlands | 1 | 3,073 | 3,073 | 2000 census- <15 km |
| Wafi Prospect Mine[b] | Morobe | 1 | 2,576 | 2,576 | 2000 census- <15 km |
| Hidden Valley Prospect[b] | Morobe | 1 | 8,729 | 8,729 | 2000 census- <15 km |
| Freida[b] | W. Sepik | 1 | 423 | 423 | 2000 census- <15 km |
| Gobe Gas Base Camp[b] | Gulf | 1 | 425 | 425 | 2000 census- <15 km |
| **LOGGERS**[c] | | | | | Reported rape of women employees, (Melick Report on Wawoi Guavi 2005); multiple reports of presence of Asian sex workers, local sex workers |
| Employees (National)[c] | | 16 | 5,250 | 5,250 | |
| Contractors (Expatriate)[c] | | 16 | 385 | 385 | |
| Kamusi[b] | Western | 1 | 1,497 | 1,497 | 2000 census- <15 km |
| Morere[b] | Gulf | 1 | 1,815 | 1,815 | 2000 census- <15 km |
| Gauri-Turama[b] | Gulf | 1 | 2,079 | 2,079 | 2000 census- <15 km |
| Siluvuti[b] | W. New Britain | 1 | 2,923 | 2,923 | 2000 census- <15 km |

*(continued)*

119

**Annex 3A. The Estimated Size of At-Risk Groups in and Near Selected Existing Enclave Developments** (continued)

| Highly vulnerable enclaves | Provinces | No. of sites | Number | Total | Comments |
|---|---|---|---|---|---|
| Ginane[b] | W. New Britain | 1 | | 1,638 | 2000 census– <15 km |
| Amio[b] | W. New Britain | 1 | | 1,638 | 2000 census– <15 km |
| Wide Bay[b] | E. New Britain | 1 | | 1,335 | 2000 census– <15 km |
| Open Bay[b] | E. New Britain | 1 | | 1,340 | 2000 census– <15 km |
| **FISHERMEN[d]** | | | | | |
| (purse seine, longline, prawn, lobster, barramundi) | Madang, Morobe, E. Sepik, Manus, Western, NCD, Milne Bay | 7 | 1,668 | 1,668 | Exposure through FSW at docks, sometimes taken for sex service on trips; exchange sex for fish |
| **Shore Bases[d]** | | | | | |
| Male | Various | Various | 250, 250 | 500 | |
| Female | | | | | |
| **Canneries[d]** | | | | | |
| Processing F | Madang, Morobe | 2 | 3,000, 400 | 3,400 | Predominantly female workforce; "wanpis, wansut"—exchange sex |
| Admin. M | | 2 | 500, 50 | 550 | Reported forced sex, commercial sex (Sullivan Report 2004) |
| **Oil Palm[d]** | | | | | |
| Hagita Oil Palm[d] | Milne Bay | 1 | | 13,248 | 2000 census– <15 km |
| **Bensbach Lodge[d]** | Western | | | 418 | 2000 census– <15 km |
| **Refugee Camp[d]** | Western | | | 1,653 | 2000 census– <15 km |
| **Total** | | | | 155,091 | |

*Data source:* a. PNG Chamber of Mines and Petroleum.
b. 2000 census—15- to 50 year-old people living within 15 km of census site.
c. Forestries Department.
d. ADB. Fisheries Project.

## Annex 3B. Main PNG HIV/AIDS Control Activities

| Name of agency | Type of agency | Main programs |
| --- | --- | --- |
| National AIDS Council and Secretariat | Government | Multisectoral coordination of the HIV/AIDS program nationwide |
| Department of Correctional Services | Government | Peer education |
| Department of Defense | Government | Home-based care, community support, returning PLWHAs |
| AusAID | Bilateral | NHASP supporting NACS, PACS, condom social marketing, surveillance, research and other activities; HSSP—procurement and distribution of condoms, STI drugs. National STI treatment project planned for initiation in 2006. |
| USAID | Bilateral | Targeted intervention, sex workers, MSM, 2–3 cities, Save the Children/Family Health International |
| British Government Community Fund | Bilateral | Community mobilization through NGOs, Madang, ETESP Elementary Teacher Education Support Program, WHP |
| Asian Development Bank | Multilateral | HIV awareness for fisheries and new cannery installation, Wewak; purchase of limited ARVs Pilot HIV/AIDS care centers HIV/AIDS Prevention and Control in Rural Development Enclaves Project |
| European Union | Multilateral | Peer education—High-risk groups: to reach 10,000 in 7 provinces |
| World Health Organization | Multilateral | Promotion of ART Health worker training—STIs |
| UNFPA | Multilateral | HIV prevention with 300 sex workers in Port Moresby (POM) through World Vision Reproductive health training Curriculum development, University of Papua New Guinea sexual health; female condom promotion |
| UNDP | Multilateral | Advocacy and policy dialogue at the national level; workplace support/legal rights for PLWHAs (International Labor Organization [ILO]); integration of gender dimensions into HIV/AIDS programs (United Nations Development Fund for Women) |
| UNICEF | Multilateral | Support for PMTCT; Village leadership, Karkar, Trobriands School-based and out-of-school education Knowledge, attitudes, and practices studies, community needs assessment Orphan studies, policies |

*(continued)*

**Annex 3B. Main PNG HIV/AIDS Control Activities** (*continued*)

| Name of agency | Type of agency | Main programs |
|---|---|---|
| UNAIDS | Multilateral | Support NSP-HIV/AIDS, M&E training; strengthening NGOs for ART |
| | | PLWHAs, health workers |
| | | Other workshops |
| International Federation of the Red Cross | International NGO | Training volunteers, AIDS awareness |
| APHEDA | Trade unions | Strategic plan, union pilot projects |
| Catholic Agencies | Faith-based | Treatment, VCT and PMTCT at few selected sites; day care for orphans and street children, Port Moresby; counseling, Wewak, Mt. Hagen |
| Catholic Medical Mission Board | Faith-based | 5 PMTCT centers, VCT, nevirapine, training |
| Caritas | Faith-based | Care centers |
| World Vision New Zealand | Faith-based | Home-based care |
| Anglicare | Faith-based | VCT w/hosp, PLWHA support; fund; youth awareness program, school, out-of-school, Port Moresby; Central; construction workers/AusAID roads & bridges; Business house awareness, Mad Lae Hagen POM; peer ed settlements, POM VCT care center opened 2004 |
| HOPE YWCA | Faith-based | Community and school awareness, Port Moresby |
| ADRA | Faith-based | Awareness, Lae |
| Mines | Private sector | Collaboration with PNGIMR-Porgera, Ok Tedi; peer education |

*Source:* Mission documentation.

**Annex 3C. Papua New Guinea's Response to the HIV/AIDS Epidemic**

| Organization | Agency | Political advocacy and multisectoral support | Surveillance, monitoring, and evaluation | Prevention | Care, treatment, and support | Health services |
|---|---|---|---|---|---|---|
| GOPNG | NACS | Technical support for advocacy and awareness events for private sector and other agencies; works with government leaders to raise priority of HIV in various government sectors; informal coordination of donors' activities; promotion of training for building local capacity; serious personnel and funding constraints | After failed attempts at sentinel surveillance between 1989 and 1994, all surveillance through passive detection of blood donors, clinical tests, voluntary tests, others; many problems with testing and delays in confirmation; collation with limited analysis by NACS ; beginning 2002—sentinel surveillance in ANC, STI, TB in POM, Lae, Goroka, Daru, and Hagen; not all sites functioning, confirmation delays, limited supervision and quality control, short of personnel and | Local distribution of condoms supplied by NHASP | Promotion of ARV treatment, support of PLWHAs | |

(continued)

**Annex 3C. Papua New Guinea's Response to the HIV/AIDS Epidemic** *(continued)*

| Organization. Agency | Political advocacy and multisectoral support | Surveillance, monitoring, and evaluation | Prevention | Care, treatment, and support | Health services |
|---|---|---|---|---|---|
| | | funds, additional sites needed in high-risk groups, no behavioral surveillance. | | | |
| NDOH | Limited | Current surveillance utilizes NDOH infrastructure and staff | Condom distribution through drug kits to health centers and Aid Post Orderlies; unknown end-user distribution; storage issues | Through the health system; constrained in infection control/ supplies; opportunistic infections drugs; treatment options, social services linked to hospitals; larger hospitals have VCT available but few support services for PLWHAs; purchase of tests | Responsible for oversight and funding of the health system through public and church institutions |
| Provincial government | Commitment varies, very limited support for PACS from some provinces | Limited involvement through health services and PACS | Very limited | None | Limited |

| | | | | | |
|---|---|---|---|---|---|
| PACS | Main implementing and coordinating agency at provincial level; main funding from NHASP, many not fully functional or staffed; little contribution from provinces, only limited success | Limited involvement in support of NDOH | Distribution of free condoms sent by NHASP to local groups, clubs, etc.; main point of contact for local community groups seeking information and funding; must apply to small grants scheme of NHASP; conducting social mapping; some developing provincial plans | In some PACS, there are counseling coordinators, but their activities are not specifically supported for VCT or care | No institutionalized association |
| PNGIMR | | HIV, STI, and behavioral surveys with AusAID funding | Maintains small intervention with sex workers in Goroka | | |
| Churches | Various efforts to advocate for humane treatment of PLWHAs, orphans | | Variable attitudes toward condoms, emphasis on abstinence and fidelity | VCT, PMTCT, support to PLWHAs at selected Catholic institutions; orphan care in Port Moresby | Major provider of health services; variable attitudes toward HIV/AIDS |
| Faith-based NGOs | Various efforts to advocate for humane treatment of PLWHAs and prevention for youth | No linkage to surveillance | Variable attitudes to condoms, emphasis on abstinence and fidelity | Youth life skills; AIDS awareness; VCT, support for PLWHAs; workplace awareness | Some provision of settlement health care in POM |

*(continued)*

**Annex 3C. Papua New Guinea's Response to the HIV/AIDS Epidemic** *(continued)*

| Organization | Agency | Political advocacy and multisectoral support | Surveillance, monitoring, and evaluation | Prevention | Care, treatment, and support | Health services |
|---|---|---|---|---|---|---|
| | | | | | campaigns in Lae, POM, Mt.Hagen, Wewak; planned youth-friendly clinics in POM | |
| AusAID | AusAID | Major donor; committed $43 million for 2000–2005 for implementation of MTP in provinces through NHASP and PACS; preparing joint strategy with World Bank (WB), ADB | Through NHASP-funded activities | Through NHASP-funded activities | Through NHASP-funded activities | Major donor through health projects |
| | NHASP | Major funds for HIV control through this AusAID project; aim to implement MTP in all provinces through PACS with emphasis on STI treatment, labs, surveillance, counseling, peer education, social marketing of condoms | Support for surveillance in MTP; procurement of HIV test kits | Social marketing of condoms, STI treatment, testing, peer education, procurement of male and yes female condoms (branded) there are male and female condoms | STI treatment, strengthening labs, training prescribers for ARVs | |

| | | | Procurement, distribution of generic male condoms | Procurement of azithromycin | |
|---|---|---|---|---|---|
| HSSP | Project to improve health services | | | Procurement of azithromycin | Major project for improving health services in provinces and national functions |
| EU | Sexual health project aims to conduct peer education activities for high-risk groups; USD3.5 million 2002–2007 | No linkage with surveillance | Lae, POM, Goroka: sex workers, truckers, etc. | Not linked | Not linked |
| USAID FHI/Save the Children | USD750,000 per annum over 2003–2006; behavioral change interventions for sex workers and MSM | Not yet linked to surveillance | Intention to work in 2–3 cities | Not linked | Not linked |
| UN UNAIDS | Support NSP-HIV/AIDS process; GFATM proposals, leadership advocacy | No involvement | None | None | No association |
| WHO | Promotion of ART | | | Development of ART program | Directly linked to major hospitals |
| UNICEF | Conducts workshops for local agencies; funds NGOs; youth, sex workers; technical support for PMTCT | Not involved | Through NGOs; with education dept., curriculum | PMTCT, technical support | Associated through workshops for PMTCT |

(continued)

**Annex 3C. Papua New Guinea's Response to the HIV/AIDS Epidemic** *(continued)*

| Organization | Agency | Political advocacy and multisectoral support | Surveillance, monitoring, and evaluation | Prevention | Care, treatment, and support | Health services |
|---|---|---|---|---|---|---|
| UNDP | | Gender mainstreaming in other projects; promotion of leadership | | | Leadership training for PLWHAs | |
| UNFPA | | Advocacy for reproductive health | No linkage with surveillance | Sex worker intervention, HIV and STI testing, STI treatment; referral; coverage of 300 sex workers in POM; tertiary education peer ed; church leaders/wives | STI treatment | Referral |
| ADB | | Prepare joint strategy with WB | | Support AIDS awareness program in new cannery at Wewak, other fisheries | Purchase of ARVs, support pilot program | Major donor through health projects |
| World Bank | | Prepare joint strategy with ADB | | | | |
| Private sector | Mines | | | | | |
| | Porgera | | With PNGIMR, research | Research, peer education | Testing | |
| | Ok Tedi | | | Awareness | Testing | |
| | Lihir | | | Awareness | Testing | |
| | Private clinics | | | | Treatment and testing | |

## Notes

1. Data collected by World Bank from PMGH ANC 2005.

2. Data collected by World Bank from Mount Hagen and Kudjip hospitals in Western Highlands and Vunapope and Nonga Base Hospitals in Eastern Highlands Province June 2004.

3. HIV can be spread in three ways—through sexual contact, through mother-to-child transmission (via birth and breastfeeding), and through the exchange of blood. The risk of transmitting HIV during sex rises when the viral load in genital secretions is high, which can occur if the blood viral load is high and/or if a genitally sexually transmitted infection is present. Risk is also greater in anal versus vaginal intercourse, and in vaginal intercourse among girls under 18 to 20 years old compared with older women.

4. Previous work by Jenkins and Robalino (2003) has shown that there is a negative relationship between increased HIV prevalence and reduced female participation in the formal workforce.

5. Previous cross-country comparisons by Over (1977) have shown that there is a direct positive relationship between the Gini coefficient and HIV prevalence; in other words, the higher the coefficient, the higher the prevalence.

6. In fact, the core of NACS staffing was established by shifting much of the NDOH disease surveillance capacity to NACS and thereby destroying much of the already limited disease surveillance capacity in PNG.

# CHAPTER 4

# Education in Papua New Guinea: A Situation Assessment and Proposed Strategic Directions

## Introduction

The MTDS 2005–2010 highlights the importance of primary education and needs of illiterate adults and out-of-school training for the sustained development of human capital in the country. Specifically, the MTDS defines its primary aim for education as being: "... *to support the implementation of reform aimed at achieving Universal Primary Education. Under the goal of Universal Education, all children will be able to complete nine years of basic education.*" The aim was to meet this development goal by 2015 consistent with the commitment of the PNG government to the MDGs and to the EFA objectives. The MTDS also argues that "*while basic education will be the foremost priority of the government over the medium term ... [it will also] ensure PNG's brightest and most talented students have the opportunity to receive a quality higher education ... [and] address the requirements of functionally illiterate adults and out-of-school youth, through community-based informal education programs.*" More generally, there is a recognition that PNG needs to emphasize training, particularly in the skills that are relevant to rural development and the informal sector, which together absorb over 80 percent of the country's workforce.

This review of the current situation in the education and skills development sectors aims to help the government of PNG to develop an education and training sector strategy consistent with the twin goals of:

(a) Achieving universal basic education (UBE); and
(b) Ensuring that postbasic education responds to formal labor market demands and that all skills development facilitates income-earning opportunities, especially in the informal rural sector of the economy.

The review starts by giving a brief overview of the education reforms that have been implemented over the past 12 years. It then explores the continuing problems of access, equity, quality, governance, and financing in the system and assesses whether the new National Education Plan (NEP 2) goes far enough to overcome the constraints facing the education sector and to solve those problems. This includes an analysis of the resource demands both on the government and on the wider community (parents, nongovernment agencies, and the private sector) and at the efficiency gains that will need to be made if PNG is to have any chance of meeting the twin goals.[1] The review also explores issues facing the skills-development postgeneral education sector. Finally, consistent with the basic purpose of the review, this chapter identifies priorities for the education and training sector, and provides a proposed strategy designed to develop and sustain a more comprehensive education and skills system for PNG.

## National Education Reform (1993)

The PNG government introduced an education reform package in 1993 in response to concerns about: (i) access, especially at the primary level and at the lower high school level; (ii) the system's general performance; (iii) poor education outcomes; and (iv) whether it was going to be possible to maintain financing for the increased enrollment rates. Gender disparities in access and educational outcomes were also substantial and needed to be addressed.

The reform fundamentally restructured the education system in PNG. It redefined schooling to consist of nine years of "basic" education (three years of elementary and six years of primary) and four years of secondary education (Grades 9 to 12). An important backdrop to the reform was the average annual population growth rate–in excess of 2.7 percent per annum. With little abatement in population growth rates, the expanding number of children to be educated continues to pose a major challenge for the education system. More generally, the

MTDS acknowledges high population growth as a key threat to growth and development.

The primary focus of the government's reform was to increase access, equity, and retention at all levels of education and, in so doing, to support the MDGs and EFA goals of achieving Universal Primary Education (UPE)—which in the case of PNG equates to nine years of UBE. A second focus of the reform was qualitative—to revise the curriculum to address concerns about the quality of the teaching and learning in PNG's schools and its relevance to real life. Particular attention was given to improving academic performance and to developing life skills that students would be able to use in their villages when they left school.

Because of the reforms, the system expanded dramatically in quantitative terms, particularly in the basic education cycle. In 2003,[2] one decade after the education reform commenced, there were about 1 million basic and postbasic students (an approximately 100 percent increase from 1993) serviced by some 33,000 teachers (a 154 percent increase) in over 7,600 institutions (a 153 percent increase).[3]

## Expenditure and Financing

The funding of the national education system is shared between government, donors, parents, and community; however, despite achievements, total funds provided from these sources have fallen well short of providing for the National Education Plan 1995–2004 (NEP 1) general education[4] targets in terms of basic education enrollment, quality, and equity.

Total government expenditure on education has, however, been significant over the last decade. Between 1996 and 2003[5] (excepting 2002)[6]:

(a) education's total expenditure, recurrent and development, grew from K 185.8 million to K 473.6 million in nominal terms and from K 185.8 million to K 215.4 million in constant (1996 prices) values, a real increase of 16 percent. Its share of total government expenditure ranged between 10 and 15 percent, being in 1996, 10 percent, and in 2003, 12 percent;

(b) education's recurrent expenditure grew from K 180 million to K 423 million in nominal terms and from K 180 million to K 192 million in constant (1996 prices) values—a real increase of 7 percent. Its share of total government recurrent expenditure ranged between 11 and 17 percent, being 11 percent in 1996 and in 16 percent in 2003;

(c) recurrent education's share of total education expenditure ranged between 77 and 95 percent, being 97 percent in 1996 and 89 percent in 2003;

(d) teacher salaries made up the biggest single item of expenditure, ranging between 67 and 85 percent of the recurrent education budget, being 85 percent in 1996 and 80 percent in 2003.

Since 2003, education appropriations seem to demonstrate an even greater commitment to education. In 2005, budget appropriations to general education had increased to 17 percent of the total budget. General education's share of GDP has ranged between 2.7 percent in 1996 to 3.2 in 2003, reaching as high as 4.8 in 2001. Based on the 2005 appropriations, it now stands at 3.5 percent of GDP. This compares with the latest United Nations Educational, Scientific, and Cultural Organization (UNESCO) figures, 2000–2002, for the region of Indonesia (1.5), Solomon Islands (3.4), Vanuatu (8.2), Tonga (5.3), Fiji (6.0), and the Philippines (3.5) (UNESCO 2004).

The contributions of donors to the education development budget have fluctuated considerably from year to year, but in recent years have steadily increased.[7] In 2002, the development budget allocation was K 1.7 million, rising to K 50.7 million in 2003 and K 107.2 million in 2004.[8] Development expenditure's share of total education expenditure in these same years was 0.3, 10.7, and 18.4 percent, respectively. Based on the figures for 2004, AusAID's contribution accounted for some two-thirds (66.4 percent) of the development budget, followed by the EU (22 percent), New Zealand (6.4 percent), and JICA (2.1 percent). In total, donor funding on average accounts for around 97 percent of the education-sector development budget, meaning that only 3 percent is financed by the government.

## The New National Education Plan: Addressing General Education Issues

The rapid expansion of the system has made it more fragile. In some respects, the resounding quantitative success in increasing access in the first decade of reform has generated additional stresses that must be addressed in the next decade. These stresses are most evident in the broad areas of access and equity, quality and relevance, governance and management, and financing. This section addresses the first three areas of concern, and the next section will deal specifically with the issue of how general education can be funded in PNG in the years to come.

NEP 2, which is designed to cover the years from 2005 to 2014, was launched in early 2005 with the goal of addressing the continuing challenges in the education sector. The situation assessment for the plan draws heavily on a number of key studies and reports. These include the NDOE's "The State of Education in PNG" (2002 and 2003); the Education Sector Affordability Study (2003); and the PERR (2003). NEP 2 takes particular note of the recommendations in the PERR paper on "Improving Education Spending" and devises strategies based on those recommendations. NEP 2 makes the crucial but unwarranted assumption that the capacity and commitment exist at all levels of governance to implement these strategies. Furthermore, as with NEP 1, NEP 2 may have underestimated the level of resources required to implement these strategies and overestimated the extent to which parents and development partners can be expected to meet the gap.

*Access and Equity.* NEP 2 aims to expand enrollments in basic education from 957,000 in 2005 to 1,370,000 in 2014[9]—a growth rate of 3.6 percent per annum—and envisages achieving universal enrollment of six-year-olds in the first year of school by 2012. Even such a rapid expansion as this would only increase the net enrollment rate for the basic cycle from an estimated 71 percent in 2005 to 80 percent by 2014 because of the sustained rate of population growth.[10] According to NEP 2 projections, simply maintaining existing enrollment proportions would require enrollment rates to grow at the same pace as the projected basic education cycle's school-age population (6 to 14 years old); in other words, by 2.8 percent per year.

In addition, a number of significant inequalities pervade the education system and need to be explicitly addressed. They are an issue in the PNG system, not only because of inequity of outcomes, but because inequities affect the capacity of regions and people to implement the education reforms. This is particularly so concerning the assumptions made in NEP 2 about the contributions that will be needed from provincial and local-level governments (LLGs) and from parents.

*Participation and Absenteeism.* Despite the rapid increase in enrollments and in transitions into Grades 7, 9, and 11, it is estimated that in 2003 some 30 percent of children of primary/basic education age were not enrolled.[11] The Mi Lusim Shul study[12] estimated that as many as 19 percent of children still never enter school at all.

Student absenteeism is also a serious issue; the Mi Lusim Skul study revealed that absenteeism on any one day in 2001 was as high as 9 to 25 percent in different provinces. The Public Expenditure and Service Delivery (PESD) study[13] estimated that student absenteeism in 2002 averaged 15 percent, with significant provincial variations ranging from 26 percent in West New Britain and 8 percent in Morobe.

Retention in the basic education cycle remains a major problem. According to NEP 2, only 53 percent of children who enrolled in Grade 1 in 1998 completed Grade 6 in 2003, a decline from an estimated 61 percent for 1995—a result counter to the objectives of the education reforms. Significant variations by province are also noteworthy—in Eastern Highlands and Sandaun, only 20–22 percent of those entering school remain until grade 8.

*Geographic Inequity.* Access to general education varies considerably from province to province. Using enrollments as a percentage of the estimated total population of provinces in 2003 as an access index,[14] the national average was 15.6 percent, ranging from the lowest— Madang, Enga, Gulf, and Southern Highlands (all under 12 percent)— to the highest—Bougainville, Manus, Milne Bay, and Western (all over 22 percent).

NEP 2 acknowledges the significant variations in access between provinces, particularly with regard to elementary schools, Grades 7 and 8, and secondary places. However, while it proposes an annual increase of 360 classes (on average) in elementary schools and 150 new Grade 7 classes, it does not explain how this expansion will be spread throughout the provinces to redress the inequity-of-access issue. Similarly, NEP 2 does not say how to control transition rates from Grade 8 to Grade 9 (already at 70 percent, or 20 percentage points over the proposed target of 50 percent) as a result of past expansion and lower-than-expected completion rates in Grade 8. While secondary school access has increased significantly, the PESD study indicates that the relatively small number of secondary schools means that the nearest secondary school is four hours away (eight hours round-trip) from the average primary school—about five hours away from schools in poor areas and about six hours away from schools in remote areas.[15]

The PESD study of 2002 showed that remote schools were at a significant disadvantage compared with more accessible schools in respect of facilities, including the state of their buildings, specialist rooms (such as science labs, technology labs, home economics rooms, and libraries), equipment, water and toilets, and electricity. Remote schools have greater difficulty in attracting and retaining teachers and tend to have higher rates of teacher absenteeism—17 percent compared with 13 percent in more accessible schools.

*Gender Inequity.* Gender equality in education remains a challenge for PNG. In 2003, girls occupied between 44 and 46 percent of school places across all provinces in the basic education cycle, dropping to an average of 40 percent by Grade 10 and 35 percent by Grades 11 and 12.[16] Female teachers accounted for 41 percent of staff,[17] and female students accounted for about 42 percent of places at teacher training colleges. Between 1996 and 2003, the proportion of females in general education enrolments did not change significantly, and although the proportion of female teachers in basic education increased from 35 to 41 percent, it only increased marginally from 34 to 35 percent at the secondary level.

*Capacity to Pay.* The PESD study also showed that schools from wealthier communities were better supported, not only in terms of revenue from subsidies (partly through reduced "leakage") but also by fees. Indeed, the wealthiest 20 percent of schools received more revenue from fees than from subsidies (see below for a discussion of fees).

However, NEP 2 does make some proposals toward addressing the problems of income inequity, such as the proposed scholarship scheme for Grades 10 to 12 (to be introduced by 2008–2009) that targets students from remote areas, promotes the value of schooling, encourages greater involvement in school management by local communities and boards of management (BOMs), and recommends better counseling services for students to improve retention.

### Quality and Relevance

NEP 2 recognizes the importance of quality inputs and commits to supporting teaching and learning materials, preservice and in-service training, the monitoring of teacher performance, improved assessment, and counseling services in schools. However, it does not appear to take into account the resource implications of making substantial curriculum changes or even of its ongoing requirements, particularly with regard to the cost of materials, including textbooks (see also the Financing Challenge, Section 4, below).

In reality, NEP 2 addresses quality and relevance primarily in terms of curriculum and teacher training. Other important factors such as leadership training for head teachers and school BOMs (e.g., to administer funds effectively and to create a school environment conducive to learning), and the inspectorate, are given less prominence in this context, the principal references in the NEP being under Management.

*Curriculum.* One of the basic assumptions of the education reform was that curriculum revision would have a positive impact on the quality-of-learning outcomes and on retention, particularly at the primary level, thereby promoting the goal of UBE. The NDOE's Curriculum Development Division, with the assistance of the AusAID-funded Elementary Teacher Education Support Program (ETESP) and the Curriculum Reform Implementation Program (CRIP), has completed the revision of the basic education curricula. Work is well under way to revise the curricula for Grades 9 and 10, which have not been upgraded since the 1980s. While the curriculum revisions include the preparation of teacher guides, there is a shortage of teaching and learning materials, including textbooks, especially at the elementary and primary levels.

Although there is considerable anecdotal evidence suggesting that the quality of education is declining, there is little reliable assessment of learning outcomes. It is reasonable to expect that as more children enter school and automatically progress to Grade 8, there is likely to be a greater proportion of students at the lower end of the intellectual ability distribution than was the case when there were significant "push-outs" at the end of Grade 6.

Apart from the paucity of materials and textbooks (the PESD study estimates that 85 percent of primary schools and about 70 percent of secondary schools do not have sufficient textbooks for students to use and, that in particular, there is a paucity of materials to support effective teaching to help students to start learning English instead of the vernacular in Grades 3–5—a critical transitional phase in the syllabus), other factors would appear to be detracting from the quality of learning. These include delayed preparation and distribution of materials to support the new syllabuses, student absenteeism, late opening of schools and teacher absenteeism (which effectively reduces the length of the school year), limited monitoring of teacher performance by head teachers and inspectors, limited in-service support for teachers, and less-than-adequate facilities.

*Assessment.* Assessment of learning outcomes remains a weakness, both at the system level and for individual students in the classroom. The only national measures of learning outcomes are the Grades 8, 10, and 12 examinations, which are, of course, not necessarily a reliable assessment of achievement levels over time. However, at the request of NDOE, AusAID has been supporting the development and trial of curriculum Standard Monitoring Tests for Grades 3, 5, and 8. Ongoing funding has not been costed in the plan.

*Teacher Development.* NEP 2 proposes an enhanced program of professional development for teachers at all levels. This will be achieved by introducing more flexible ways of providing these services, including strengthening the role of the Papua New Guinea Education Institute (PNGEI) and by conducting programs at regional and provincial levels. Some cost-recovery measures are proposed, including the option of teachers paying for their own professional development (if it should lead to a professional qualification) or the option of this being covered by provincial budgets, which, based on experience to date, is problematic.

Provision for in-service training and development in reality is limited and largely ad hoc. In the past, the government has relied heavily on donors to finance teacher in-service training. Budget allocations for this work remain seriously inadequate. Furthermore, there are no structures or regular training posts at the provincial or district level to support teachers in schools, other than the inspectorate, which is not fully functional (see below).

*The Inspectorate.* Within the national context, the inspectorate has a key role in assessing teacher performance and the standards of school achievement. NEP 2 proposes a major revamp of the inspectorate, including involving BOMs in elementary schools (for example, in monitoring teacher attendance); greater participation of head teachers (and also BOMs) in primary schools; and annual reporting by inspectors on all secondary schools. Historically, the inspectorate—particularly for primary schools—has long suffered from limited resources that have restricted its ability to visit schools on a regular basis, particularly those in remote areas. Specific proposals to reverse this lack of resources are not evident in the new plan.

*Facilities.* There is widespread concern that school facilities and infrastructure are generally in a state of disrepair. According to the PESD study, there are, on average, 3.5 classrooms per 100 students, but, when accounting for those in disrepair, the average ratio of effective classrooms per 100 students drops to 2.3. Only 50 percent of all classrooms contain a desk and chair for teachers, and 40 percent do not have enough chairs for students. Without a concerted change in current domestic financing arrangements, it seems likely that PNG will have to continue to depend on donor support to assist in expanding, upgrading, and maintaining buildings (see Chapter 5 on Cross-Cutting Issues).

*HIV/AIDS.* Nowhere is the issue of quality and relevance more important than in how the national education system responds to the HIV/AIDS epidemic discussed in Chapter 3. Many young people are sexually active, including those in schools,[18] but they generally know very little about HIV/AIDS, STDs, and reproductive health in general. Although many children do not attend school or complete the basic cycle of education, the majority do attend school at some time. Therefore, schools are an enormously important place to educate young people about HIV/AIDS and reproductive health and could play a critical part in the overall national response to HIV/AIDS, reproductive health, and health status more generally.

While NEP 2 acknowledges that education has a role to play in the response to HIV/AIDS, it does not elaborate a strategy, although it does commit to operationalizing such a strategy in 2007. A comprehensive response should at least include the following elements:

(a) A revision of the "personal development" elements of the curriculum of each level of schooling to include knowledge of HIV/AIDS, how it is contracted, and how to prevent transmission of the virus. This could be developed within the context of "healthy lifestyles" and within the framework of lessons about reproductive health;[19]

(b) The development of relevant material and pamphlets for children (and their parents and communities) to support the revised curriculum;

(c) A revision of the preservice teacher education syllabus to ensure that teachers who are entering the teaching service are equipped to teach the revised school curriculum. This would also involve training the staff of teacher training colleges to teach the revised teacher education syllabus;

(d) Putting HIV/AIDS on the agenda for in-service training for all teachers in the school system to increase their own knowledge of HIV/AIDS and how to protect themselves from the disease and ensure that they are equipped to teach the revised syllabus and are familiar with the supporting materials; and

(e) Consideration should also be given to providing special training for school inspectors and other senior education staff who support teachers and schools.

*Prerequisites for Realizing Quality Improvements.* The realization of the quality output objectives will depend in large measure on:

(a) Ensuring the relevance of the curriculum, which will entail substantial revision at the postbasic level;

(b) Building the capacity of teachers who will require extensive in-service training, particularly given the proposals in NEP 2 to increase student/teacher ratios and to introduce multigrade teaching;

(c) Providing appropriate teaching and learning materials (including textbooks);

(d) Implementing the proposal for school managers and principals to become more involved in appraising teachers, which will require a substantial in-service program;

(e) Revisiting the approach to monitoring elementary schools (which currently involves the traditional format for inspections);

(f) Reviewing the role of inspectorate and assessing the scope for reducing the size of the cadre and using the "saved" funds for training principals and for operational expenses (particularly travel);

(g) Ensuring that provincial and district education advisors have the capacity and facilities to fulfill their management-related responsibilities, including making visits to schools; and

(h) Ensuring effective monitoring and assessment of the performance of students, teachers, and schools.

Given the current, relatively low quality of education provided across the sector, there is a strong case for adopting the proposed NEP 2 strategies to improve the quality and for finding the resources that will be necessary to implement them.

## Governance, Management, and Community Participation

*Governance.* A major constraint on education functioning, and therefore on the implementation of NEP 2, is the fragmentation of governance and the system's demonstrated weakness in (i) ensuring the sustainability of reforms and initiatives in a time of financial hardship, including having to take account of the costs of new initiatives; (ii) establishing organizational systems to meet new demands; (iii) planning at all levels for increasing numbers of students, teachers, and classes; (iv) providing planning expertise and commitment at the provincial level; and (v) strengthening the capacity of national and subnational authorities to monitor and evaluate the reforms and to measure progress against the targets.

The fragmentation arises significantly from (i) the failure of PNG to implement or enforce the mechanisms needed for the effective support and monitoring of the decentralized system of public service (including general and vocational education) delivery at provincial and local government levels as provided for under the 1995 NOL, and (ii) the "silo mentality" of the different agencies and levels of government involved.

NEP 2 acknowledges the difficulties involved in complying with the decentralization provisions of the NOL and meeting the associated costs, as well as the human resource management and financial management challenges that this presents. In the education sector, the NOL assigned the authority and responsibility for implementing national general education and vocational school policies to provincial and LLGs.; however, the law did not require provinces to report to the NDOE at the national level so there is no line of accountability. This has led to marked variations across and within provinces in terms of equity and resource allocation. These differences are particularly marked in secondary education, where the number of places proportionate to the population is grossly uneven.

In contrast, the limited interchange between the NDOE and other central agencies—particularly with Department of Treasury (DOT), Department of National Planning and Rural Development (DNPRD), Department of Prime Minister (DPM), and Department of Provincial and Local Level Government (DPLLG)—has been more a matter of practice than of legal limitations. Instead of coordinating their plans and budgets, different agencies and levels of government have a "silo mentality," which leads them to operate independently of each other. Of particular concern is the fact that the NDOE has traditionally been excluded from the provinces' discussions about provincial budgets and expenditure, which jeopardizes effective planning and implementation at all levels.

The eventual overcoming of these weaknesses—as acknowledged in the MTDS—requires reform of the NOL and a "whole-of-government" approach. In the meantime, the national government does have a number of financial tools to enable it to control key aspects of the education sector. For example, teacher positions are created at the national level and teachers' salaries are paid through the national budget. Also, more than half the subsidy amount funded through the national budget is administered through the NDOE.[20,21] The national government needs to use these and other mechanisms to ensure that it exercises due control over the expansion of the education system in accordance with national policy and plans; however, these administrative controls also touch on political matters that can only be solved with high-level political integrity and support for senior management.[22]

*Management capacity* across the system is limited or inhibited, and because of the decentralized system under the NOL is a concern at all government levels. The NEP 2 at the outset acknowledges that "The education reform process started in 1993 (. . .) has not always been supported by the required management and institutional strengthening reform."[23]

The NDOE recognizes the need to upgrade its structures and systems, and considerable progress has been made on strengthening central management capacity as a result of the AusAID-funded Institutional Strengthening Project and the more recent Education Capacity Building Project (ECBP). Nevertheless, there is still an ongoing need to consolidate the NDOE's capacity and at the same time upgrade capacity at the provincial and local levels, including in schools and vocational colleges.

One issue with considerable financial implications[24] is the weak management of the employment and deployment of teachers and the lack of an entity accountable for teachers' performance and attendance.[25] The responsibility for establishing teaching positions; for hiring, paying, and deploying teachers; and for monitoring their performance is shared among different agencies within and across national and provincial governments. Recent work (supported by AusAID) has been done to improve the management of the public sector payroll, and this has gone some way toward improving personnel-related policies and systems.[26] In addition, an interagency Position Allocation Committee (PAC), arising from NEP, for deploying teachers to provinces has been established. Other related NEP proposals include introducing an annual audit of teachers, conducting reviews of teacher and inspectorate absenteeism, and giving greater responsibility for managing teachers to head teachers and BOMs. The challenge now for all parties across the sector is to implement these improvements in a timely and consistent way. The NDOE has also completed a review of the size of its administrative and support staff, in accordance with government requirements.

*Community and parental support* for education is variable. Traditionally, parents, school communities, and agencies such as churches and NGOs, have contributed to the cost of providing general education through the payment of schools fees and through in-cash or in-kind support for managing, constructing, and maintaining school facilities (at the elementary and primary levels) and for teacher housing (at the primary level). However, anecdotal reports suggest that more than 50 percent of secondary school fees remain unpaid and that the majority of communities make little or no contribution to building and maintaining the infrastructure of their schools, with the exception of some church agencies. Nevertheless, the PESD study estimates that contributions from parents in 2001 amounted to K 68 million (some 10 percent of the total education budget, excluding higher education), while a similar amount was raised from other private sources, namely, development partners, NGOs (including churches), and local communities.

The NEP emphasizes the importance of the continuing involvement of parents (by way of fees) and communities (presumably including agencies) in constructing and maintaining elementary and primary schools (whether in cash or kind). The plan suggests that the NDOE should hold regular forums with church agencies and NGOs and increase the capacity of community organizations at the provincial and district level to raise the awareness of community members of the need to contribute to maintaining schools.[27]

## General Education Challenges: The Need to Enhance the NEP 2 Framework

### Key Implementation Challenges

Government reform initiatives in education, including responses to the recommendations embodied in the PERR study, are set out in NEP 2. Most of the key individual reform actions required to be undertaken are well-known, are long-standing, and have been mutually agreed as necessary between government and the Joint Donors both in the past, and as part of the dialogue underpinning this review. However, it is the assessment of this review that, given implementation capacity constraints, NEP 2 seriously underestimates the implementation challenges of the plan and the need to sequence reforms. This is of great significance, because the expenditure estimates underpinning NEP 2 (see below) assume these reforms are in place and that the implied significant efficiency gains have been made.

Many of the reforms will require a coordinated and sustained effort and commitment of the central agencies of government to give effect to the plan. A few key examples of key reforms illustrate this point:

*Control of Teacher Employment and Deployment.* There are significant variations from the national policy on student/teacher ratios in the current employment and deployment of teachers between and within provinces. It is reassuring to note that the long-standing problem of ghost teachers has recently been addressed, with some measure of success, through the AusAID-funded Payroll and Personnel Project.

In addition, as noted above, the teacher PAC, as recommended under NEP 2 (comprising NDOE, the Teaching Service Commission [TSC], DOT, DNPRD, and provincial government representation) has been established. This provides for an annual agreement on teacher allocations, employment, and budgets consistent with national policies. It will be critical for the PAC to be linked to the budget processes (see below).

*Increases in Student-Teacher Ratios.* In order to effect cost savings, the plan proposes to increase student-teacher ratios (STRs) and class sizes at each level—including the institutionalization of multigrade teaching in the basic cycle. This will only be feasible if teacher employment is controlled and teachers are deployed according to need.[28]

*Containing Secondary School Construction and Enrollment Growth.* NDOE, and the national government more generally, has only limited and indirect control over school construction by provinces. Once constructed, provinces deploy teachers paid from the national-government-financed teacher payroll. Given the high social demand for secondary school education, it will be very difficult for NDOE, without the full and active support of the central agencies of government, to restrict support through subsidies and teachers to only approved schools. A failure to control school construction by collective action by national authorities will also mean provincial equity objectives will be hard to achieve.

*Establish Mechanism for Reviewing Adequacy of National and Provincial Budgets.* Over recent years (with the exception of efforts to prepare the 2006 budget) there has been only limited discussion between DOT (or other central agencies) and the NDOE on provincial budgets. Since the new NOL, NDOE has had no involvement in reviewing provincial budgets and being able to advise on their adequacy and consistency with national policy objectives—notwithstanding that the vast majority of recurrent expenditure is financed by the national government.

*Review of the Organizational Capacity of NDOE and Provincial Offices of Education.* Currently under way, this review is an opportunity to relate the NDOE structure to the outcomes and strategies in the plan, including consideration of core business and outsourcing, particularly for major procurement and printing.

This report recommends that these actions need to be sequenced within the order in which they are raised. Control of teacher employment and deployment is critical. Implementing policies on teacher-student ratios is not feasible without being able to control the number of teachers. Containing construction programs for high schools to be consistent with expansion targets will reduce pressure on additional teachers to staff empty classrooms and enable increased fiscal space for basic education. Ensuring that additional schools, consistent with agreed policies, are allocated to provinces with the lowest access to secondary schools will be a serious challenge—but a critical challenge. Controlling teacher growth with limited budgets will enable critical quality issues to be addressed. Settling how to do the above will have implications for how NDOE and provincial education authorities are organized and how they interact with the central agencies.

## The Financing Challenge

In aggregate terms, NEP 2 estimates the costs to the government-financed budget of achieving its targets for the general education sector, including vocational schooling, as K 545 million in 2005, rising to K 726 million in 2014 (in 2003 prices)—an increase of 3.2 percent per annum.[29] Significantly, the costs of achieving the proposed basic education goals (i.e., universal entry by 2012) are expected to rise from K 421 million to K 560 million, implying that the basic education budget, while the largest share of the education budget at 76 percent, would also increase at 3.2 percent per annum (i.e., the share proposed for basic education financed by government is not expected to increase faster than the rest of the education sector). On the other hand, the increased enrollments, particularly at the basic level, are expected to be feasible in financial terms because the efficiency gains (discussed above) that will result in a fall in costs per student in the basic cycle from K 435 to K 409 per annum, and a reduction for those in the postbasic system from K 1,051 to K 1,030 (in real 2003 prices)—representing falls of 6 percent and 2 percent, respectively.

It is expected that the cost of the basic education system would rise from 15.8 percent of the national recurrent budget in 2005 to 18.3 percent in 2014 (assuming forward budget growth projections of 2.5 percent per annum in real terms). This, in accordance with the MTDS, represents a shift in government priorities toward basic education. But it also represents (and this is not in accordance with the MTDS) an equal shift in priority toward postbasic, as over this period, basic education's share of general education remains the same, at 76 percent.

The costings underpinning the proposed NEP 2 program are reasonably detailed; however, the framework for the costings is very partial in that they only cover the costs expected to be financed by the government-financed budget and by no means cover all education needs. From an expenditure and financing perspective, the NEP has five significant limitations that need to be addressed:

First, the plan does not adequately cost a minimum package of quality inputs (e.g., curriculum materials, including teacher materials and textbooks, and elementary-teacher training workshops). The review estimates that a "quality-enhanced" package such as this would cost K 39 million in 2005 and K 54 million in 2014 (in real 2003 prices), an increase of 7.3 percent in the overall education budget.[30]

Second, the plan does not include school operational costs, which are meant to be covered by school fees. These fees are set annually by the National Education Board (NEB) as guidelines to the provinces and are supposed to cover school operational costs that are not financed directly by government. If all fees were collected (it is estimated that less than half the amount owed by parents is collected), they would amount to K 221 million, or 27 percent of the estimated cost of a full "quality-enhanced" education program in 2005.[31]

Third, although less important in quantitative terms, the plan does not include (i) the cost to higher education of the expansion of secondary teacher training, (ii) the full cost of in-service teacher training (which is at least in part financed by fees), (iii) the full cost of examinations and the operational cost of the inspectorate, and (iv) the operational cost of education administrative staff employed and located in the provinces on the provincial payroll.

Fourth, except as noted below for expenditure on school infrastructure, the NEP costings do not include development expenditures that are largely financed by PNG's development partners. In recent years, these have represented about 11 to 18 percent of education expenditure and have largely focused on (i) technical assistance, (ii) curriculum development activities, and (iii) system capacity building, including staff development and training. Development partners have also financed significant recurrent expenditures outside the education budget,[32] but this support has been piecemeal and not part of an agreed systematic expenditure plan jointly financed by the government and its development partners.

Fifth, the NEP lays out the maintenance and infrastructure costs for (i) secondary schools, which are the responsibility of the provinces; and

(ii) those of elementary and primary schools, which are the responsibility of LLG. These costs, which amounted to K 53 million in 2005, rising to K 70 million in 2014 (in 2003 prices), are probably reasonable estimates of the burden of costs on provincial and local governments. However, the NEP makes no assessment of whether or not provincial and local governments have the financial capacity or willingness to finance either the maintenance or the capital costs.[33] Over the past decade, it has become clear that provinces and local governments have not been financing school maintenance at the levels needed or implied by the plan. Furthermore, to meet equity objectives, it is critical that secondary school construction, in particular, be targeted to provinces where there are currently insufficient secondary school places; however, the "own revenue" capacity of provinces varies enormously, and it is not clear that some of the poorer provinces have the capacity to finance schools in the manner implied by the plan. On the other hand, richer provinces have considerable capacity to finance new schools, and often do so. Thus, senior high school growth in the last plan was over 300 percent faster than planned, with the result that enrollments already exceed the plan's totals for the next decade (see Chapter 5).

There are a number of key assumptions underlying the NEP 2 costings, outlined in part in the previous section, that if not implemented will undermine the validity of the costing—particularly the achievement of the expected "efficiency gains" that drive the reduced annual student unit costs. Specifically, the NEP 2 costings assume, among others mentioned:

(a) That there is no real increase in teacher remuneration;
(b) That there is no "leakage" of central education funds from subnational distribution agencies, such as provincial and local governments and parliamentary member fund accounts. In reality, the PESD study estimated that 16 to 29 percent of fee subsidies did not reach schools in 2001;[34] and
(c) That postbasic education enrollment rates and continuation rates stay within the plan policy framework proposed. The NEP assumes that continuation rates are contained within the national policy limits (50 and 25[35] percent, respectively, from the preceding Grades 8 and 10).

These are both significant and difficult challenges: NDOE, the central agencies, and provinces have not been able to deal with these "inefficiencies" in the past.

*School Fees and the Feasibility of Parental Funding.* It is appropriate to explore some of the issues related to school fees. School fees, as discussed, are set at a level designed to ensure schools can finance adequate operational costs (excluding textbooks and curriculum materials which should be financed by Government). The NEP 2 costings do not contain the cost of fee-funded services in any of its estimates. Further, NEP 2 adopts the principle that, as elementary education becomes increasingly universal, it should become free.[36] It does not disclose how these services would be provided should fees be abolished.

*School fees are a significant share of the financing* of education services at the school level. If all parents paid in full the NEB-recommended maximum school fees, fee income would be financing 24 percent of the cost of a "quality-enhanced" basic education, 40 percent of a "quality-enhanced" secondary education, and 28 percent of a "quality-enhanced" total general education.[37]

However, it is well known that at present parents do not pay fees in full and that what they do pay differs according to their capacity to pay. For example, the PESD study estimated that in primary schools in 2001, families in the bottom 40 percent of the income distribution paid an average fee of K 4, the middle 40 percent paid an average of K 30, and the top 20 percent paid an average of K 115.

It would seem evident from these data that schools make allowances for the capacity of parents to pay fees. However, given that fees are established to finance the operational costs of schools, the low amount of per student fees collected by many poor schools means not only that they can provide only substandard services but also that these services are distributed on an inequitable basis from school to school. Therefore, the fee subsidy scheme should be adjusted to reflect the capacity of schools to raise revenues.

Considering the rights of all citizens to a basic education, and the external social and economic benefits to society at large of having an educated population,[38] the appropriateness of charging any fees at the basic level can be questioned. The levying of fees beyond basic education is a separate issue. The government needs to contain the total education budget, and the levying of fees at postbasic levels not only contributes to revenue, but also restricts the number of participants (albeit non-equitably). The scholarship scheme for secondary education proposed in the NEP could address this problem at least partially. Fees or levies also help society, at large, to claw back some of the income benefits that graduates obtain from the state-provided education. Nevertheless, again, it is important that compensation for income differences is made in the form of scholarships or subsidies so that all students, regardless of society's income differentials, have equal access to further government education.

## NEP 2 and Achieving Universal Basic Education

The fundamental challenge remains of reaching the goal of UBE emphasized in the MTDS, the MDGs, and the EFA. The NEP 2 implied proposal to have no fees for elementary grades by 2011 is the first stage in moving toward free UPE. Given the resource constraints and population growth, PNG will continue to have a major challenge to achieve the MTDS objective of UPE. The recent initiative of the Minister for Education in establishing a task force to address the issue is commended.

Because of dialogue between the NEP Steering Committee and Treasury during plan preparation, the education targets were lowered,[39] in part because of concerns about resource constraints and in part because of the implementation issues that had been fully identified. While the net primary enrollment rate[40] is expected to increase over the life of the plan, the basic education target for 2014 is still only 80 percent (up from 71 percent in 2005).

This review argues that the overriding challenge and primary priority for the next 10 to 15 years for the PNG education sector, consistent with the stated objectives of the MTDS, is how to ensure that every child completes the basic education cycle.[41] This is seen as a minimum objective to ensure that society and individuals can adapt to the vast social changes that are under way globally and in PNG. This is a huge task; it is a stated PNG objective, but it is going to be a stretch to achieve it, given the demand-side constraints, supply-capacity constraints, and, not least, fiscal constraints.

Without a special effort, PNG will not be in a position to move decisively toward UBE until 2020 or 2025 at the earliest. This would leave PNG and its people well behind the rest of the world. The current NEP 2 has set completion targets for basic education by 2014 that are significantly below current achievements in almost all regions of the world. In 2000 (14 years prior to the end of the NEP 2 period), Africa already had a basic cycle completion rate of 45 percent; South Asia, 70 percent; Latin America and Caribbean, 85 percent; and Middle East and North Africa, 74 percent. By 2015, it is expected that all regions will have made further decisive progress given the goals set by the EFA initiative and the push for achieving the MDG of universal completion of basic education.

To this end, this report advocates that PNG should seriously consider developing a new initiative over the next two to three years designed to enable it to achieve universal completion of basic education consistent with the proposed sector strategy outlined below and using the public expenditure framework suggested in Chapter 6 to work in partnership with development partners. This approach is consistent with proposals in the MTDS that expenditure priorities should be consistent with the Medium-Term Fiscal Framework. There are possible expenditure savings and efficiency gains to be made within the overall education sector. Further, as discussed above, the NEP 2 does not envision that the share of education expenditure on the basic cycle financed by government should increase faster that the remainder of the education sector. There is scope to shift relative education expenditures priorities toward the basic cycle. Finally, the medium- to longer-term fiscal outlook discussed in Chapter 5 suggests government may have more fiscal space for high-priority development options such as basic education in the medium to longer term arising from the new mining and the gas pipeline venture.

According to a simulation of the costs of universal completion of basic education (with a "quality-enhanced" basic education package) real cost (at 2003 prices) of basic education would increase from the K 421 million in 2005 to K 983 million in 2014, an increase of 133 percent over the plan period. The difference between this amount for 2014 and the K 560 million costed in NEP 2 comes from including (i) an additional K 41.6 million for improved quality provision, (ii) an additional K 185 million for taking over the cost of fee-funded school operational costs, and (iii) an additional K 197 million for extending this package from the NEP 2 projected enrollment of 80 to 100 percent of the 6-to-14 age group. This full cost would raise the share of basic education from 15.8 percent of the projected recurrent budget in 2005 to 32.1 percent in 2014 (assuming that the recurrent budget grows by 1.6 percent in real terms). However, if revenues from the new mining and gas ventures only increase government revenues a conservative 20 percent, the full costs of UBE would be less than 20 percent of the budget. If we assume that GDP grows by 2.5 percent in real terms per year, basic education as a share of GDP would rise from 3.5 percent in 2005 to 5.1 percent in 2014.

*The Issue for Development Partners.* Unless the economy of PNG significantly improves, the recurrent funding of free UBE by 2015 or even soon after is clearly beyond the present public budget without donor support, even allowing for further systemic reforms and a change in overall priorities (see sector strategy proposals below). Given the size of the funding task, the issue for donors is how much they are prepared to help the government to achieve its millennium goals, not only in terms of the amount of funds they provide, but also in terms of the allocation of those funds between development and recurrent expenditure.

Over the past four years, the principal donors in the education sector have been AusAID, the EU, New Zealand, and JICA (see Section 3, above). They have supported a wide range of activities in relation to capacity building, curriculum reform, elementary teacher training, primary and secondary teacher education, upgrading of primary school facilities, and the provision of school supplies. Historically, development partners have also supported vocational education and training in both formal and informal sector skills (see Section 6, below).

However, over the same period, the government has frequently failed to support or follow up on their commitment to many of these donor-funded programs.[42] Furthermore, development partners and government have failed to take a coherent approach to the sector as a whole. A suggested set of priorities and a proposed strategy are discussed below, and how government donor collaboration could be organized to reach agreement on the financing of an initiative to achieve universal completion of the basic cycle of education is discussed in more detail in Chapter 6.

## Vocational Education and Skills Development

There is an urgent need for the Government of Papua New Guinea (GOPNG) to review both its skills development (including literacy programs) and tertiary sectors. These two sectors, along with basic education, are necessary for PNG's economic growth and health—a necessity that is now accentuated in the light of what HIV/AIDS is doing in deskilling the labor force of a number of African nations, and could do the same in PNG, if not contained. Furthermore, the expansion of the basic education is not only increasing financial pressure upon these sectors, but the high per capita cost of these sectors means that a more efficient use of the resources they use and a shift of costs onto the users could release funds back to basic education.

Both NEP 2 and the MTDS acknowledge the essential connection between general and skills development/vocational education. Nevertheless, what little planning there is for the skills development sector is fragmented, and the plan recognizes the need for coordination.

In the skills development area, there is a need to find ways to identify the skill gaps of the labor market and to provide the skills development and vocational training to ensure that there are enough workers to fill that demand. To make this happen, consideration will need to be given to find ways to:

(a) Establish a new agency, or empower an existing agency, to coordinate and regulate training for the formal and informal economic sectors. This agency will need to be at minimal bureaucratic cost, but nevertheless, on the basis of experience in other countries, have real authority, a balanced representation of all stakeholders, and an independent source of funding;

(b) Encourage greater involvement of private providers in the national training system and make it more responsive to market and community needs;

(c) Make the national training system more cost-effective and less a burden on the public purse;

(d) Establish a national qualifications framework, or an appropriately modified version thereof, that will enable workers with the most basic or the most sophisticated of vocational skills to move laterally and vertically between and within economic sectors; and

(e) Establish a labor market information system that provides appropriate signals for adjusting training and labor market supply to labor market demand.

Similarly, a review is required in the tertiary education sector, where success in planning requires a restoration of cooperation, trust, and transparency between the parties involved. The current fragmentation of the sector, which accounts for over K 116 million or 4 percent of the overall government budget, is costly, and the current ineffective coordination mechanisms mean that many of the tertiary institutions are decaying and that both their internal efficiency (cost structures) and external efficiency (relevance to the labor market) are declining.

The funding of postbasic education is also an important issue for the government and for parents, and for private industry, which has a material stake in the creation of vocational skills. Given the high per capita cost of much of tertiary education,[43] it is tempting to argue that in terms of value for money, much of this public funding should be reallocated to the basic education sector;[44] however, any reallocation should only be done on the basis of a sound cost-benefit analysis.

## Where to from Here? Proposed Priorities and Strategic Directions

Based on PNG's goals as expressed through the MTDS, NEP 2, the MDGs, and EFA, and in regard to the situational assessment outlined in this review, four key priorities have been identified for the education and training (skills development) sectors.

The *first priority* for the education sector, over the next 10 to 15 years, should be to ensure that every child completes the basic education cycle and that the education that he or she receives is of decent quality. As such, the system should be providing an education that ensures both literacy and numeracy for all, together with a sound preparation for citizenship and for participation in the world of work in the traditional and informal economy or further education. This is an absolute minimum objective to ensure that society and the workforce are able to adapt and respond adequately to the major structural and social changes and challenges that PNG will face over the coming decades. On equity and reducing the barriers to schooling grounds (and given the now extremely high positive externalities arising from completion of basic education), the reduction and eventual elimination of school fees warrant serious consideration. As discussed, there is scope to increase the relative share of the education budget allocated to basic education and to ensure that a more-than-proportionate share of increased domestic revenues also goes to basic education.

The *second priority* should be to provide for a gradually increasing number of students to enter and complete secondary education over the next decade. Significant challenges will continue to confront policy makers and implementation agencies in trying to make this happen. First, the extremely high social demand for secondary education needs to be carefully managed in order to ensure that the overall growth is contained within the NEP 2 targets, and that there is equity of access across provinces. In particular, there is a need to redress large provincial and gender inequalities in access to secondary education. Second, it is critical that public resources allocated to secondary education do not constrain the capacity of the government to finance universal completion of basic education. Within secondary education, it is also critical—from the perspective of both development and resource constraints—that Grades 9 and 10 not be disadvantaged in terms of the demand of Grades 11 and 12. Third, it is important that basic standards of quality be achieved and maintained in secondary schools. This will require a determined effort to train well-qualified teachers, particularly for senior secondary grades, and to ensure an adequate supply of quality-enhancing inputs. On the other hand, there are likely to be important linkages between the probability of getting a place (or being able to attend because of distance) in a secondary school and staying in and completing the basic cycle. This will require judicious expansion of the secondary system.

The *third priority* should be to reform the skills-development programs (including literacy programs) and vocational and technical college programs to ensure that they are demand-oriented, have strong links to both the world of work and income-earning opportunities, including the informal economy, and become more cost-effective and efficient. The basic challenge is to bring the relevant labor market stakeholder and educational authorities together to address the much agreed need for a regulatory and coordinating framework, under whose aegis not only are public and private training providers regulated, but labor market analyses conducted, and a national certification and testing framework established.

The *fourth priority* should be to reform the tertiary sector, including universities and the array of pre-employment training institutions (including teacher training colleges and health training facilities) to provide strategic coherence and oversight. Trust, cooperation, and transparency needs to be restored between the Commission and Office of Higher Education and the educational institutions to make the system more cost-efficient, more directed to labor market needs, and more self-generating of funding.

The key government support agencies in PNG—NDOE, Treasury, DPM, DNPRD, the DOF, the provincial governments, and the district governments—have been unable to ensure that the education system functions to ensure education objectives are met—particularly in achieving basic education goals and labor market needs. Therefore, new arrangements are necessary.

Given the limited capacity of the public sector to deliver services, the central aim of any new strategy will be to reduce the government's direct responsibility for service delivery by diversifying the range of providers—albeit with appropriate subsidies. In identifying these options, policy makers must take into account the need for accountability and transparency and the limited integrity of existing government systems, but despite these problems, they must ensure that high-quality education and training is provided.

It is critical that a consensus is developed on the overall priorities for education. The MTDS and government's commitment to both the MDGs and the EFA initiative all point in a similar direction. An approach to establish viable strategic directions for education is outlined below. Each of the six elements of the proposed package is necessary for a coherent approach to education development that is implementable with appropriate development partner support; however, none of them is sufficient in itself. The education and training outcomes prioritized by the government in the MTDS can only improve if the government's expenditure priorities are adjusted accordingly. This means that fiscal space must be created to allow the changes in expenditure priorities and requires that the funds thus allocated are used in an efficient and transparent manner. Therefore, it is critical that the government and its development partners achieve a consensus on the six elements. The strategy could be implemented using a dual-track approach that will simultaneously:

(a) Address issues that can be dealt with within the national and provincial Departments of Education to improve the ability of education to provide quality learning, and

(b) Help the central agencies (Treasury, DOF, the DNPRD, the DPM, the AGO, and the Department of Intergovernmental Relations) to strengthen their capacity to support the NDOE and the provinces.

The key elements of the proposed strategic directions for education are:

1. **Set priorities for the subsectors.** Government is responsible for setting priorities for the education and training sectors. Considerable progress has already been made through MTDS and NEP 2 in terms of declared priorities, particularly for the general education sector. It is now timely for government to make a clear and unequivocal statement on priorities for the sector as a whole, regarding not only general education, but also skills development. The priorities proposed in this review provide a baseline for early consideration by government. In designing the details of how to put government's declared priorities into practice, it is important that government pays particular attention to the following :

   (a) **Identify the technical options for achieving the education and learning outcomes and the ways in which the options might be packaged for delivery.** This would include consideration of ensuring that key teaching and learning materials (including textbooks) and general school supplies are available to all students and teachers and improving, markedly, retention rates, a key prerequisite for achieving UBE.

   (b) **Set priorities for public expenditure using public finance criteria** (equity, feasibility, and alleviation of market failure) within the context of a rolling public expenditure planning process (MTEF).

This would include ensuring that any school fees are affordable, particularly for the poor. Options exist to use public financing to resolve equity issues arising from relatively high and inequitable school fees at lower levels of the system and from scholarships at the postsecondary-school level.

(c) **Commit to monitoring and evaluating progress toward the agreed education and training targets, learning outcomes, and the education MDGs.** This will involve ensuring that the Education Information System is revitalized and sustained and that information systems of other agencies involved in postsecondary education and training are also developed. This would include establishing standardized achievement tests to measure learning outcomes, and undertaking studies to inform decision making, including to find out why some children never enter school, why they drop out, and how charging fees affects school attendance and are affected by poverty.

2. **Public-private interface: Identify ways to:**

   (a) **Focus the public sector on those public goods that it can effectively deliver.**

   (b) **Promote involving the private sector in the delivery of private goods, such as vocation and technical training, for the formal sector.** Private providers are already operating in technical and business training; however, the GOPNG has caused the failure of private providers by not honoring payment of contracts on time. This can also involve communities and school BOMs in managing and operating schools. Local communities are more likely to provide voluntary services and help raise funds if they are involved in local-level planning and management.

   (c) **Strengthen the collaboration between the public and private sectors.** The inability of the government sector to effectively run and manage vocational schools, print and distribute textbooks and teaching materials in a timely manner, deliver the full range of technical courses demanded by the formal sector, and church management of almost half of the schools are examples of where these considerations are relevant.

3. **Prepare an expenditure and an implementation plan** for the whole of the publicly funded part of the education sector (covering all programs financed by the PNG government and its development

partners) based on the priorities and activities identified in the preceding steps and consistent with available resources. Understandably, in the process, full account will need to be taken of provincial plans and financing proposals and the role of school fees. Further, there is a need to fill the gaps in the costing of the NEP 2, particularly the financing of textbooks and school materials.

4. **Create fiscal space.** This can be achieved in three ways—achieving savings in the sector, making more efficient use of existing funds, and increasing sectoral allocations.

   (a) **Savings** can be sought in a number of different areas. A very important contribution has been the attempt to clean up the payroll. In an earlier section of this document and in the PERR, evidence was cited of problems with the education sector payroll and the likely savings that could be achieved by a physical audit of all staff and facilities and adjusting the payroll as needed. Improving procurement procedures, particularly for school materials and textbooks, housing rentals, office supplies, travel, civil works, and the hiring of casual staff would also achieve savings, as would the prevention of theft. Outsourcing and other ways of cooperating with the nongovernment sectors could also produce savings.

   (b) **Increased efficiency of expenditures.** Significant increases in efficiency are possible in a range of areas of the education and training system. NEP 2 particularly emphasizes this approach in the general education sector and in the vocational sector. As teacher salaries comprise between 70 and 80 percent of the education and 10 and 13 percent of the total national recurrent budget, the NEP also proposes increasing STRs at all levels of the system. This has the potential, if implemented, to reduce the per-student costs of teachers. Efficiency might also be obtained by increasing competition between providers, both public and private, and replacing guaranteed funding through, say, subsidies, with grants, such as vouchers, dependent upon demand.

   (c) **Increased sectoral allocations.** Increased sectoral allocations are also important in creating fiscal space, particularly if the appropriate reforms to increase efficiency have already been undertaken. For example, the present allocation of 4 percent of the recurrent budget to the tertiary education sector makes this sector a possible starting point for reallocation of public funds, particularly if more of the funding can be shifted to private beneficiaries, such as graduates and employers. Sectoral allocations could also be increased by judicious increases in the level of cost recovery for postsecondary education and training. Already, steps are proceeding in this direction, with increasing of fees for Tertiary Education Scholarship Assistance Scheme (TESAS) and other students; however, fee increases and TESAS need to be administered with the guidance of labor market analysis and monitoring of the impact on economic requirements and social equity. Some tertiary education programs might also recover costs through providing fee-financed services. While there are a number of ways for education to tap other nongovernment resources in order to give effect to the declared priorities in the education and skills development sectors, government resources will still have to be augmented.

5. **Prepare a financing plan.** Having decided on the programs that it wants to emphasize and implement and having prepared an expenditure and implementation plan, the NDOE (and other agencies, where appropriate) must find the resources to put it into practice. This will mean adopting a medium-term financing plan in which the national government, the provincial governments, and the major development partners declare what resources they will be able to make available for the education sector over the next specified number of years. This will then allow the NDOE to make realistic plans that are tied to the actual amount of resources that will be available. It has not been possible to do this before as the resource flows over time have not been clear. For the general education sector, this would be a necessary complement to and elaboration of the current NEP. Present ongoing reforms to the budget process are a significant move in the right direction, but they also need to cover all public expenditures at both the national and provincial level, including development assistance.

6. **Restore and guarantee the integrity of government processes.** The progressive erosion of the integrity of government processes, especially as decentralization was implemented, was a major factor in why all PNG's development partners decided to move their funds off-budget in an effort to ensure adequate transparency. This move has itself created other problems in the education sector. It is important to bring these funds back on-budget in due course so that the NDOE can take into account the full level of resources available

to the education sector from all sources. Restoring and maintaining the integrity of government processes is the first step in this process. This governmentwide issue is further discussed in Chapter 5.

## Conclusion

Each of the elements of the strategy outlined above is necessary for improving education and training outcomes in PNG: none is sufficient in itself. Outcomes based on the government's declared priorities will only be achieved if there is a systematic and coordinated approach to the inherent challenges, the resolution of which will require a "whole-of-government" intervention, together with development partner support. Accordingly, it is critical that the government and its development partners reach a consensus on the elements of the strategy to be pursued. Chapter 6 discusses how government and development partners might better work together.

## Annex 4A: Principal Responsibilities of the Key Stakeholders in the PNG Education and Skills Development System

### Overview

The National Education System (NES) of PNG is usually defined in terms of its formal structure; however, given the Human Development (HD) Mission's emphasis on the twin goals of providing a basic education and skills development for the PNG populace, the "national system" has been defined to embrace:

a. general education,
b. pre-employment education and training, and
c. employment-located training.

The *general education* sector includes basic and secondary education; *pre-employment* includes vocational centers, technical and teacher colleges, colleges of nursing and allied health sciences, other single occupation training centers, and the public and private universities; and *employment- located training* includes industry-based training and training in village and rural communities. *A summary of the key stakeholders and their responsibilities is given in the attached Table 4A.1.*

## A. General Education Sector

The general education sector consists of basic and secondary, with basic comprising elementary (age six to eight years) and primary (age nine to 14 years) over nine years, beginning in preparatory and ending in Grade 8. The key stakeholders are the Ministry of Education (MOE), the provincial and LLGs, churches, DOT, and DNPRD, as well as students, parents, and local communities. The MOE comprises the NDOE and the TSC.

NDOE is responsible to the GOPNG for:

- developing national policies and plans and coordinating their implementation in provinces and districts;
- supporting provinces with planning, professional services, and standards;
- managing preservice training for basic teachers, and coordinating in-service training;
- controlling curriculum at all levels;
- distributing school-fee subsidies in the first and third quartiles of each year;
- managing all government schools within the National Capital District (NCD) and all national high schools; and
- managing teacher payrolls.

The TSC is the employer of teachers in the NES and sets salaries, conditions of employment, approves the appointment of teachers to positions, and handles industrial relations.

The provinces, through divisions of education, are given overall responsibility for teacher management, including deployment and in-service training, and for capital works and maintenance of secondary schools. The education function grants paid by the national government to the provincial treasuries in the second and third quartile of each year are administered through the divisions. The provincial education advisors heading the divisions of education are appointed by, and answerable to, the provincial administration, and not to the national secretary of education. All provinces have districts education offices.

LLGs have responsibility for capital works and maintenance at elementary and primary school levels.

For historical reasons, some 51 percent of general education schools and 47 percent of student enrollment within the NES are also part of a church agency system. Church agency schools conform to national

**Table 4A.1. Key Responsibilities of Stakeholders in General Education and Skills Development in PNG**

| | | Stakeholders | | | | | | | | | | |
| | | Regulatory/provider/support agencies | | | | | | | | | | |
| Goal orientation subsectors | Institutions | MOE | Prov./LLG | CHE/OHE | NATTB/ NTC/DPM | DCD | DOH | Church and other agencies | DOT/ DNPRD | Students/ Parents | Community | Industry/ NGO |
| 1 | 2 | 3 | 4 | 5 | 6 | 7 | 8 | 9 | 10 | 11 | 12 | |
| A. General education | (1) Basic education | Central support/ appoint teachers/ school subsidy | Infra/maint, local support/ teacher management | | | | | Partnership with government | Budgetary approp. to (a) NDOE, (b) provinces for teachers/ function grant | Fees and services in-kind | Memberships of BOMs, Provision of labor. | |
| | (2) Secondary education | Central support/ appoint teachers/ school subsidy | Infra/maint, local support/ teacher management | | | | | Partnership with government for teachers/ | Budgetary approp. to (a) NDOE, (b) provinces for teachers/ function grant | Fees and Services in-kind | Memberships of BOMs. Provision of labor. | |
| B. Pre-employment | (1) Vocational | Central support/ appoint teachers/ school subsidy | Infra/maint, local support/ teacher managemt. | test skills. | Register training providers, certify and | Set One | | Partnership with government for teachers/ | Budgetary approp. to (a) NDOE, (b) provinces function grant | Fees and services in-kind | Memberships of BOMs. Provision of labor. | |
| | (2) Technical colleges | Central support/ salaries/infra/ mainten. | Central support/ staffing infra./maint. | Tertiary coordination/ scholarships | Register training providers, certify and test skills. | | | | Budgetary approp to NDOE | Fees | | Participates in governing councils |
| | (3) Teacher colleges | Central support/ salaries/infra/ maint. | | Tertiary coordination/ scholarships | | | | Partnership w/ government. University affiliations. | Budgetary approp. to NDOE | Fees | | |

| | | | Management role | Partnership | | Fees | Involvement |
|---|---|---|---|---|---|---|---|
| (4) Nurse/AHS | Tertiary coordination/scholarships | | | Partnership with govt. University affiliations. | Budgetary appro. to NDOH. | Fees | |
| (5) Other single occupations | Tertiary coordination/scholarships | Register training providers, certify and test skills. | | | | Fees | |
| (6) Universities | Tertiary coordination/scholarships | | | | | | |
| (6a) Public | Tertiary coordination/scholarships | | | | Budgetary approp. | Fees | |
| (6b) Pvt. | Tertiary coordination/scholarships | | | Sponsorship | | Fees | |
| C. Employment located (1) Formal economy | | Register training providers, certify and test skills. DPM—Pub. sector | Executing agency of EOSDP | | Budgetary approp. | | Apprenticeships and training sponsorship. Participate in apprenticeship and trade-testing panels. |
| (2) Informal economy | | | | · Involvement | Budgetary approp. | | Involvement NGO involvement |

**Source:** Mission Documents.
**Abbreviation:** CHE = Commission for Higher Education; DCD = Department of Community Development; NDOE = National Department of Education; NDOH = National Department of Health; DNPRD = Department of National Planning and Rural Development; DPM = Department of Personnel Management; EOSDP = Employment-Oriented Skills Development Project; LLG = Local-level government; MOE = Ministry of Education; NATTB = National Apprenticeship and Trade Testing Board; NGO = Nongovernmental Organization; NTC = National Training Council; OHE = Office of Higher Education.

curriculum and standards, and their teachers are employed by the state. All students are required to meet fees set by the provincial education boards, under guidelines set by the NEB.

## B. Pre-Employment Sector

The key stakeholders for the vocational centers are much the same as for secondary schools. The national and provincial levels of government have the same responsibilities. Church agencies and communities may take a more active role in the managing these centers.

**Technical and Business Colleges:** There are four state technical and three state business colleges. NDOE is responsible for providing central support services (including management and coordination, research, curriculum, and inspectoral services), staffing, and capital provision and maintenance. Additional resources are largely provided through fees. The TESAS provided by government through the Office of Higher Education largely subsidises the fees of the scholarship holders undertaking the Technical Training Certificate courses, while parents and industry pay fees of self-sponsored students. The technical colleges have also been recently equipped as the principal testing centers for the National Apprenticeship Trade Testing Board (NATTB) competency-based trade testing programs.

**Primary teacher colleges:** Six church and one government-agency primary teacher colleges exist. Four are now affiliated with universities: Madang and Balob with the University of Goroka, and St. Benedict's and Kabaleo with Divine Word University. NDOE remains the key stakeholder, with responsibility for coordination and payment of staff, and support services and operational and messing (accommodation) funding is largely through TESAS; however, "partnerships" also exist between the college administrations, church agencies,[1] and affiliated universities, which raises the question of what the present role of NDOE is.

**Nursing and other single-occupation institutions:** Some pre-employment institutions, such as colleges of nursing within the aegis of NDOH and of church agencies, have a similar relationship between key stakeholders, as do the primary teacher colleges. Likewise, students are largely funded through TESAS or by self-sponsorship.

**Universities:** PNG has four government and two private universities. Those set up under their own statutes with the GOPNG are the universities of PNG, Technology, Goroka, and Vudal. The private ones are the Pacific Adventist University and the Divine Word University. Students at all six universities receive government-funding assistance through TESAS, but in addition, the government universities receive budget appropriations for staffing, capital, and maintenance, and some operational costs.

**Commission for and Office of Higher Education:** The Commission for Higher Education (CHE) and its Office of Higher Education (OHE) secretariat are responsible for the administration of TESAS and planning and coordination within the tertiary education sector.

### C. Employment-Located Training

**Formal Sector:** The main government stakeholders in the area of employment-located training are:

- *for the private sector:* the National Training Council (NTC) and the NATTB, each with administrations answerable to the Department of Labour and Industrial Relations (DOLIR); and
- *for the public sector:* the DPM.

The NTC, a statutory body set up in 1991, arose out of the National Training Policy (NTP) adopted in 1989. It is funded directly by a government grant. The Council is chaired, and its director and secretariat appointed, by the minister and secretary of DOLIR, respectively. The NTC is a tripartite organization, with representation from the public and private sectors and from NGOs. The responsibilities of the NTC include preparing annual national training plans and priorities, setting training standards and accrediting and monitoring training providers, determining the distribution of overseas training places through donor-funding, and managing the internally funded National Scholarships Fund.

The NATTB, like the NTC, consists of government and industry representation, but is administered by a unit within DOLIR. NATTB is responsible for the regulation of apprenticeship training and testing and certifying apprenticeships; however, since 1999, it has also been involved, through AusAID-funded programs, with the development of competency standards for trades and other occupational areas. These programs also involve testing of standards at three different levels (the highest being level three at the tradesperson standard).

Training by private industry is encouraged by imposing a training levy on companies with annual payrolls of K 200,000 or more that do not expend at least two percent of the payroll figure on training. Approved training expenditure by companies is tax-deductible. Under the NTP, the training levy was meant to help fund NTC programs, but, because the NTC was established after the levy, it is still collected by Internal Revenue. The DPM takes responsibility for in-service training within the government public sector.

### Informal Sector

The NTC was given responsibility, under the NTP (1989), for coordinating training in the informal as well as formal sectors; however, its capacity to do so is very limited.

Key stakeholders within this area include line departments engaged in rural and fisheries development, NGOs (such as women's organizations), and the Department of Community Development (DCD).

## Annex 4B: Teacher Workforce

## Part A: Teaching Service and Student: Staff Ratios

The following summarizes system wide aspects of the teaching service and student: teacher ratios.

### Context

The TSC, as the employer of teachers, is responsible for setting teacher salaries and emoluments, terms and conditions of employment, and resolving major industrial disputation. The Secretary is responsible for: determining the qualifications and standards for registration of teachers; inspecting teachers for registration; and certifying and assessing teachers. Provincial authorities, operating in the context of national policies and plans, are responsible for appointing teachers through provincial education boards and managing the deployment of teachers in a cost-effective manner.

### Key Policies

Table 4B.1 summarizes current (2004) staffing policies for the National Education Department by school level and/or type of educational facility.

**Table 4B.1. Key Staffing Policies by Level in 2004 (NEP 1)**

| Level | Class size | Teachers per class | STR |
|---|---|---|---|
| Elementary | 28/30 | 1 | 30:1 |
| Primary | G1: 45; G3: 40; G7: 35 | G1—6:1; G7—8:1.5 | 33:1 |
| Lower secondary | 45 | 1.5 | 26:1 |
| Upper secondary | 30 | 1.75 | 20:1 |
| Vocational | Variable | Variable | 18:1 |
| Technical | Variable | Variable | 15:1 Trade; 20:1 Bus. |

Source: NEP 1.

**Table 4B.2. Staff Cadre by Level, Selected Years**

| Level | 1997 | 2002 | % F 2002 | STR 2002 | % Growth 1997—2002 |
|---|---|---|---|---|---|
| Elementary | 801 | 7,553 | 41 | 29.6 | 843.0 |
| Primary | 16,143 | 16,596 | 39 | 35.5 | 2.8 |
| Secondary | 2,874 | 3,299 | 33 | 24.5 | 2.1 |
| Vocational | 711 | 1,085 | 30 | 15.0 | 45.1 |
| Technical | 194 | 229 | 30 | 7.8 | 18.0 |

Source: NDOE statistics.

## Strategic Data and Observations

Table 4B.2 presents information on trends in teacher numbers by level 1997–2002 and 2002 key statistics on the teaching workforce.

### Observations

- **Elementary:**
  - Teacher numbers have increased by 843 percent, from 801 in 1997 to 7,553 in 2002.
  - The STR at 29.6:1 is below the NEP 2 policy target of 32:1 by 2014.
  - The cadre is 41 percent female.

- **Primary:**
  - Teacher numbers have decreased by 2.8 percent, from 16,140 in 1997 to 16,596 in 2002.
  - The STR at 35.5:1 is below the NEP policy target of 37:1 by 2014.
  - The cadre is 39 percent female.

- **Secondary:**
  - Teacher numbers have increased by 2.1 percent, from 2,874 in 1997 to 3,299 in 2002.
  - The STR at 24.5:1 is below the NEP policy target of 26:1 by 2014.

- ▪ The cadre is 33 percent female.
- ▪ In 2001, there were 157 expatriate staff (66 contract teachers and 91 volunteers) accounting for some 4.8 percent of the cadre.

- **Vocational:**
  - ▪ Teacher numbers have increased by 45 percent, from 711 in 1997 to 1,085 2002.
  - ▪ The STR at 15:1 is below the NEP policy target of 18:1 by 2014.
  - ▪ The cadre is 30 percent female.
  - ▪ There is an inequitable deployment of staff among colleges.

- **Technical:**
  - ▪ Teacher numbers have increased by 18 percent, from 194 in 1997 to 229 in 2002.
  - ▪ The STR at 7.8:1 is below the NEP policy target of 15:1 by 2014.
  - ▪ The cadre is 30 percent of female.
  - ▪ There is an inequitable deployment of staff among colleges.
  - ▪ The large number of expatriate staff (some 21 percent) adds to the cost and reduces employment opportunities for nationals (if available).

## CODE:

- While reliable data on College of Distance Education (CODE) staff numbers are not available, it is generally argued that it is under-staffed in the professional cadre. The shortfall is met in part by the employment of some 100 nonprofessional casuals at an annual cost of around K 600,000.

## Main Issues and NEP Response

- The rapid, yet planned, growth in elementary enrollments has required a corresponding growth in the teacher cadre. It is important to note that the growth is in line with the NEP as adopted by government in 1997. Further, the unit cost of elementary teachers was around 45 percent of their primary counterparts in 2003; however, this will increase over time as elementary teachers reach their salary ceiling of around K 7,000 per annum.

- Some elementary schools have been established outside national policy and provincial plans. Adherence to agreed national and provincial plans is essential. In addition, there is scope for greater use of multigrade teaching, especially in the smaller schools, which is now to be institutionalized under the NEP.

- Grades 7 and 8 have had a high teacher-class ratio at 1.5:1. The initial rationale was based on the need for specialists by level at a time when most schools had only a single stream for each level; however, in support of the increase in the number of streams in many schools, a review of the ratio is warranted. The NEP has changed the policy to accord with other primary grades (i.e., a generalist primary teacher per class, yielding a class ratio of 1:1).

- The higher-than-expected growth in upper secondary enrollments has placed considerable pressure on the demand for teachers for that level. This could explain in part the continuing dependence on expatriate teachers, especially in higher grades. The NEP projections allow for only a modest growth in secondary enrollments, with a wind-back in current transition rates for Grades 8 and 9 from over 60.0 percent in 2005 to 50 percent by 2011. In the case of Grades 10 and 11, the 2005 rate is given as 29 percent, rising to nearly 32 percent in 2008 and reaching just under 29 percent by 2014.

- Overall, the percentage of female teachers is low, even at elementary and primary levels, with marked variations across provinces. Strategies for encouraging greater participation of females as stated in NEP are general in nature and require greater specificity. The planned increase in female-student participation in upper secondary from 37 to 45 percent by 2014 could help.

- Vocational and technical colleges have limited scope for flexibility to meet emergent needs or to encourage entrepreneurial initiatives. Significant governance and structural changes are required in the subsector, including greater provision of shorter courses to meet national and local needs and involvement of the private sector. The NEP has responded to this challenge by changing the focus of vocational colleges to be more responsive to community needs, including provision of short courses, and by promoting greater entrepreneurial activity in both vocational centers and technical colleges. Technical colleges will also be required to be more responsive to national skill needs.

## Part B: Teacher Demand, Supply, and Qualifications

The following summarizes key aspects of the teacher traing program and the supply and demand for teachers.

### Context

**Elementary:** the mixed-mode training program extends over three years, leading to a Certificate of Elementary Teaching (CET) through PNGEI. Entry can be from Grade 10.

**Primary:** the two-year program (six semesters), through primary teachers colleges requires a Grade 12 entry, there being some exceptions for special circumstances.

**Secondary:** the secondary program is provided through four-year B.Ed. program at the University of Goroka. Grade 12 entry is required. There is also provision for a degree plus a postgraduate teaching diploma. There have been increasing numbers of students studying through Lahara (summer) sessions. The Pacific Adventist University also offers teacher education.

**Vocational:** There is only limited provision for preservice for instructors in traditional trade-related areas. Training for new staff is provided through the Diploma in Vocational Education and Training (DOVET), which is a mixed-mode program for instructors already working in centers. There is a three-year preservice program in Home Economics at PNGEI and provision for training in hospitality and tourism. The University of Goroka (UoG) also offers a one-year Diploma in Technical and Vocational Education (DTVE) for vocational teachers. Don Bosco (in conjunction with Divine Word University) offers a B.Ed. majoring in vocational and technical education. As this is a preservice program, trade experience tends to be limited.

**Technical:** While there is no regular preservice course for the training of lecturers in technical colleges, UoG's one-year DTVE is relevant. Vocational instructors, however, have limited access to full-time training. Lecturers may also enroll in the DOVETcourse.

The ETESP has provided extensive support for the training of elementary teachers. Concurrently, the Primary and Secondary Teacher Education Project (PASTEP) has supported the upgrading of training for primary and secondary teachers.

## Key Policies

Table 4B.3 set out current entry level requirements for various categories of teachers and the length of training for the desired formal requlifications for each category of teacher.

## Students in Training

The NDOE is responsible for teacher training at all levels, except for secondary, which rests with universities. In the case of elementary, while NDOE is responsible, some provinces have made local arrangements for training. Table 4B.4 documents the number of teachers (by category) under training by year of the course in 2003.

## Strategic Data and Observations

The following teacher demand projections are taken from the NEP 2005–2014. The assumptions are included here for ease of reference (as these are demand projections, there is no gender breakdown and

**Table 4B.3. Preservice Training Requirements by Level**

| Level | Entry | Length | Desired qualification |
|---|---|---|---|
| Elementary | Grade 10 | 3 years (mixed-mode) | CET |
| Primary | Grade 12[1] | 2 years (6 semesters) | Dip.Ed. (Primary) |
| Lower secondary | Grade 12 | 4 years | B.A./B.S. Dip.Ed.; B.Ed. |
| Upper secondary | Grade 12 | 4 years | B.A./B.S. Dip.Ed.; B.Ed. |
| Vocational | 5 years in trade | 3 years[2]; 1 year (UoG) | DOVET or DTVE |
| Technical | 5 years in trade | 1 year (UoG) | DTVE, DOVET B.Ed. |

*Source:* NDOE Statistics—1. Some exceptions in special circumstances;
2. For females only—males only mixed-mode DOVET, while employed.

**Table 4B.4. Students in Training by Year 2003**

| | Year 1 | Year 2 | Year 3 | Year 4 | Total |
|---|---|---|---|---|---|
| Elementary | 594 | 421 | 326 | 0 | 1,351 |
| Primary | 1,170 | 1,107 | 0 | 0 | 2,277 |
| Secondary[1] | 183 | 142 | 138 | 125 | 588 |
| Vocational | | | | | 77 |
| Technical[1/2] | | | | | 58 |
| Other[1/3] | | | | | 29 |

*Source:* Various.
1. University of Goroka only;
2. Postgraduate Diploma: 23 doing technical and 13 business studies;
3. PGD: 22 agriculture and seven expressive arts.

**Table 4B.5. Staff Projections by Level—Selected Years**

|            | 2005   | 2008   | 2011   | 2014   |
|------------|--------|--------|--------|--------|
| Elementary | 11,262 | 14,533 | 16,680 | 18,673 |
| Primary    | 18,858 | 19,211 | 19,765 | 20,805 |
| Secondary  | 3,292  | 3,355  | 3,585  | 3,982  |
| Vocational | 1,050  | 1,215  | 1,407  | 1,629  |
| Technical  | 211    | 202    | 233    | 269    |

Source: NEP 2 database.

attrition rates have not been built-in). Table 4B.5 projects teacher requirements by category over the period 2005–2014 presented in the National Education Plan.

## Assumptions

The assumptions underlying the projection presented in Table 4B.5 are set out below:

**Elementary:**
- Prep class size: 30, rising to 32.4 by 2014
- New prep classes per year: 360 on average until 2012
- STR: 29:1 in 2005, to 32:1 by 2014

**Primary:**
- Grade 1 class size: 45
- Grade 3 class size: 40, rising to 42 after 2012
- Grade 7 class size: 35, rising to 37 afte 2012
- Teachers per class in Grades 7 and 8: 1.5 reduced to 1 by 2009
- STR: from 33:1 in 2005 to 37:1 by 2014

**Secondary:**
- Lower secondary (LS) class size: 45
- Upper secondary (US) class size: 30
- LS/US teachers per class: 1.5
- Transition Grade 8 to Grade 9: 50 percent by 2014
- Transition Grade 10 to Grade 11: 25 percent by 2014
- STR: 26:1

**Vocational:**
- STR 18:1

**Technical:**
- STR 15:1
- Localization of staff to 95 percent by 2014

### Observations on Demand/Supply (Figures Rounded):
The following key observations about the demand/supply projections are highlighted:

**Elementary:**
- Some 41 percent of students in training are female (41 percent in teaching cadre in 2002).
- Based on the NEP projections, there will continue to be a marked increase in the cadre from nearly 11,300 in 2005 to some 18,700 by 2014 (some 7,400).

**Primary:**
- Some 45 percent of students in training are female (39 percent in teaching cadre in 2002).
- The percentage of Grade 12 trainees increased from 70 percent in 1999 to 94 percent in 2001.
- The number of primary teachers is projected to increase gradually, from some 18,860 in 2005 to just over 2,080 by 2014 (some 1,940).
- Current training capacity is around 1,100 per year (including day students, who tend to be from the immediate vicinity of colleges and who are required to pay fees if not selected on national merit). Under NEP, the intake will increase marginally: 1,200, on average, to meet demand.
- NDOE is encouraging colleges to seek accreditation of courses through universities (Madang has already gained accreditation through UoG and is reported to have been invited to seek affiliation).

**Secondary:**
- Percentage of females in training not known (33 percent in teaching cadre in 2002).
- The number of secondary teachers is projected to grow steadily over the period, reflecting the stabilization of enrollments. The cadre is planned to increase by nearly 700 from 3,290 in 2005 to 3,980 by 2014 (some 700).

**Vocational:**
- Some 30 percent of students in training are female (30 percent in teaching cadre in 2002).
- There is projected increase in staff from 1,050 in 2005 to 1,630 in 2014 (some 580).

**Technical:**
- Some 25 percent of students in training are female (30 percent in teaching cadre in 2002).
- There is a projected increase in staff from 210 in 2005 to 270 in 2014 (some 60).

### Qualifications of Teaching Cadre

Reliable data on teacher qualifications are not readily available. A major initiative is currently being undertaken (through the PNG Personnel, Payroll Project, funded by AusAID) to "cleanse" teacher data for both payroll and personnel files. Available databases should contain information on qualifications. Anecdotally, it is thought that the level of unqualified staff is quite low (probably nil in the elementary and primary sectors); however, there is a much higher proportion of staff who are underqualified for the levels at which they are required to teach. In general, nonnational staff in schools (4.8 percent) are working in upper secondary grades or in the technical subsector (23 percent).

### Main Issues and NEP Response

**Elementary:** Flexibility in the application of criteria at the local level can affect quality of those who are entering the service. Some provinces are making local arrangements to meet unplanned expansion outside NEP and provincial education plans. The NEP provides for a controlled and reasonably constant growth over the next decade. Adherence to national and provincial plans is essential and will be a critical challenge to communities and authorities.

**Primary:** Under NEP, provision is being made for enrollment of a quota (unspecified) of Grade 10 students from remote areas, in teachers colleges, as a strategy to staff their local schools.

**Secondary:** There is a shortfall in the supply of teachers for upper secondary in specialist areas, currently being filled by untrained graduates, with provision for Lahara courses. In 2004, 40 untrained teachers were enrolled in UoG (as a one-off program). Under NEP, it is proposed that the postgraduate diploma in education be offered by a mixed mode of delivery.

**Vocational:** There is limited provision for preservice training (in home economics and tourism/hospitality). The DOVET program is available, on a fee-for-service basis, for those in the service seeking to gain a teaching qualification. Under NEP, the residential component of DOVET will be offered by distance mode similar to that of the elementary teacher education program. Accreditation through UoG will be considered.

**Technical:** It is difficult to attract and retain well-qualified national staff due to the demand from the private sector. Housing is often only available on the open market, and staff are not eligible for the domestic market allowance or the "expertise" allowances. Training opportunities, which traditionally have been quite limited, will be expanded under NEP, including access to a mixed-mode preservice course.

**Employment/Deployment:** Teachers are not distributed equitably between or within provinces. In addition, some teachers have been paid while not in the school to which they have been posted. Further, there has been evidence of "ghost" teachers on the payroll. As indicated above, these and other related matters are being addressed through the personnel payroll project. It has long been recognized that more stringent and consistent measures are required to control staffing numbers and deployment, both in the interests of student learning and resource utilization. To this end, NEP proposes establishing the PAC to determine and monitor provincial staffing entitlements according to agreed criteria.

**In-service:** NDOE funding for in-service has been minimal over recent years, a significant source being through donor-funded projects, particularly CRIP, and, in the case of college lecturers, through PASTEP. NEP refers to the need for and provision of professional development across all subsectors. Funding projections include an annual allocation for in-service initiatives, although this appears to fall short of the resources required to update teachers, particularly in light of a major curriculum revision at primary and secondary levels.

**Expatriate Contract Teachers:** There are a significant number of contract teachers in secondary schools (4.8 percent) and technical colleges (23 percent). There is need for a policy on phasing out of the majority of such positions, both in terms of employment opportunities for nationals and for cost-effectiveness. While the NEP does not specifically refer to phasing out expatriates from the secondary cadre, there is provision for additional preservice positions and for upgrading of qualifications. There is specific reference to localization of position in the technical subsector, the target being to reach 95 percent by 2014. Constraining the rate of secondary growth in upper secondary grades, combined with improved access to training for nationals, should help.

## Annex 4C: Geographic, Income, and Gender Inequities in PNG Education

### Background

Inequities are an issue in the PNG system, not only because of inequity of outcome, but because inequities impact upon the capacity of regions and people to implement the education reforms. Particularly this is so in regard to commitments, anticipated in the NEP, for contributions from provinces and LLGs and from parents. Inequities in the system are a combination of geography, health factors, social and political organization, problems with law and order, and income. Consequently, required strategies for addressing the inequities go well beyond reform of the education system. Transport and communication facilities need to be improved, but first, in some regions, law and order needs to be strengthened, so that facilities can be established and maintained. Income disparities between communities and governments affecting both the input and output of the education system require addressing issues of support and redistribution. Finally, pronounced gender differences reflect problems concerned with cultural differences.

### Gender Inequities

Female participation in education is lower than males at virtually all levels and in all provinces (Table 4C.1); however, there are noticeable provincial variations, due probably to cultural differences.

Nationally, the highest female participation rate is 46.3 for elementary, and then declines for each successive higher level. Furthermore, although some provinces such as Bougainville approach a 50 percent rate, none reaches it, and some provinces, such as Enga (37.9 percent) fall well short (Table 4C.1).

**Table 4C.1. Females as Percentage of Total General Education Enrollments by Level and Province, 2003**

|  | Elementary | Primary | Basic | Secondary | General |
|---|---|---|---|---|---|
| Bougainville | 48.4 | 48.5 | 48.4 | 45.6 | 48.3 |
| Central | 47.5 | 44.8 | 46.3 | 40.9 | 45.7 |
| East Sepik | 47.3 | 44.9 | 45.8 | 42.6 | 45.6 |
| EHP | 46.2 | 40.5 | 43.1 | 34.4 | 42.6 |
| ENB | 47.9 | 48.6 | 48.3 | 45.1 | 48.0 |
| Enga | 40.4 | 37.4 | 38.7 | 31.5 | 37.9 |
| Gulf | 45.0 | 45.3 | 45.1 | 42.2 | 44.9 |
| Madang | 45.8 | 43.9 | 44.9 | 39.0 | 44.4 |
| Manus | 47.3 | 47.4 | 47.3 | 44.8 | 47.0 |
| Milne Bay | 47.5 | 49.6 | 48.7 | 47.8 | 48.7 |
| Morobe | 46.2 | 44.1 | 45.0 | 41.7 | 44.7 |
| NCD | 47.9 | 47.3 | 47.5 | 48.0 | 47.5 |
| New Ireland | 48.1 | 47.8 | 47.9 | 48.4 | 48.0 |
| Oro | 47.6 | 45.8 | 46.6 | 46.3 | 46.6 |
| Sandaun | 44.8 | 42.7 | 43.6 | 36.2 | 43.2 |
| SHP | 43.4 | 39.9 | 41.6 | 28.6 | 40.5 |
| Simbu | 45.6 | 41.1 | 43.4 | 31.9 | 42.6 |
| Western | 46.8 | 47.4 | 47.2 | 39.6 | 46.6 |
| WHP | 46.8 | 43.2 | 44.8 | 37.6 | 44.3 |
| WNB | 46.9 | 44.8 | 45.8 | 39.8 | 45.3 |
| PNG | 46.3 | 44.4 | 45.2 | 39.9 | 44.8 |

*Source:* NDOE School Census, 2003.

Females as a percentage of teachers have a similar trend[45] (Table 4C.2), and indeed the correlation between the patterns across the provinces is 0.77 (see Figure 4C.1 below).

However, again the participation declines at secondary level, and three provinces, Simbu, Southern Highlands Province (SHP), and Enga, have lower than 30 percent female representation.

Females are also underrepresented in the alternative postprimary route into vocational education. In 2004, of 13,860 vocational center students, 3,850 (27.8 percent) were female (source: Technical and Vocational Education Training Division, NDOE). As Tables 4C.3 and 4C.4 indicate, females fall further behind in the progression from junior to senior secondary education.

Although, at the tertiary education level, females, while still under-represented, have improved their representation from 34 percent of students (Table 4C.3) at senior secondary to 41.8 percent of those awarded the Tertiary Education Scholarship Assistance Scheme

**Table 4C.2. Females as Percentage of Total General Education Teachers by Level and Province, 2003**

|  | Elementary | Primary | Basic | Secondary | General |
|---|---|---|---|---|---|
| Bougainville | 56.2 | 48.9 | 52.0 | 36.3 | 51.0 |
| Central | 33.8 | 41.0 | 39.1 | 28.7 | 37.1 |
| East Sepik | 39.9 | 41.0 | 40.3 | 28.9 | 38.6 |
| EHP | 39.0 | 33.3 | 35.2 | 32.1 | 34.9 |
| ENB | 61.5 | 60.7 | 61.0 | 45.7 | 58.9 |
| Enga | 31.5 | 27.5 | 28.9 | 18.6 | 28.4 |
| Gulf | 36.1 | 37.8 | 36.8 | 40.0 | 37.2 |
| Madang | 32.6 | 29.7 | 30.7 | 35.7 | 31.5 |
| Manus | 51.1 | 54.0 | 53.1 | 27.8 | 49.6 |
| Milne Bay | 45.0 | 52.5 | 49.4 | 39.9 | 48.5 |
| Morobe | 39.7 | 44.6 | 43.1 | 33.6 | 42.2 |
| NCD | 56.3 | 63.7 | 61.1 | 50.4 | 59.4 |
| New Ireland | 46.2 | 63.5 | 60.3 | 46.4 | 58.4 |
| Oro | 29.5 | 49.5 | 39.6 | 35.5 | 39.3 |
| Sandaun | 33.8 | 32.6 | 32.9 | 32.2 | 32.9 |
| SHP | 38.4 | 22.7 | 27.3 | 17.1 | 26.0 |
| Simbu | 23.0 | 21.0 | 21.7 | 24.6 | 21.9 |
| Western | 39.9 | 31.5 | 35.9 | 30.0 | 35.4 |
| WHP | 34.4 | 37.3 | 36.6 | 33.6 | 36.2 |
| WNB | 54.0 | 48.1 | 50.2 | 33.3 | 49.0 |
| PNG | 41.6 | 41.8 | 41.7 | 34.3 | 40.9 |

*Source:* NDOE School census 2003.

scholarship (Table 4C.5), their representation follows the traditional gender stereotyping, with the highest representation being in nursing and the lowest in technical colleges.

Table 4C.5 present information on scholarships by type of education institution and proportions female.

## Provincial Disparities

Figures 4C.2 and 4C.3 show considerable disparity between provinces in respect to per capita revenue and enrollments in basic education. The correlation of education participation with total revenue per capita is 0.43 compared with only 0.02 with internal revenue—indicating that the national provision of grants is having some equitable effect. As noted below, in the case of Simbu, disparities in income can override the advantage a province might otherwise have in respect to access to schools through better-developed road networks. On the other hand, Western Province, despite its relative per capita wealth, is still considerably disadvantaged by the relative inaccessibility of communities.

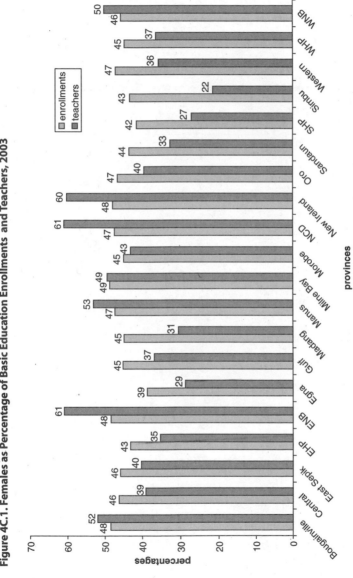

**Figure 4C.1. Females as Percentage of Basic Education Enrollments and Teachers, 2003**

*Source:* NDOE School Census, 2003.

**Table 4C.3. Grade 10 Examinations for Entry into Senior Secondary**

|  | 2001 | 2002 | 2003 | 2004 |
|---|---|---|---|---|
| Schools | 177.0 | 181.0 | 187.0 | 180.0 |
| Candidates awarded certificates | 21,586.0 | 23,299.0 | 24,312.0 | 24,111.0 |
| Male | 12,645.0 | 13,482.0 | 13,985.0 | 14,167.0 |
| Female | 8,941.0 | 9,817.0 | 10,327.0 | 9,944.0 |
| Percentage female | 41.4 | 42.1 | 42.5 | 41.2 |

*Source:* Monitoring and Standards Unit, NDOE.

**Table 4C.4. Grade 11 Students as Proportion of Grade 10, 2003 by Gender and Province**

|  | Males | Females | Total |
|---|---|---|---|
| Bougainville | 20.8 | 16.4 | 18.7 |
| Central | 15.7 | 14.1 | 15.0 |
| East Sepik | 24.8 | 18.5 | 21.8 |
| EH | 8.1 | 11.5 | 9.3 |
| ENB | 13.6 | 9.5 | 11.6 |
| Enga | 28.1 | 21.2 | 25.9 |
| Gulf | 13.1 | 8.9 | 11.2 |
| Madang | 18.0 | 19.7 | 18.7 |
| Manus | 39.5 | 31.5 | 36.0 |
| Milne Bay | 33.2 | 24.5 | 28.9 |
| Morobe | 25.4 | 23.7 | 24.7 |
| NCD | 18.2 | 25.7 | 21.8 |
| New Ireland | 14.8 | 11.8 | 13.3 |
| Oro | 32.5 | 17.8 | 25.3 |
| Sandaun | 21.3 | 14.3 | 18.8 |
| SH | 50.8 | 30.6 | 44.4 |
| Simbu | 27.7 | 25.1 | 26.8 |
| Western | 43.6 | 31.0 | 38.2 |
| WH | 51.4 | 25.4 | 41.1 |
| WNB | 22.7 | 26.2 | 24.1 |
| National | 26.0 | 20.3 | 23.6 |

*Source:* Special NDOE boarding census run, 2003.

## Remoteness, Isolation, and Geographic Inequities

The percentages of arable land in Figure 4C.4 give some indication of the differential barriers to accessibility created by mountainous and swampy terrain.

The fact that less than 5 percent of Western, the largest province, is arable is some indication of the difficulty of providing and servicing schools in this province and provinces like it. In many districts in these

**Table 4C.5. Distribution of Tertiary Education Scholarship Scheme First-Year Scholarships by Gender and Type of Institution, 2004**

| Distribution of TESAS | Female | Male | Total | Female % |
|---|---|---|---|---|
| Universities | 528 | 824 | 1,352 | 39.1 |
| Teacher Colleges | 372 | 419 | 791 | 47.0 |
| Nursing Schools | 99 | 60 | 159 | 62.3 |
| Business Colleges | 107 | 126 | 233 | 45.9 |
| Technical Colleges | 84 | 230 | 314 | 26.8 |
| Total Nonuniversity | 662 | 835 | 1,497 | 44.2 |
| Total | 1,190 | 1,659 | 2,849 | 41.8 |

Source: Office of Higher Education.

provinces, there are no roads accessing the provincial centers and servicing can only be done by walking track, water, and plane.

The district of Telefomin in Sandaun requires either long walks or access by plane. Unfortunately, the cost of flying makes the cost of servicing and inspecting these schools very difficult.

Rivers as the Sepik, can provide avenues for communication; however, the location of settlements on firmer grounds means that schools have to be accessed along minor waterways, frequently blocked by floating vegetation. In addition, access might only be seasonal, depending upon whether it is the wet or dry season.

Roads, where available, are the best option for supporting schools. An unpublished survey for AusAID in 2001 of 18 districts in five provinces[46] shows accessibility to schools by road is closely correlated with density of population (.72) and with density of road networks (.82). Schools with greater access to roads are advantaged over those with less access by having less expensive facilities costs (−.64). Elementary (.45) and primary schools (.77) also tend to be larger, permitting greater economies of scale. There is also an interesting association between accessibility of schools by road and the districts' size of health centers and the number of population they serve—suggesting schools and health centers share similar restrictions through lack of road access.

Table 4C.6 present information on correlations between different variable related to school accessability.

The inclusion of Simbu districts in the survey, which have low per capita income and high population density (see Figure 4C.4), helps explain why correlations of inaccessibility by road with measures of disadvantage and of health servicing in the chart above are much lower

**Figure 4C.2. Basic Education Enrollments as Percentage of Population, 2003**

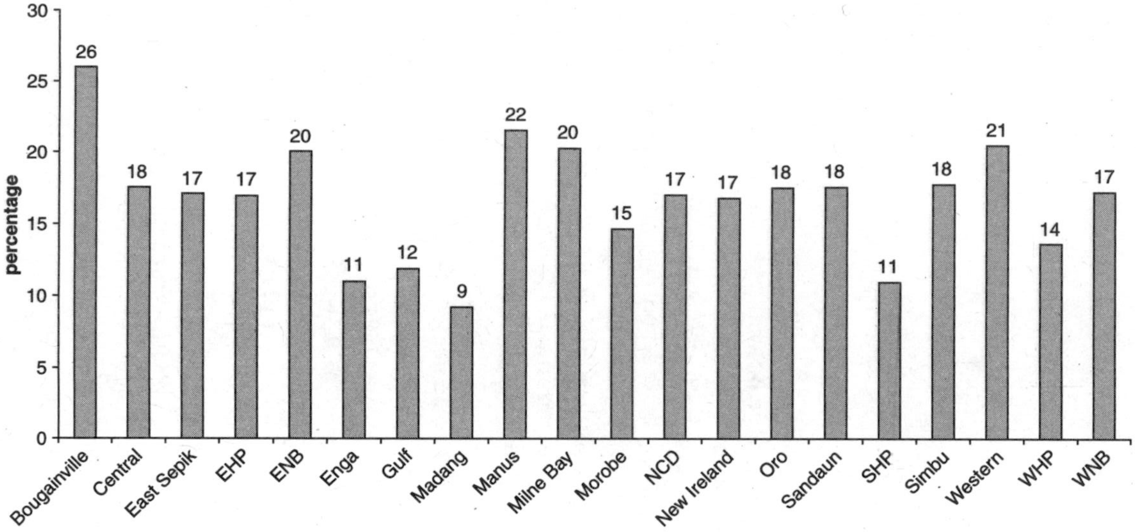

*Source:* Mission Estimates based on NDOE and Census Data.

**Figure 4C.3. Internal and Total Provincial per Capita Government Budget Revenue, 2005**

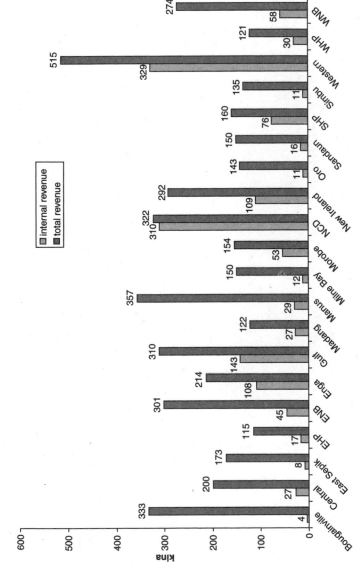

*Source:* Mission Estimates based on National Budget Estimates and Census data.

**Figure 4C.4. Percentage of Arable Land by Province**

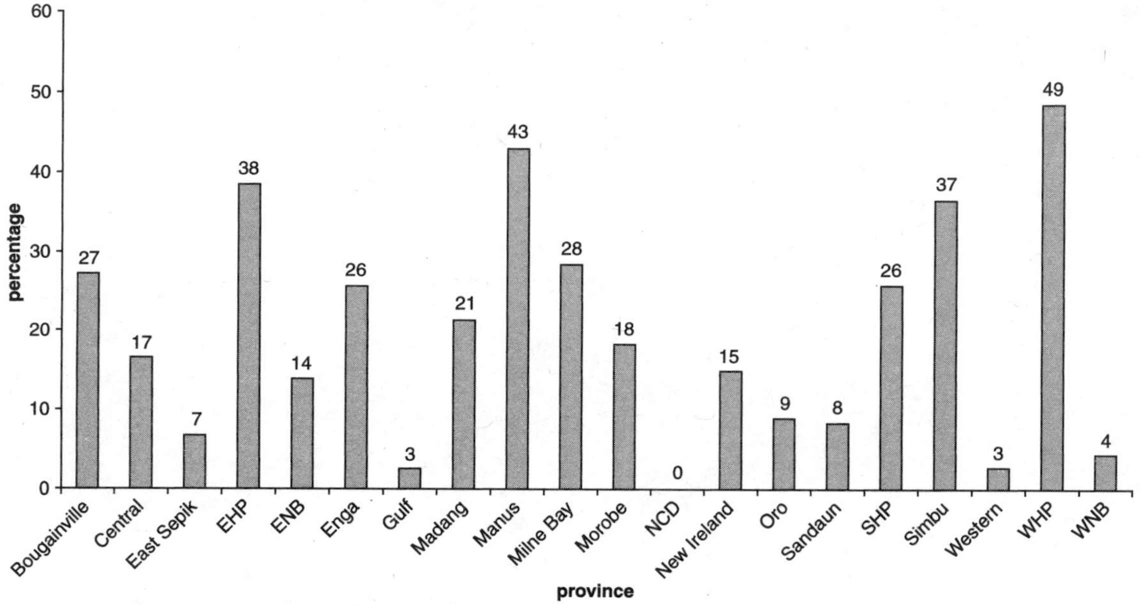

Source: Census data.

**Table 4C.6. Correlation of School Accessibility by Road with Education and Other Related Variables**

| Variables | Correlation |
|---|---|
| Persons per km$^2$ | 0.72 |
| Percent of primary schools classified as disadvantaged | −0.14 |
| Number of elementary and primary students per 100 persons in district | 0.09 |
| Number of students per elementary school | 0.45 |
| Elementary student-teacher ratio | 0.33 |
| Number of students per primary school | 0.77 |
| Primary student-teacher ratio | −0.18 |
| Kilometers of road to 100 K$^2$ of area | 0.82 |
| Percent of schools accessible by road | 1.00 |
| Roads (km) | −0.25 |
| Persons per health facility | 0.78 |
| Persons per health worker | 0.57 |
| Health workers per facility | 0.37 |

*Source:* Field analysis on AusAID mission; see text.

than would otherwise be expected. The impact of lack of income on disadvantage is described below.

Even though accessibility by road is important for reducing infrastructure costs and improving servicing, this does not mean that these features are as good as might be anticipated. For example, the roads in Simbu and the Highland provinces are subject to landslides and banditry, frequently causing disruption. In addition, in many districts, roads are impassable in the wet season.

Maritime provinces, such as Milne Bay, have an additional problem. Schools within maritime districts may be separated by large expanses of ocean, whose crossing by light craft is both slow and dangerous. The cost of hiring craft and of fuel can also be prohibitive.

Consistent with the AusAID survey cited above, showing the rising cost of building classrooms, the PESD study[47] showed that remote schools were at a significant disadvantage compared with more accessible schools in respect to the proportion of classrooms:

- made of permanent materials;
- needing to be completely rebuilt;
- with leaking roofs;
- with a chair and table for the teacher;
- with lockable storage capacity; and
- with electricity that works.

**Table 4C.7. Nongrant Revenues (by Quintiles of Nongrant Revenue per Student), 2001 (Kina per Student in the Year)**

*(nongrant revenues per student quintiles conditional on revenues being more than zero)*

|  | Bottom 40% | Middle 40% | Top 20% | Total |
|---|---|---|---|---|
| Total | 17 | 58 | 160 | 60 |
| Fees | 7 | 33 | 132 | 40 |
| Subsidies | 11 | 25 | 28 | 20 |

*Source:* PESD Study 2002.

Also, such schools were significantly less likely to have adequate or good provision of administration blocks; clear radio reception; school vehicles; agricultural areas for student or teacher use; land for expansion; sports areas; sports equipment; and specialist science, technology and home economics classrooms. Such schools were also significantly less likely to be provided with electricity, water, or toilet facilities.

According to the PESD study, schools in remote areas compared with those in less remote areas are more likely to have less financial support, from "leakage" of government subsidy; however, the study did not show any greater delay in receiving subsidies. The PESD study also noted that revenue from fees declines with increasing remoteness.

### The Impact of Income on the Quality of Provision and on Education Enrollment

As with respect to remoteness, the PESD study showed that schools in poorer districts were more likely to be at a disadvantage compared with those from wealthier communities in respect to some facilities; however, this was not always the case, as there was a general overall paucity of facilities.

The PESD study also showed that schools from wealthier communities were better supported not only in revenue from subsidies (partly through less "leakage") but also in that from fees. Indeed, for the wealthiest 20 percent of schools, revenue from fees was greater than from subsidies (Table 4C.7).

In 2002, when the national government fully subsidized fees, enrollments increased, indicating, as the PESD notes, some sensitivity of participation with cost; however, the study survey also showed very strong overall support for the payment of fees.

### Notes

1. The review primarily focuses on the general education sector in part because of the importance of achieving UBE and the demand for resources that this

will produce; however, the skills development, literacy, and tertiary sectors also play an important role in PNG's development and consume considerable resources. Further information on and analysis of these diverse and institutionally fractured sectors, beyond the scope of this report, is required.

2. Although the NDOE annual report contains 2004 data, the latest school census data available at the time of writing was for 2003.

3. See NDOE 2004, Annual Report.

4. For the purpose of this discussion, general education refers to that section of government-funded education, funded through the NDOE and, in the form of teacher salaries and education-function grants, through the provinces. This includes the salaries of teacher and technical colleges and funding of certain support services in the tertiary sectors, but funding in the tertiary sector is otherwise separate.

5. Also see other details in Annex A to Chapter 5.

6. In this year, the GOPNG provided a full-fee subsidy. General education's share of total government recurrent expenditure (including debt financing) was 20.8 percent.

7. The following data are taken from the 2005 budget papers.

8. Fluctuation, as demonstrated in the range of these figures, is common because of project funding being spread over time, and irregularity in the time in which projects are completed and others come onstream. Problems with government recording of aid received in the budget has also been a problem, particularly in 2001.

9. NEP 2 database.

10. This falls significantly short of the MTDS and EFA UBE targets (preparatory through Grade 8) by 2005, and also of the NEP Steering Committee's original intention of compulsory education through Grade 5.

11. NEP database.

12. Mi Lusim Skul, Participation and Retention in Primary and Secondary Schools in Papua New Guinea, National Research Institute, 2001.

13. In 2002, the PESD study surveyed 214 schools in 19 districts in eight provinces (Gulf and NCD in the Southern region; Enga and EHP in the Highlands region; Sandaun and Morobe in the Momase region; and WNB and ENB in the Islands region). The PESD measured remoteness on a scale of zero to one in terms of a school's access to up to 16 commonly used "facilities." Accessible equaled a measurement of up to 0.29, and remote equaled a measurement of 0.29 and above.

14. Age specific population estimates by province are not available. Care needs to be taken in drawing conclusions because of some differences in age distribution among the provinces can be expected.

15. World Bank 2004, Table 3.2.

16. Also see Annex C Table 1.

17. Also see Annex C Table 2. .

18. This needs to include students in the newly reformed primary schools, which now contain students in their early teens (Grades 7 and 8 from the old provincial high schools).

19. The new Grades 7 and 8 text "Personal Development," Book 2, Kenneth Rouse, refers to HIV/AIDS and safe sex on pp. 42, 44, 120, and 128–131.

20. The remainder is administered through the provinces.

21. There is provision under the OLPLLG for a National Monitoring Authority (NMA) to advise the government on the performance of provinces against nationally agreed indicators. Regrettably, due to limitations in resources and skills, the NMA has had little impact to date.

22. For example, although the Secretary of Education can refuse to approve the registration of new schools falling outside the NEP guidelines, she/he can be put under considerable political pressure to do so, particularly if school infrastructure has been built by provinces (or financed by a development partner).

23. PNG Department of Education (2004), pp. 38.

24. Teachers' remuneration represents 90 percent of total recurrent expenditure on education.

25. The PESD study estimated that 15 percent of posts were occupied by "ghost" teachers, with rates varying across provinces from a high of 30 percent in Morobe to 6 percent in Enga. Absenteeism is also rampant, estimated at 15 percent for all PNG. Teachers reported taking up their posts on average 10 days late, 17 in more remote areas. Removing head teachers from this calculation would increase the average to 27 days. In short, in recent years, an average of 13 percent of the school year is lost to late starts and absenteeism. In those extremely remote community schools that have remained open, the average teacher missed up to one-third of the school year.

26. Under this initiative, around 6,000 teachers were to be suspended from the payroll for not reporting for duty on time; however, the success of this initiative depends upon heads of school not being intimidated when completing the attendance forms.

27. One interesting partnership being developed in education, with the support of the World Bank, is in energy. Efforts are being made to enable teachers to finance portable solar power mechanisms to enable lights and other appliances to be powered in their homes, typically located in areas without power. Efforts are also being made to use coconut oil to run generators at schools to lower the significant costs of diesel fuel to school

BOMs. Parents in many areas will be able to pay fees or part of fees through donation of coconuts for fuel.

28. Between 2005 and 2014 the elementary student-teacher ratio is intended to rise from 29.6 to 32.4, the primary from 33.2 to 36.8, and the secondary to remain at 26.0; however, given high student and teacher absentee rates, the targeted student-teacher ratios may be more nominal than real, and the feasibility of raising real student-teacher ratios questionable.

29. Data obtained, and calculations made, from NEP 2 Table 55 and NEP database.

30. The term "quality-enhanced" refers to the increased costs (relative to the NEP 2 costings, which are based on current reality) of an education that provides students with appropriate curriculum and teacher support materials. The term "full quality enhanced" adds in to the "quality-enhanced" package the support income to schools for school materials and other school-running costs that are meant to be provided through school fees, but are not.

31. The provision of a full "quality-enhanced" education in 2005 would represent an additional 47 percent of the expenditure program as presented in the plan.

32. The PNG-AusAID Affordability Study, September, 2003, estimated that between 1997 and 2003, "off-budget" donor funding ranged between 3 and 52 percent of total donor funding, averaging 32 percent.

33. Discussions with the NEFC raised strong doubts about the capacity of more than but a few of the provinces to meet the NEP plans for capital and maintenance funding from subnational sources, and it may be necessary for the central government to take over this commitment directly. Variations in provincial capacity have implications for equity and the level of standards.

34. World Bank, 2004.

35. Although the NEP 2 report, p. 63, states a transition rate of 25 percent, the NEP statistical database assumes a transition rate of 30.

36. As suggested from Table 57 of NEP 2 database, which from 2009 removes the parental contribution to elementary education. Free education is targeted in PNG EFA, National Action Plan, 2004–2015 as a policy for all basic education by 2015; however, this document was prepared during the period of the Morauta Government's budgeting in 2002 of a full-fee subsidy, which was withdrawn in the following year.

37. Table 57 of the NEP 2 indicates that elementary education will be free when it becomes universal.

38. Proven correlations between the education of women and better health and population control and increased productivity in agriculture are just two examples.

39. In its recommendations for the NEB, the NEP Steering Committee reaffirms a commitment for compulsory education for all to Grade 5 by the end of the planning period; however, it did make this subject to affordability. Further discussions with finance officials led to a revision of this commitment. According to the data provided, the targeted basic education enrollment for 2014 was 7 percent higher in the earlier than in the later year.

40. The enrollments in Grades 3–8 as a percentage of the 9- to 14-year-old population.

41. For instance, support for basic education is the principal purpose of AusAID's education program. See AusAID 2000, and Draft Concept Paper, A Program Approach to Education in Papua New Guinea, 2006.

42. For example, problems with the provision of counterpart staff have inhibited skills transfer and continuation of initiatives after the end of projects; also, lack of provision for maintaining donor-funded assets. See ADB, Impact Evaluation Study of the Technical and Vocational Education Projects in Malaysia, Pakistan, Papua New Guinea, and Sri Lanka. December 1999, IES, Reg. 99035 for the problems arising from dependence on GOPNG funding.

43. The cost per student rises as the level of education and training rises, and the government provides a considerable amount of support to tertiary education. In 2005, an additional K 117 million (4 percent of the total government recurrent budget) was budgeted for tertiary education. This included grants to universities and expenditures on the legal training institute, on the Office of Higher Education, and on the Tertiary Education Study Assistance Scheme (TESAS).

44. See WB, 1994:3; PNG MHERST, 2004.

45. According to NDOE census data, between 1996 and 2003 the level of representation of females in general education enrollments made no advance, and although the proportion of female teachers in basic education increased from 35 to 41 percent, at the secondary level it only improved marginally from 34 to 35 percent.

46. This survey was undertaken in the course of designing a follow-up project for the AusAID Basic Education Infrastructure and Curriculum Materials project.

47. In 2002, the PESD study surveyed 214 schools in 19 districts in eight provinces (Gulf and NCD in the Southern region; Enga and EHP in the Highlands region; Sandaun and Morobe in Momase region; and WNB and ENB in the Islands region). The PESD measured remoteness on a scale of zero to one in terms of a school's access to up to 16 commonly-used "facilities." Accessible measured up to 0.29, and remote 0.29 and above.

# CHAPTER 5

# Common Cross-Cutting Themes

## Introduction

A cursory review of the situational assessments and proposed strategies for health, HIV/AIDs, and education (Chapters 2 to 4) indicates that each of the sectors, while exhibiting features unique to itself, also face a range of common challenges. This should not be surprising, as each of the sectors has to operate within some common parameters, namely: (i) the formal structure of government, which assigns a range of the health and education sector powers and responsibilities to provinces and districts, as well as to the national government; (ii) the general operational structures of government (for example, for budgeting, accounting, planning, and personnel management); (iii) declining growth and rapidly falling per capita incomes; (iv) a significant deterioration in the composition and quality of public spending in the 1990s and the emergence of both unsustainable fiscal policy and significant budget overruns in the early 2000s, resulting in a rapid increase in public debt, which further constrained expenditures; (v) significant political instability and a lack of a consensus on strategic development issues; and (vi) growing uncertainties and concerns between both government and development partners and among development partners on how best to assist and work together in a situation of problematic development outcomes. Further, as discussed in the previous chapters, the economy is impacting each sector in critical ways and government systems are themselves facing critical problems, not the least of which is a crisis of integrity.

PNG's medium- and longer-term economic and fiscal performance is also a critical backdrop to the challenges facing the health, HIV/AIDS, and education sectors. Economic growth has been volatile over the past 10 to 15 years. While GDP is estimated to have grown by about 2.8 percent in the last two years (thus sustaining real per capita GDP), this was preceded by a six-year period (1997–2002) during which real GDP declined by an average of 1 percent per annum, resulting in a protracted decline in real GDP per capita.[1]

Between 1991 and 1996, however, real GDP grew by 7.5 percent annually, fueled by the expansion of the mineral sector. The proximate cause of the subsequent negative growth was the resource depletion of a majority of the large mineral projects and the absence of any new projects; however, formal-sector employment is estimated to have increased by only 1.5 percent since 1996. Furthermore, agricultural production, which is critical to the incomes and work opportunities of the vast majority of the population, stagnated during most of this period due to the falling and fluctuating prices of traditional smallholder crops (coffee and cocoa) and the collapse of the copra plantations. Reinforcing this trend was the rapid and extensive deterioration of transport infrastructure, particularly roads and coastal shipping.

The present government inherited a difficult economic and financial situation, but has made commendable progress over the past two to three years in controlling overall spending by introducing expenditure control measures and further compressing nonwage expenditures. However, the compression of nonwage expenditures has undermined efforts to increase expenditures on the critical inputs needed to improve the quality of service delivery in the health and education sectors.

The government has also started to reform procurement arrangements and personnel management systems (including the payroll) to increase "value for money" and to constrain unplanned growth in public sector employment. However, as discussed in Chapters 2 to 4, restoring the integrity of the budget, accounting, procurement, and personnel management systems remains a critical challenge while the quality of social-sector outputs remains poor, and this makes PNG's development partners wary of working with the government in these sectors.

The recent improvement in economic performance is fragile, and medium-term growth prospects remain uncertain at best, particularly in the nonmineral sectors. Evidence suggests that general private-sector activities remain depressed, particularly in rural areas, where 85 percent of the population live and rely on the private agricultural sector for their cash incomes. Foreign- and domestically financed investment in the non-mineral formal sector remains limited, with little or no signs of this turning around in the near future. Prospects for employment growth in the formal private sector are also weak, especially for women, who account for only 20 percent of the formal-sector workforce. Estimates suggest that at present, only one in 10 school graduates are likely to find a job in private business. As discussed in Chapter 4, two-thirds of PNG's population is under 30 years old, which means that youth issues will continue to pose important policy challenges for the country.

One ray of hope is that two major projects—the proposed Papua New Guinea Gas Project and the Ramu (nickel/cobalt) Project—may begin to be implemented soon, which will improve the government's revenue position. On estimates prior to the recent dramatic increases in petroleum prices, the gas project would increase government revenues by 10 to 20 percent. The anticipated increase in revenues should enable the government to focus on its development priorities; however, as discussed in the previous chapters, in the past public expenditures have not been well targeted to the government's high-priority development goals.

PNG's past economic performance, future prospects, and rapid population growth rate have led to a dramatic increase in the level of poverty in PNG since 1996, and little likelihood that recent trends will be reduced quickly. A recent report concludes ". . . There are indications that poverty levels have increased sharply in recent years, and are unlikely to climb down in the immediate future . . . Using a poverty line that allows 2,200 calories per adult equivalent per day and an allowance for basic nonfood expenditure, the projections of poverty measures indicate that the proportion of population in poverty has increased from 37.5 percent in 1996 to about 54 percent by 2003. The trends are no different for the international poverty line of '$1 per day,' using which the incidence of poverty is estimated to have risen from about 25 percent to just under 40 percent over the same period."[2] The report further estimates that 70 percent of the population (or 3.9 million Papua New Guineans) now live on less than US$2 per day, up from 54 percent in 1996.

Clearly, these trends represent real problems for clients of PNG's health and education services. For a majority of the population, their disposable cash incomes, never very large, have been severely squeezed, making it harder than ever to pay for school fees, to access health facilities and schools, and to pay for health care. Transport infrastructure, particularly roads, has deteriorated significantly, with one assessment indicating that over 50 percent of the rural roads that were operational two decades ago are unusable now and that there is little likelihood that they can be rehabilitated in the foreseeable future. This has effectively increased the cash and opportunity costs of accessing health and education facilities.

Increasing poverty, the lack of growth in both formal-sector jobs and in income-earning opportunities for women, and the proliferation of enclave development sites, as discussed in Chapter 3, have been critical underlying factors in the increasing spread of the HIV/AIDS virus.

It is central to each of the proposed strategies for health, HIV/AIDS, and education (outlined in Chapters 2, 3, and 4 respectively) that there is a consensus among government policy makers in PNG (and as reflected in official documents such as the MTDS) that the core objective of each sector should be to improve sectoral outcomes consistent with the objectives of the MDGs, in order to achieve the MDGs.

## The Fragility and Inequity of Current Outcomes

A central theme of the sectoral chapters of this Human Development Strategy has been the fragility and inequity of current health, HIV, and education outcomes. The fragility of these outcomes is manifest in a number of ways in each of the sectors, and, while a lack of data makes it difficult to do a detailed analysis of inequities of outcomes, it is clear that these inequities are very significant.

In health, as discussed in Chapter 2, the IMR is probably the best overall single indicator of the performance of the health systems of low-income countries. The IMR for PNG dramatically declined between 1970 and 1980 from more than 130 to 72 deaths per 1,000 live births. This happened in response to the expansion of the basic primary health care system dominated by frontline workers with minimal amounts of training, some basic drugs, and an expanded network of primary health care facilities (health centers at the district level and basic hospital services at the provincial level). These facilities were able to provide immunization against the major communicable diseases to children and pregnant women through outreach activities. However, by 2000, 25 years after independence, the IMR had only fallen to 64 deaths per 1,000, and there is no indication that it has fallen significantly since 2000.

The key health problems in PNG are overwhelmingly high maternal and infant death rates, and high rates of communicable diseases. Together, these problems account for 60 percent of the disease burden in PNG. Poor reproductive health, in which only limited gains have been made in the last 30 years, is at the core of the low maternal health status.

Underlying this, faltering in the earlier trend of improvements in health status has been a decrease in the performance of the health system. This has happened despite the fact that the government has significantly increased expenditures on health, particularly in recent years. Health care infrastructure and management capacity, as discussed in Chapter 2, particularly in rural areas, is declining, maternal and child health services are inadequate and showing few signs of improvement, vaccine coverage in rural areas is very low, TB control is poor (partly a consequence of the burgeoning HIV/AIDS epidemic), malaria treatment and prevention remains problematic despite its significance for general health, and ambulatory care is in a state of long-term decline—annually, outpatient visits per capita are declining.

The available information on the performance of the health system indicates that it is in greater decline in remote areas, where the lack of access to income-earning opportunities and of transport infrastructure is most pervasive, which is a strong indication that the faltering health system is causing particular problems for the poor.

The HIV/AIDS epidemic clearly highlights the fragility of health outcomes in PNG and the impact that this fragility is already having on the rural poor. Due to the lack of a coherent policy response to the epidemic (as discussed in Chapter 3), the virus has now spread throughout the country, with more than 60 percent of people with the virus to be found in rural areas. Further, all the evidence suggests it is spreading, and will continue to spread, without a clear and decisive response to the disease.

In the last decade, PNG has made considerable progress in increasing the access of young people to education. Despite considerable population growth, the gross enrollment rates of 6- to 18-year-olds in general education rose between 1997 and 2003 from 43 to 55 percent. With donor assistance, considerable effort has also been put into the planning of this expansion, with an extensive restructuring of the education system, so that a nine-year basic education program (from preliminary through to Grade 8) has now been developed with a newly developed vernacular elementary and a restructured primary system.

However, under its current plan, PNG will fail to meet its commitment under the 2000 Dakar Agreement to provide education for all by 2015. The latest targets would, if achieved, only raise the gross enrollment rate of 6- to 14-year-olds in basic education from 71 percent in 2005 to

80 percent in 2014. Also, retention, although improving, remains a problem; by 2014, only just over half (54 percent) of those who started school eight to nine years before will complete Grade 8. Absenteeism is also a problem, and partly because of remoteness, nearly 20 percent of children currently do not attend school at all.

National enrollment data conceal the considerable variation in education participation between provinces, and that access to general education is greater for males, for the wealthier, and for those in urban areas. The enrollment data also conceal the need to raise the quality and standards of education, as well as the means of assessing those standards. The latest plan notes the concern with equity and with standards, but sets aside no additional funds for addressing either.

Funding is the major constraint upon achieving UBE. The present targets were cut back because of funding constraints, and even to achieve these, the GOPNG will need improvements in cost-efficiency and reforms to the administration of funds to schools that have not been achieved before. To achieve higher standards and quality the government will also depend upon donor and parental contributions, which makes a commitment to "free" compulsory basic education problematic. Furthermore, progress in achieving UBE depends not only on spending on education directly, but on spending to overcome remoteness and civil disorder. Cultural traditions, which in some provinces also restrict the representation of females as students and as part of the teaching force, also need to be addressed.

Apart from the issues arising to expand basic education, account has to be taken also of the impact this expansion has upon the rest of the education and skills development sectors. This expansion, along with "credential inflation" in the labor market, creates additional private demand for further qualifications. This brings planning of education expansion within the context of the needs of the formal and informal labor-market sectors, and raises further issues of labor market mobility, equity, and sources of funding. Unfortunately, despite much discussion in this area, the regulation and planning that exists is uncoordinated and piecemeal.

## The Need for a "Whole-of-Government" Approach

A key issue adversely affecting service delivery and outcomes in all three human development areas is the fragmentation of government's approach to policy that results in policy incoherence. Indeed, this problem may extend beyond these sectors. Policy incoherence is manifested when national policies and goals are not (a) articulated in a manner consistent with achieving agreed objectives; and/or (b) effectively translated at the subnational levels into policies and goals. The resulting inconsistency between national and subnational policies can be costly in terms of wasting scarce budgetary resources and failing to meet human development goals. This is certainly the case in PNG where, for a variety of reasons, including the decentralization reforms of 1995, there has been a strong disjunction between national and subnational policies. Differing technical and implementation approaches and priorities by donors active in these sectors has also tended to reinforce the policy incoherence at the national levels. Therefore, as discussed in each sectoral chapter, there is a need to draw up a clear delineation of responsibilities for the formulation and oversight of policies in health, HIV/AIDS, and education. Responsibility for implementing and sustaining these policies must then be clearly vested at the national levels in the relevant line agencies, with other central agencies having a supporting role as appropriate. Development partners also need to be part of this effort to harmonize policy making and implementing interventions.

Central to the proposals in this report is the notion of a need for a "whole-of-government" approach to

(a) Developing a national vision for each sector and for the outcomes desired consistent with the MDGs and the MTDS.
(b) Establishing enforceable policy oversight arrangements at the national government and subnational government levels.
(c) Setting priorities for sectoral reforms that are based on a consensus between the national and provincial authorities and other stakeholders.
(d) Identifying both implementation and financing constraints at each level of government and ensuring that their implications are embodied in the priorities for sectoral reforms.
(e) Developing implementation plans and arrangements for monitoring and evaluating progress over time, including for national and provincial authorities.

These themes are further discussed in Chapter 6.

## Decentralization and Devolution

The fact that responsibility for health and education service delivery is held by many different entities that are isolated from each other is a critical problem with the institutional landscape of governance in PNG. There is little doubt that the current devolution arrangements in PNG are a major cause of this isolation and fragmentation and at least one of the deep-seated causes underscoring the fragile health, HIV/AIDS, and education outcomes.

Following the establishment of the provincial government system in 1978, both the education and the health system became highly decentralized. Political responsibility for managing primary and secondary schools, vocational centers, and the primary health care system (including health centers and health posts) was devolved to the provinces, albeit within the concept of a unified budget and accounting system subject to the national government's Finance Management and Audit Acts.

The revised decentralization arrangements embedded in the NOL of 1995 significantly altered the devolution arrangements in PNG. Behind the revised arrangements was a political concern at the national level that national parliamentary members (particularly those who were not ministers) were unable to influence the allocation of resources by the provincial and district governments for the main devolved functions—particularly primary education, health, and rural transport infrastructure. Unfortunately, the current devolution arrangements make it almost impossible for PNG to reap any significant benefits from decentralization because they are not organized on sound principles.[3] As presently organized, devolution has led to waste due to ineffective deployment of resources and at times been the cause of perverse outcomes, as, for example, when provincial and district spending patterns have deviated significantly from nationally agreed policies. Specifically, the Organic Law:

(a) Established LLGs that became responsible for elementary schools (newly created under the 1993 Education Reform Act), primary schools, health centers, and health posts; in other words, the backbone of the health and education systems.

(b) Replaced directly elected provincial governments with a provincial governance structure comprising nationally elected provincial members of parliament and elected heads of local-level councils in the province. Now these provincial members of the national parliament are expected to represent national, provincial, and district-level functions and interests and also to chair district planning and budget committees. One consequence of these arrangements is that members of parliament can now lobby for funds for their province directly from the national government and have some influence over the amount and flow of revenue available to provinces and districts. This is not desirable and in many respects goes counter to the very principles of decentralization.

(c) Established financing arrangements for provincial governments and LLGs that have proved to be unaffordable and unsustainable given the current and likely future fiscal positions.[4] This has created significant tension between national and provincial governments and has given provincial governments a "justification," at times, for ignoring nationally determined policies and priorities.

(d) Assigned to provinces (and LLGs) the administrative authority to make and execute budgets, with the national sectoral departments providing only general policy oversight and monitoring and technical support. Furthermore, the Organic Law established a National Monitoring Authority (NMA) to monitor outcomes in provinces and at the local level, but this has never been done. The NMA's role relative to other central agencies of government, provinces, and national line departments remains unclear. An important consequence of this is that national departments, which have the policy-making authority and the technical knowledge of what indicators should be monitored, have no line authority over the provinces for the devolved sectors. However, the Organic Law does allow the Minister of Finance to approve or reject provincial budgets, which gives the national government one important but underused lever to influence the activities of provincial governments and LLGs.

(e) Removed provincial governments and LLGs from being subject to the national government's Finance Management and Audit Acts and providing for provincial legislation instead. This led to a discontinuity in accountability arrangements across provinces, even though the provincial legislation had to be developed within national guidelines.

(f) Required national sectoral departments to sponsor amendments of national legislation governing specific sectors and to provide guidance to provinces to establish provincial legislation for sector governance. This proliferation of acts and schemes of arrangements, while developed within national guidelines, generated unprecedented disruption and unnecessary complexity in a system that was already confronting severe capacity constraints. A decade after the establishment of the revised Organic Law, much of the enabling legislation and rules and regulations at both the national and provincial levels remains to be enacted or put in place.

(g) Caused the responsibility and accountability for workforce employment and deployment to be fragmented between national sectoral departments, the provinces, and the central agencies responsible for public-sector employment (such as the DPM for public servants and the TSC for teachers). One major consequence of this fragmentation is that most staffing decisions are now taken independently of the budget framework.

The overriding implication of this fragmentation is the absence of uniform, clear oversight arrangements for programs delivered at the provincial and local government levels. Furthermore, the financing arrangements embodied in the Organic Law reinforce this structural fragmentation and create significant inequalities among provinces in terms of their capacity to finance and carry out their assigned sectoral priorities, including the provision of health and education services. Also, in part because of a lack of consensus over the roles and responsibilities of different levels of government, the resources made available to provincial governments and LLGs are not used as originally intended by national government and many of those who supported the current decentralization arrangements. Under these financing arrangements:

(a) The fragmentation of financing sources available to provinces has prevented them from preparing efficient and coherent expenditure plans and has been an obstacle to consolidation and monitoring at the national level. A complex array of different grants is available to finance provincial budgets. Some of this money is earmarked to pay for sectoral staff, provincial staff, and local government staff, and for social sector and infrastructure services. The provinces can also draw on their "own revenues" from goods and services taxes, mining and petroleum royalties (where applicable), and tax-credit-scheme income. Also, development partners provide provinces with funds on-budget or off-budget, or in the form of goods or services supplied either through national departments or directly from the donor agencies themselves.

(b) Provincial governments have considerable discretionary expenditure[5] at their disposal. In 2005, budgeted discretionary expenditure was K 374 million, or about 34 percent of total budgeted nonwage, non-interest recurrent spending for PNG as a whole. Despite this level of discretionary expenditure, very little is spent on the main sectors for which the provinces have constitutional responsibility—particularly health and education (and rural transport infrastructure)—even though there are clearly critical deficits in each of these sectors. As we have seen, there is a lack of clarity and consensus about the financial roles and responsibilities of the national and provincial governments. Currently, the central agencies of the national government do not actively work with provinces on these issues.

(c) As a matter of policy, the NDOH tries to ensure that provinces allocate 6 percent of their total resources to health programs. Despite this effort, this does not always happen and this continues to be a matter of contention and tension between levels of government and PNG's development partners in the health sector. Provincial officials often argue that donors provide adequate financing for health services, thus freeing up the provinces to finance other activities and priorities, but they are not always correct in this respect and so priority services remain unfunded—a classic illustration of fungibility. The National Department of Education (NDOE) does not formally attempt to ensure a comparable compact to that tried by NDOH with provinces. Provinces, on the other hand, as discussed in Chapter 4, often allocate resources to finance high school construction or expansion (due to high private demands for secondary education) outside the policy framework on high school expansion plans that they agreed to with the NDOE. This leads to schools being constructed even though no provision has been made to finance their staffing and operational costs, which are then presented to the national government as a *fait accompli*. It is all but impossible for the national government to refuse to finance the operational costs of these schools. Consequently, 70 percent of children graduating from Grade 8 now have access to a Grade 9 class even though national policy currently restricts the continuation rate to 50 percent as a means of ensuring enough funds are available for basic education.

(d) Budgetary resources are very inequitably distributed among the provinces. This is true for both for recurrent revenue (which primarily consists of remuneration from the national government for the costs of teachers and health workers) and the provinces' own revenues. The provinces' development expenditures, which are largely financed by development partners, also vary quite significantly, at least those that can be separately identified in budget papers and from project documents as being provincial expenditures. The average amount of per capita recurrent revenue provided to the provinces by the national government in 2005 is K 108; however, there is considerable provincial variation around this average—from Manus, with K 268 per capita and Southern Highlands, with K 76 per capita. The average amount of per capita revenue raised by the provinces themselves (a measure of their discretionary expenditure capacity) in 2005 was K 65, ranging from a low of K 4 per capita in Bougainville to a high of K 329 per capita in the Western Province. Overall, the total amount of per capita resources available to the provinces in 2005 is K 195, ranging from a low of K 115 per capita in the Eastern Highlands Province to a high of K 515 per capita in Western Province.

The NEFC is attempting to tackle many of these issues; however, given the enormous agenda faced by the NEFC and the need for political consensus on the many difficult issues relating to resource allocation, devolution, and autonomy, it is not likely to have any impact before the medium term. Given the urgency of the unmet needs in the human development areas, this time frame is not a luxury that the country can afford. This means short-term direct actions are required. It needs to be understood and acknowledged by the national government and provinces that these actions may not always be consistent with the Organic Law. Therefore, the line agencies and central agencies, in consultation with the NEFC, will need to work out what are the most appropriate interim arrangements; in other words, whether this should be done by reaching mutual agreements with provincial governments or by amending legislation. Some of the urgent direct actions that the national government has already taken include (i) establishing health and education function grants; (ii) taking over the direct financing of grants to mission health services, (both of which are contrary to the provisions of the Organic Law on Provincial and Local level Government (sometimes called NOL). Establishing strategic guidelines for the preparation of sectoral budgets by both the national sectoral departments and the provinces and working out arrangements to ensure appropriate funding by provincial governments of health, HIV/AIDS, and education should be done as a matter of urgency. These actions are critical and will require joint action by the Minister of Finance and Treasury and the Minister for Inter-Governmental Relations, in cooperation with other relevant ministries and provincial governments.

## The Long-Term Decline in the Integrity of Core Government Systems

Underlying the fragility of social-sector outcomes and the fragmentation of responsibility for service delivery are two important long-standing governance failures:

(a) The failure to control the size of the civil service and to ensure that payroll expenditures stay within budget allocations, and
(b) A long-term and deep decline in the integrity of budget institutions and systems.

The need to correct the serious decline in the governance of the payroll and budget institutions was a central theme of the recent PERR exercise. The PERR argues that PNG has tended to resort to short-term solutions to weather its past fiscal crises, typically by cutting core operational and staff budgets, and these were not sustainable. Typically, any attempt to make structural reforms was not made sustainable after the crisis had passed, which meant that subsequent fiscal crises were subject to the same short-term fixes. The PERR argues that the scope for these short-term solutions has been exhausted: "The growing burden of debt, poor prospects for growth and PNG's vulnerability, as a small commodity-producing open economy, to exogenous shocks underscore the need for effecting a sharp turnaround through a sizeable fiscal adjustment, and importantly, sustaining the effort over the medium term. . . . Furthermore, there is a need to allocate a higher share of public expenditures to goods and services and infrastructure to build up the long-term potential of the economy."[6]

### The Reform of the Payroll System
Payroll costs in PNG are high and have been steadily rising. Wage and salary costs have taken up an increasing share of the recurrent budget in recent times, from 42 percent in 2002 to an estimated 45 percent in 2005. Despite the recent fall in interest rates and, therefore, in interest payments on the public debt, this trend looks likely to continue, with wages projected to rise to 48 percent of recurrent expenditure in 2009.

These payroll increases are due both to increases in public-sector employment and to increases in wages that have exceeded the rate of inflation, which are continuing to squeeze the discretionary resources that are available for spending on goods and services.

According to the PERR, public-sector employment accounts for at least 30 percent of total expenditures. Between 1999 and 2002, the number of staff on the central payroll increased from 69,840 to 77,785— an increase of 11.4 percent. The salaries and wages of national and provincial departments grew by 30 percent, about 10 percentage points above inflation. This rapid increase in payroll costs is one of the chief pressures on the budget that is accentuating the public debt. It is also a major reason why expenditures on important goods and services needed for health care and education are being displaced. During this period, expenditures on goods and services grew by only 5 percent, which was significantly below the rate of inflation.

The education and health sectors together accounted for about 46,400 public sector employees in 2002, or about 60 percent of the public sector workforce. Therefore, they are a major and increasing component of the public-sector payroll. During the period 1999 to 2002, the education and health workforce increased by approximately 4,000 and 780 respectively, thus accounting for 63 percent of the increase in public-sector employment during this period.

Chapter 4 discussed the significant inefficiencies in the deployment of teachers by province and level of schooling that exist in PNG, and the NEP has proposed several strategies for dealing with the problem of teacher deployment. These include reform of the teacher payroll, as well as giving greater responsibility for teacher activities to school BOMs, establishing a teacher PAC (comprising representatives of the central agencies, the provinces, and the NDOE) to deploy teachers to the provinces, producing an annual teacher audit, conducting a review of teacher absenteeism, and reviewing the inspectorate. Current reforms of the payroll to associate payment of salaries with approved school-staffing positions should remove "ghosting" and ensure schools have the appropriate number of teachers for their enrollment size.

The NEP 2 has proposed increasing the student-teacher ratio as a way to reduce unit costs and increase the affordability of education. The failure to make these changes will cause the teacher budget to increase by another K 58 million, an additional 3.6 percent.

In 2004, the national health workforce totaled 12,355. The health workforce had grown more than 14.5 percent between 1998 and 2005, almost twice as fast as it had grown between 1988 and 1998 (see Table 1, Chapter 2). Furthermore, as noted in Chapter 2, this growth was significantly faster than the growth in the number of graduates of health-training schools. This suggests that there are potential savings of close to K 28.6 million that could be realized in the health sector, comprising K 15 million on nurses' salaries and K 13.6 million on CHWs, due to duplications of staff or to unqualified staff being on the payroll. Meanwhile, health outcomes have been declining, and budgets for important nonsalary expenditures, including operational costs for outreach services and pharmaceuticals, were being severely constrained.

Reducing health staff costs is clearly an area where involving the central agencies of government, the NDOH, and provinces in the budget preparation process could yield positive results. Such an arrangement would work only if the NDOH was empowered to reduce salary costs and reallocate the savings to support key health program priorities; however, this would require a strong commitment by the NDOH, the provinces, and the central agencies to address governance issues and implement payroll reform.

Actions as outlined above, to control employment and payroll costs will require a concerted effort by both the respective line agencies and the central agencies or payroll costs will continue to balloon. In addition, given the scale of potential savings (and, conversely, of fraud), the need to conduct physical audits of the workforce is pressing, which once again will require line agencies and central agencies to work together. The fiscal space that could be created by making these savings would make it possible to redirect funds to high-priority areas.

## Restoring the Integrity of Budget Systems and Institutions

The PERR highlighted the need to restore the integrity of budget systems as the cornerstone of efforts to improve public expenditure management and, ultimately, service delivery. As a rule, budgets need to reflect the policy intentions of the government. They also need to be accounted for, and the spending needs to be carried out efficiently. The accounts and accounting function need to provide the government with the necessary reassurance that its policies are being implemented according to its wishes. The basic structure of the accounts themselves and of the central and subnational agencies that handle budgets—need to be organized so that they provide clear and comprehensive information about whether resources are being deployed according to PNG's policy priorities. Achieving this will not be easy because the reality in PNG at the moment is that the budget system is considerably fragmented. Furthermore, PNG's development partners will continue to insist on providing support only off-budget, which in itself will reinforce the underlying fragmentation, unless they are satisfied that the government is adhering to and implementing its Public Finance Management and Audit Acts.

Restoring the integrity of budget systems is critical to improving overall budgetary performance and to delivering public services for which the line agencies are responsible. Yet, in some respects, this is the most challenging element of the agenda as it encompasses both the concrete and the intangible. As identified in the PERR exercise, the root cause of this long-term deterioration is poor governance. This poor governance has fostered and enabled a number of bad habits to flourish, mainly because the government has failed to enforce the rules and regulations of the public service, principally the Public Finances (Management) Act, which, in turn, has caused a breakdown in accountability. Conversely, as individuals have not been held to account for their actions or their lack of action, this has in turn reinforced the breakdown in the enforcement of the relevant laws. Reversing this decline in governance standards will require strong and persistent leadership from the top, and the senior staff of government departments will need to be transparent in practicing what they preach. After the strengthening of governance and accountability and greater compliance with the Public Finances (Management) Act, it will become easier to tackle some of the specific areas where action is needed. For example, it will become easier to control wasteful spending on goods and services, to strengthen public procurement processes to ensure value for money, to ensure more prudent and transparent management of trust accounts, and to enforce greater budget control and accountability at the provincial levels. Budget preparation and monitoring will be greatly improved in the process.

### Other Expenditure Priorities

Shortcomings in the areas of health, HIV/AIDS, and education are not just the result of failures in the respective systems, but also a combination of geography, health factors, social and political organization, problems with law and order, and culture. Consequently, required strategies for addressing the inequities go well beyond reform of the education and health systems. Inaccessibility to population is a shared constraint upon provision of both education and health support. Transport and communication facilities need to be improved, but first, in some regions, law and order needs to be strengthened, so that facilities can be established and maintained. Income disparities between communities and governments affecting both the input and output of the education and health systems require addressing issues of support and redistribution. Finally, pronounced gender differences reflect problems concerned with cultural differences.

## Budget Allocations and Their Composition: Less Than Optimal

Papua New Guinea accords a relative high priority to the human development sectors. Total health, HIV/AIDS, and education expenditures (excluding postsecondary education and training expenditures[7]), while fluctuating have increased from 22.2 percent of total government expenditures in 1997 to 27.6 percent in 2004 (Table 5.1). Including postsecondary education and training expenditure of K 110 million in 2004 with general education expenditure would bring the share of total expenditure on the human development sector to 31.6. That is almost one in every three kina, or one-third of total government expenditure allocated to the human development expenditures. The increased level of fiscal effort (greater growth in expenditures on human development relative to total government expenditures) over this period is quite

**Table 5.1. Human Development Expenditures as Share of Total Expenditures and of GDP, 1997–2004**

*(percent)*

|  | 1997 | 1998 | 1999 | 2000 | 2001 | 2002 | 2003 | 2004 |
|---|---|---|---|---|---|---|---|---|
| **Education** | | | | | | | | |
| As share of total expenditure | 12.1 | 15.0 | 14.7 | 14.0 | 15.4 | 14.4 | 12.4 | 14.6 |
| As share of GDP | 3.4 | 4.1 | 4.7 | 4.7 | 5.5 | 4.8 | 3.9 | 4.6 |
| **Health** | | | | | | | | |
| As share of total expenditure | 9.9 | 11.3 | 10.0 | 10.5 | 10.9 | 11.4 | 10.8 | 11.9 |
| As share of GDP | 2.8 | 3.1 | 3.2 | 3.5 | 3.9 | 3.8 | 3.4 | 3.8 |
| **HIV/AIDS** | | | | | | | | |
| As share of total expenditure | 0.2 | 0.2 | 0.2 | 0.3 | 0.6 | 0.7 | 0.9 | 1.2 |
| As share of GDP | 0.1 | 0.1 | 0.1 | 0.1 | 0.2 | 0.2 | 0.3 | 0.4 |
| **Human Development Sector** | | | | | | | | |
| As share of total expenditure | 22.2 | 26.5 | 24.8 | 24.8 | 27.0 | 26.5 | 24.2 | 27.6 |
| As share of GDP | 6.3 | 7.2 | 7.9 | 8.3 | 9.6 | 8.9 | 7.5 | 8.8 |

*Source:* Education; annual budget appropriations and detailed costing analysis prepared for the New Education Plan 2005–2014; Health: Ministry of Health Analysis of Health Expenditures—various years. HIV/AIDS: annual budget appropriations—various years and data collected from development partners.

remarkable given the fiscal problems (discussed above) the government has had over this period.[8] Human development expenditures, as a result of this increased fiscal effort and the decline in real GDP, have increased significantly from 6.3 percent of GDP in 1997 to 8.8 percent in 2004— a not insignificant achievement in aggregate terms.

Over this period, both education and health expenditures have increased as both a share of total government expenditure and of GDP (Table 5.1). General education accounted for 12.1 percent of total government expenditure in 1997, and this had increased to 14.6 percent in 2004. As a share of GDP, general education increased 1.2 percentage points from 3.4 percent in 1997 to 4.6 percent in 2004. Total health expenditures increased from 9.9 percent of total government expenditures to 11.9 percent over this period, and health's share of GDP increased from 2.8 percent to 3.6 percent in 2004. As discussed in Chapter 3, HIV/AIDS expenditures did not increase in the early years of this period and it was not till 2001 that expenditures increased as a share of government expenditures—from 0.3 percent of total government expenditures in 2000 to 1.2 percent in 2004; although, as also discussed in Chapter 3, this growth was from a low base and the quality of the expenditures is problematic given the scale of the disease in PNG.

The level of aggregate expenditure effort by the PNG government can be compared (Table 5.2) to the Pacific Islands and to "low- and middle-income countries" and to countries in "East Asia and the Pacific countries" (as classified by the World Bank). As a share of total government expenditures, human development expenditures in PNG in 2004 of 31.6 percent (including postsecondary expenditures), compares well with other Pacific island countries. Only Kiribati (35.9 percent), Samoa (39.7 percent), Solomon Islands (32.4 percent), and Vanuatu (37.6 percent) allocate a greater share of government expenditures to the human development sectors. For both health and education, PNG expenditures as a share of total government expenditures are around the average of other Pacific island countries.

PNG expenditures on the human development sectors, as a share of GDP, is at 8.8 percent, which is above that of three Pacific Islands countries (Fiji, 8.0 percent; Tonga, 8.2 percent; and Vanuatu, 8.6 percent), but below the other six countries (Table 5.2). However, compared to the share of GDP allocated by all "Low- and Middle-Income Countries" as a whole to the human development sectors—6.7 percent—or for the "East Asia and Pacific Region" as a whole—4.5 percent—PNG's expenditures on human development equivalent to 8.8 percent of GDP is significant. But

**Table 5.2. Pacific Island, Low- and Middle-Income, and East Asia Country Expenditures on the Human Development Sectors, 1997–2003**
(constant 2000 USD)

| | Average annual government expenditure (1997–2003) | | | | | |
|---|---|---|---|---|---|---|
| | Share of GDP (constant 2000 USD) | | | Share of Gov't expenditure | | |
| | Education | Health | Total | Education | Health | Total |
| Fiji | 5.2 | 2.8 | 8.0 | 16.5 | 8.8 | 25.3 |
| Kiribati | 17.8 | 12.5 | 30.3 | 21.1 | 14.8 | 35.9 |
| RMI | 13.1 | 11.3 | 24.5 | 15.3 | 12.8 | 28.0 |
| FSM | 10.5 | 5.8 | 16.2 | 16.0 | 8.8 | 24.8 |
| Palau | 7.7 | 8.2 | 15.9 | 12.2 | 13.1 | 25.3 |
| Samoa | 5.3 | 4.1 | 9.4 | 22.2 | 17.5 | 39.7 |
| Sol. Islands | 7.3 | 5.1 | 12.4 | 19.4 | 13.0 | 32.4 |
| Tonga | 4.9 | 3.2 | 8.2 | 16.7 | 11.1 | 27.8 |
| Vanuatu | 5.7 | 2.9 | 8.6 | 25.0 | 12.6 | 37.6 |
| LIC & MIC | 3.9 | 2.8 | 6.7 | n.a. | n.a. | n.a. |
| EAP | 2.6 | 1.8 | 4.5 | n.a. | n.a. | n.a. |

*Source:* Budget Books, World Development Indicators, as presented in World Bank (2006), p.19.
*Notes:*
* Compact countries (RMI, FSM, Palau): government expenditure includes (1) general fund, and (2) special fund (including compact fund and the federal grant). Compact capital fund is excluded. Expandable trust fund is included for RMI because of the Health Care Fund.
** Kiribati, Solomon Islands, and Vanuatu: government expenditure excludes government capital expenditure and any donor fund.
*** Fiji, Samoa, and Tonga: government expenditure excludes any donor fund.

questions remain about the quality of this expenditure and whether it is sustainable. It is thus appropriate to view trends in and the overall composition of both recurrent and development expenditures on the human development sectors.

### Recurrent Budget Trends

The recurrent budget is financed by government while over 95 percent of development expenditures are financed by development partners. The primary purpose of the recurrent budget is to finance all recurrent inputs—remuneration and necessary quality-enhancing inputs—required to deliver quality services. In nominal terms, human-development-sector recurrent expenditures have increased from K 383.4 million in 1997 to 800.8 million in 2004. In 1997, recurrent expenditures on human development represented 21.1 percent of total government recurrent expenditures, rising to 29 percent in 2004 (Table 5.3). In other words, human development expenditures have been increasing faster than total recurrent expenditures; however, for each of the subsectors, recurrent expenditures have declined significantly as a share of total sector expenditures. Over

**Table 5.3. Trends in Human Development Recurrent Expenditures, 1997–2004**
*(percent)*

|  | 1997 | 1998 | 1999 | 2000 | 2001 | 2002 | 2003 | 2004 |
|---|---|---|---|---|---|---|---|---|
| **Education** | | | | | | | | |
| Recurrent as % Total Education Expenditure | 89.1 | 87.0 | 85.2 | 78.9 | 71.1 | 99.7 | 89.3 | 81.6 |
| Recurrent as % Total Recurrent Expenditure | 11.9 | 14.3 | 16.9 | 15.0 | 16.1 | 20.8 | 15.7 | 17.2 |
| **Health** | | | | | | | | |
| Recurrent as % Total Health Expenditure | 83.3 | 75.9 | 69.8 | 73.0 | 71.8 | 57.7 | 68.1 | 68.4 |
| Recurrent as % Total Recurrent Expenditure | 9.1 | 9.3 | 9.5 | 10.4 | 11.5 | 9.5 | 10.4 | 11.8 |
| **HIV/AIDS** | | | | | | | | |
| Recurrent as % Total HIV/AIDS Expenditure | 14.0 | 13.0 | 15.9 | 7.4 | 4.0 | 3.1 | 2.3 | 2.4 |
| Recurrent as % Total Recurrent Expenditure | 0.0 | 0.0 | 0.0 | 0.0 | 0.0 | 0.0 | 0.0 | 0.0 |
| **Human Development Sector** | | | | | | | | |
| Recurrent as % Total Human Development Expenditure | 85.8 | 81.7 | 78.5 | 75.6 | 70.0 | 79.0 | 76.5 | 72.6 |
| Recurrent as % Total Recurrent Expenditure | 21.1 | 23.6 | 26.4 | 25.5 | 27.6 | 30.4 | 26.1 | 29.0 |

*Source:* Education; annual budget appropriations and detailed costing analysis prepared for the New Education Plan 2005–2014; Health: Ministry of Health Analysis of Health Expenditures—various years. HIV/AIDS: annual budget appropriations—various years and data collected from development partners.

the period 1997–2004, recurrent education expenditure declined from 89.1 percent of total education expenditures to 81.6 percent in 2004. Health recurrent expenditures declined from 83.3 percent of total health expenditures to 68.4 percent, and for HIV/AIDS the decline was from 14.0 percent to 2.4 percent. The corollary of this is that the share of development expenditures, and thus the share of sector expenditures financed by development partners increased very significantly over the same period.

It is also true that the share of education and health recurrent expenditures as a share of total recurrent expenditures has increased significantly—for education from 11.9 percent to 17.2 percent and health from 9.1 percent to 11.8 percent (Table 5.3). On the other hand, it is particularly noticeable that HIV/AIDS recurrent expenditure has remained less than 0.1 percent of the total recurrent budget—a woefully small amount given the seriousness of the epidemic.

In real terms, recurrent expenditures on education increased 1.3 percent between 1997 and 2004, while real health recurrent expenditures declined 9.4 percent over this period and HIV/AIDS real recurrent expenditures fell 15.2 percent—albeit from a very low original base (Table 5.4). The 21.4 percent increase in real expenditure on education in 2001–2002 was associated with the one-off "full free education subsidy" in 2002, discussed in Chapter 4. The 13.4 percent real increase in health expenditures in 2003–2004 was in large part associated with government taking over increased financing of the procurement of pharmaceuticals from development partners who had been progressively financing pharmaceuticals in earlier years.

It is very notable that real total recurrent expenditure fell significantly over the seven-year period 1997–2004—by almost 30 percent—which was a significantly faster decline than that for real total human development expenditure, which declined 3.3 percent (Table 5.4). This reinforces the point made that the government has made considerable effort to maintain expenditures on the human development sector in the face of declining recurrent expenditures.

One of the key issues identified in both Chapter 2 and Chapter 4 on health and education respectively is that quality health and education services require significant nonsalary recurrent expenditures. To this end, it is important to note that while the share of recurrent education expenditures allocated to nonsalary budgets more than doubled over the period 1997–2002 to 38.5 percent, the share allocated in subsequent years has fallen significantly so that the share spent on nonsalary budget items in 2004 was only 26.7 percent—although this was 10 percentage points above that recorded in 1997 (Table 5.5). Thus, expenditure on salaries

**Table 5.4. Real Human Development Sector Recurrent Expenditure Growth Rates 1997–2004**

*(percent)*

|  | 97–98 | 98–99 | 99–00 | 00–01 | 01–02 | 02–03 | 03–04 | 97–04 |
|---|---|---|---|---|---|---|---|---|
| Education | 13.1 | 9.3 | −12.6 | 0.7 | 21.4 | −30.2 | 9.9 | 1.3 |
| Health | −3.5 | −6.4 | 8.7 | 3.7 | −22.1 | 0.8 | 13.4 | −9.4 |
| HIV/AIDS | −12.0 | 1.5 | −13.5 | 4.6 | −10.6 | −12.8 | 34.6 | −15.2 |
| Total Human Development Recurrent | 5.9 | 3.1 | −5.0 | 1.9 | 3.2 | −20.4 | 11.3 | −3.3 |
| Total Government Recurrent | −5.5 | −7.9 | −1.5 | −5.7 | −6.2 | −7.6 | 0.4 | −29.6 |

*Source:* Education: annual budget appropriations and detailed costing analysis prepared for the New Education Plan 2005–2014; Health: Ministry of Health Analysis of Health Expenditures—various years. See detailed note on sources Chapter 2, Annex 2; HIV/AIDS: annual budget appropriations—various years and data collected from development partners.

**Table 5.5. Trends in Composition of Education and Health Recurrent Expenditures, 1997–2004**
*(percent)*

|  | 1997 | 1998 | 1999 | 2000 | 2001 | 2002 | 2003 | 2004 |
|---|---|---|---|---|---|---|---|---|
| **Education** | | | | | | | | |
| Emoluments: percent share | 84.0 | 64.3 | 68.1 | 66.6 | 69.4 | 61.5 | 80.2 | 73.3 |
| Nonemoluments: percent share | 16.0 | 35.7 | 31.9 | 33.4 | 30.6 | 38.5 | 19.8 | 26.7 |
| Total Education | 100 | 100 | 100 | 100 | 100 | 100 | 100 | 100 |
| **Health** | | | | | | | | |
| Emoluments: percent share | 55.1 | 61.4 | 62.8 | 65.6 | 66.3 | 76.9 | 73.0 | 67.0 |
| Nonemoluments: percent share | 44.9 | 38.6 | 37.2 | 34.4 | 33.7 | 23.1 | 27.0 | 33.0 |
| Total Health | 100 | 100 | 100 | 100 | 100 | 100 | 100 | 100 |

*Source:* Education: annual budget appropriations and detailed costing analysis prepared for the New Education Plan 2005–2014; Health: Ministry of Health Analysis of Health Expenditures—various years. HIV/AIDS: annual budget appropriations—various years and data collected from development partners.

as share of recurrent education expenditures is now only 73.3 percent. For the health sector, trends are very disturbing. Salary expenditure as a share of recurrent expenditures has systematically increased over the seven-year period from 55.1 percent of health recurrent expenditures to 67 percent. As a corollary to this, nonsalary expenditures have declined from almost 45 percent of the total health recurrent budget to 33 percent.

## Development Budget Trends

The overall rise in human development expenditures—as a share of government expenditure and in real terms—has largely been driven by the dramatic rise in development expenditures over the period 1997–2004, which as noted above, is almost wholly financed by development partners. Education development expenditure as a share of total education expenditures rose from 10.9 percent in 1997, peaked at 28.9 percent in 2001, dropped precipitately to less than 1 percent in 2002, and increased to 18.4 percent in 2004. In real terms, education development expenditure has grown 8.9 percent per annum over the 1997–2004 period—notwithstanding the volatility of the expenditures. Real education development expenditures in 2004 were 87 percent higher than in 1997 (Table 5.6). These trends also highlight the dependence of total education development expenditures on development partners. In 2002, there was almost no education expenditures financed by development partners and, consequently, education expenditures fell dramatically.

**Table 5.6. Trends in Real Human Development Recurrent and Development Expenditures, 1997–2004**

*(1996 = 100) (kina million)*

| | 1997 | 1998 | 1999 | 2000 | 2001 | 2002 | 2003 | 2004 | Annual growth rate | | |
|---|---|---|---|---|---|---|---|---|---|---|---|
| | | | | | | | | | 97–01 | 01–04 | 97–04 |
| **Education** | | | | | | | | | | | |
| Development | 25.6 | 35.1 | 44.8 | 60.1 | 92.3 | 0.8 | 23.1 | 47.8 | 32.1 | –21.9 | 8.9 |
| Total Education Expenditure | 234.2 | 271.2 | 302.7 | 285.5 | 319.3 | 276.4 | 215.4 | 259.1 | 7.7 | –7.0 | 1.4 |
| % Development | 10.9 | 13.0 | 14.8 | 21.1 | 28.9 | 0.3 | 10.7 | 18.4 | | | |
| % Recurrent | 89.1 | 87.0 | 85.2 | 78.9 | 71.1 | 99.7 | 89.3 | 81.6 | | | |
| **Health** | | | | | | | | | | | |
| Development | 31.9 | 49.0 | 62.5 | 57.9 | 63.7 | 92.6 | 59.7 | 66.9 | 17.3 | 1.6 | 10.6 |
| Total Health Expenditure | 191.5 | 202.9 | 206.6 | 214.6 | 226.1 | 219.2 | 187.3 | 211.5 | 4.2 | –2.2 | 1.4 |
| % Development | 16.7 | 24.1 | 30.2 | 27.0 | 28.2 | 42.3 | 31.9 | 31.6 | | | |
| % Recurrent | 83.3 | 75.9 | 69.8 | 73.0 | 71.8 | 57.7 | 68.1 | 68.4 | | | |
| **HIV/AIDS** | | | | | | | | | | | |
| Development | 3.6 | 3.4 | 2.7 | 5.5 | 11.3 | 13.3 | 15.5 | 20.0 | 28.9 | 19.0 | 24.7 |
| Total HIV/AIDS Expenditure | 4.1 | 3.9 | 3.2 | 6.0 | 11.8 | 13.7 | 15.8 | 20.5 | 26.2 | 18.4 | 22.9 |
| % Development | 86.0 | 87.0 | 84.1 | 92.6 | 96.0 | 96.9 | 97.7 | 97.6 | | | |
| % Recurrent | 14.0 | 13.0 | 15.9 | 7.4 | 4.0 | 3.1 | 2.3 | 2.4 | | | |
| **Human Development Sector** | | | | | | | | | | | |
| Development | 61.1 | 87.5 | 110.0 | 123.6 | 167.3 | 106.7 | 98.2 | 134.7 | 25.2 | –7.2 | 11.3 |
| Total HD Expenditure | 429.9 | 478.0 | 512.6 | 506.1 | 557.2 | 509.3 | 418.5 | 491.2 | 6.5 | –4.2 | 1.9 |
| % Development | 14.2 | 18.3 | 21.5 | 24.4 | 30.0 | 21.0 | 23.5 | 27.4 | | | |
| % Recurrent | 85.8 | 81.7 | 78.5 | 75.6 | 70.0 | 79.0 | 76.5 | 72.6 | | | |
| **Memo Items** | | | | | | | | | | | |
| HD as % Gov. Expenditure | 22.2 | 26.5 | 24.8 | 24.8 | 27.0 | 26.5 | 24.2 | 27.6 | | | |
| HD as % Total Gov. Dev. | 33.1 | 58.1 | 20.3 | 22.8 | 25.6 | 18.0 | 19.4 | 24.6 | | | |
| HD Rec. as % of Total Gov. Rec. | 21.1 | 23.6 | 26.4 | 25.5 | 27.6 | 30.4 | 26.1 | 29.0 | | | |

*Source:* Education: annual budget appropriations and detailed costing analysis prepared for the New Education Plan 2005–2014; Health: Ministry of Health Analysis of Health Expenditures—various years. See detailed note on sources Chapter 2, Annex 2; HIV/AIDS: annual budget appropriations—various years and data collected from development partners.

Health development expenditure also increased dramatically from 16.7 percent of total health expenditure in 1997 to peak at 42.3 percent in 2002 and subsequently declined to still be almost one-third of expenditures in each of 2003 and 2004. In real terms, health development expenditures have grown 10.6 percent per annum over the years 1997–2004. Development-partner-financed development expenditure has accounted for the lion's share of all expenditure on HIV/AIDS over this period—well over 90 percent since 2000 and reaching 97.6 percent in 2004 (Table 5.6).

Overall, development-partner financing of development expenditures for education, health, and HIV/AIDs, and thus of overall human development expenditures, have been very significant. Over the period 1997–2001, total expenditures on these sectors grew 6.5 percent in real-terms and development, expenditures grew at over 25 percent per annum (Table 5.6). Notwithstanding the slump in development expenditures in 2002–03 and in recurrent expenditures in 2003 (Table 5.4), overall expenditures on the human development sector grew 1.9 percent in real terms over the period 1997–2004. Development expenditures over this period grew 11.3 percent in real terms.

It is unfortunate that detailed breakdowns of development expenditures by input categories or by subsector or program category of the sectors is not available. Nevertheless, a number of observations can be made based on the breakdown available. About one-third of the education development budget is allocated to postsecondary training—a very large proportion of which is for overseas scholarships. It is known that development budgets finance a significant proportion of education operational expenditures associated with (a) training, workshops, and community-school-teacher training; and (b) teacher materials and textbooks. A significant proportion of development expenditure is also for technical assistance associated with quality enhancements, including curriculum reforms and for management and planning advice and capacity building.

In health, more detailed information is available. Real development expenditures on goods and services increased from K 26.7 million in 1997 to K 52.8 million in 2004, a real increase of over 100 percent. In 2004, development-budget-financed expenditures on goods and services represented almost 50 percent of total expenditures on goods and services on health compared to 30 percent in 1997. Thus, the development budget is financing an increasing amount and an increasing share of quality-enhancing health expenditures, which should be, in the medium term at least, recurrent-budget-financed. From a subprogram perspective, it is noteworthy that the health development budget finances over one-third of general administration, well over 90 percent of family services and disease control activities, and two-thirds of health promotion activities.

In HIV/AIDS, development partners finance well over 90 percent of all activities, including a significant share of PNG staff working on the program. As noted in Chapter 3, we have argued too much attention is spent on treatment and inadequate attention is being given to surveillance, prevention, and behavior change and monitoring and evaluation of programs.

Another important feature of the development budget has been the large number of specific development-partner-financed projects in each of the human development sectors. While there have been four or five fairly large projects in education, since 2000 there have been about 20 other projects financed by development partners, and a number of technical-assistance and smaller projects financed by the UN system in operation at any one time. A similar picture is also true for the health sector, although, as discussed in Chapter 2, the NDOH, working with major development partners has made progress toward reducing the number of projects and mechanisms are emerging to build a basis for a sectorwide approach. For HIV/AIDS, there was one major project financing a very large share of total expenditures through 2004, with another Global Fund project coming on-stream in 2005/06. There are, however, over 30 projects under implementation in 2005. This number of projects is clearly a burden on the departments of education and health and the NACS management capacity. It also means there is considerable fragmentation of financing and accountability arrangements as previously discussed.

In summary, over the period 1997–2004, PNG has increased the level of fiscal effort in support of the human development sectors—albeit within declining real growth in total public expenditures. Compared to the Pacific Islands, "East Asia and the Pacific," and "Low- and Middle-Income Countries," PNG affords a relatively high level of GDP to the human development sectors. However, the share of the recurrent budgets expended on staffing has increased systematically over the period and the share of recurrent budget resources allocated to critical quality-enhancing nonsalary expenditures has declined. As discussed in the sectoral chapters—particularly health and education—there is considerable evidence that staffing levels are too high relative to workload and student numbers and that staff are very inefficiently deployed. It is also argued, consequently, that there is considerable savings to be made on salary expenditures, which could be used for significant nonsalary budget enhancements. A large share of development expenditure is currently financing nonsalary items, which should and could be financed by the recurrent budget if problems with staffing and staffing expenditures were dealt with. There are also opportunities to better align development expenditures with desired outcomes in health, HIV/AIDS, and education. There is also a need to reduce the number of development projects and better align them with government systems and within a consistent accountability framework. An approach to ameliorate these problems is developed in Chapter 6.

## Conclusion

This chapter highlights the important cross-cutting issues that adversely affect sectoral performance and outcomes in the human development sectors, in addition to the sector-specific issues identified in Chapters 2–4.

Improved outcomes will not be attainable unless the following issues receive attention as a matter of priority; (a) the need to focus on sectoral outcomes, and the inequity of current outcomes; (b) the need for a "whole-of-government" approach to policy development and implementation arrangements; (c) the need for reduced sectoral fragmentation and isolation; (d) the need for improved oversight and decentralization arrangements; (e) the need for decisive actions to redress the long-term decline in the integrity of government systems; and (f) the need to improve the quality of expenditures in support of sectoral objectives. Given the cross-cutting nature of these issues—across sectors, across levels of government, and across line departments and the central agencies of government—national leadership, particularly by the central agencies, is critical. There is need for a new partnership between government and development partners. This will require change in how all do business with one another.

The next chapter considers possible next steps to create compacts between (a) line departments and the central agencies; (b) the national government and provinces; and (c) between government and development partners in support of a decisive attempt to improve health, HIV, and education outcomes and the lives of Papua New Guineans. Critically, the development of these compacts will require the proactive support of the central agencies to provide the framework within which this can be achieved.

## Annex 5A. Human Development Expenditures 1996–2004

### Table 5A.1. Social Sector Expenditures 1997–2004
(unit: kina million)

|  | 1997 | 1998 | 1999 | 2000 | 2001 | 2002 | 2003 | 2004 |
|---|---|---|---|---|---|---|---|---|
| **Education[1,2]** | | | | | | | | |
| Recurrent | 216.9 | 278.7 | 350.0 | 353.6 | 389.3 | 528.3 | 422.9 | 474.8 |
| Development[3] | 26.6 | 41.5 | 60.8 | 94.3 | 158.2 | 1.6 | 50.7 | 107.3 |
| Total | 243.5 | 320.2 | 410.8 | 447.9 | 547.5 | 529.9 | 473.6 | 582.1 |
| **Health** | | | | | | | | |
| Recurrent | 165.9 | 181.8 | 195.6 | 245.8 | 278.5 | 242.5 | 280.5 | 324.9 |
| Development | 33.2 | 57.8 | 84.8 | 90.9 | 109.2 | 177.6 | 131.3 | 150.3 |
| Total | 199.1 | 239.6 | 280.4 | 336.7 | 387.7 | 420.1 | 411.8 | 475.2 |
| **HIV/AIDs** | | | | | | | | |
| Recurrent | 0.6 | 0.6 | 0.7 | 0.7 | 0.8 | 0.8 | 0.8 | 1.1 |
| Development | 3.7 | 4.0 | 3.7 | 8.7 | 19.4 | 25.4 | 34.0 | 44.9 |
| Total | 4.3 | 4.6 | 4.4 | 9.4 | 20.2 | 26.2 | 34.8 | 46.0 |
| **Total Human Development Sector** | | | | | | | | |
| Recurrent | 383.4 | 461.1 | 546.3 | 600.1 | 668.6 | 771.6 | 704.2 | 800.8 |
| Development | 63.5 | 103.3 | 149.3 | 193.9 | 286.8 | 204.6 | 216.0 | 302.5 |
| Total | 446.9 | 564.4 | 695.6 | 794.0 | 955.4 | 976.2 | 920.2 | 1,103.3 |
| **Government Expenditure** | | | | | | | | |
| Recurrent | 1,816.7 | 1,950.7 | 2,065.7 | 2,352.2 | 2,424.9 | 2,541.7 | 2,695.3 | 2,763.3 |
| Development | 191.9 | 177.9 | 735.7 | 848.8 | 1,119.3 | 1,139.8 | 1,112.3 | 1,229.6 |
| **Total Government** | | | | | | | | |
| **Expenditure** | 2,008.6 | 2,128.6 | 2,801.4 | 3,201.0 | 3,544.2 | 3,681.5 | 3,807.6 | 3,992.9 |
| **GDP** | 7,063.7 | 7,789.0 | 8,781.0 | 9,515.0 | 9,948.0 | 10,992.0 | 12,204.0 | 12,596.0 |

Source: Education: annual budget appropriations and detailed costing analysis prepared for the New Education Plan 2005–2014; Health: Ministry of Health Analysis of Health Expenditures—various years. HIV/AIDS: annual budget appropriations—various years and data collected from development partners.

### Table 5A.2. Social-Sector Expenditure Shares—Key Aggregates 1997–2004
(percent)

|  | 1997 | 1998 | 1999 | 2000 | 2001 | 2002 | 2003 | 2004 |
|---|---|---|---|---|---|---|---|---|
| **Education** | | | | | | | | |
| Recurrent as % Total Education | 89.1 | 87.0 | 85.2 | 78.9 | 71.1 | 99.7 | 89.3 | 81.6 |
| Development as % Total Education | 10.9 | 13.0 | 14.8 | 21.1 | 28.9 | 0.3 | 10.7 | 18.4 |
| Recurrent as % Total Recurrent | 11.9 | 14.3 | 16.9 | 15.0 | 16.1 | 20.8 | 15.7 | 17.2 |
| Development as % Total Development | 13.9 | 23.3 | 8.3 | 11.1 | 14.1 | 0.1 | 4.6 | 8.7 |

(continued)

**Table 5A.2. Social-Sector Expenditure Shares—Key Aggregates 1997–2004** (continued)
(percent)

|  | 1997 | 1998 | 1999 | 2000 | 2001 | 2002 | 2003 | 2004 |
|---|---|---|---|---|---|---|---|---|
| Total as % |  |  |  |  |  |  |  |  |
| Total Expenditure | 12.1 | 15.0 | 14.7 | 14.0 | 15.4 | 14.4 | 12.4 | 14.6 |
| Total as % of GDP | 3.4 | 4.1 | 4.7 | 4.7 | 5.5 | 4.8 | 3.9 | 4.6 |
| **Health** |  |  |  |  |  |  |  |  |
| Recurrent as % |  |  |  |  |  |  |  |  |
| Total Health | 83.3 | 75.9 | 69.8 | 73.0 | 71.8 | 57.7 | 68.1 | 68.4 |
| Development as % |  |  |  |  |  |  |  |  |
| Total Health | 16.7 | 24.1 | 30.2 | 27.0 | 28.2 | 42.3 | 31.9 | 31.6 |
| Recurrent as % |  |  |  |  |  |  |  |  |
| Total Recurrent | 9.1 | 9.3 | 9.5 | 10.4 | 11.5 | 9.5 | 10.4 | 11.8 |
| Development as % |  |  |  |  |  |  |  |  |
| Total Development | 17.3 | 32.5 | 11.5 | 10.7 | 9.8 | 15.6 | 11.8 | 12.2 |
| Total as % |  |  |  |  |  |  |  |  |
| Total Expenditure | 9.9 | 11.3 | 10.0 | 10.5 | 10.9 | 11.4 | 10.8 | 11.9 |
| Total as % of GDP | 2.8 | 3.1 | 3.2 | 3.5 | 3.9 | 3.8 | 3.4 | 3.8 |
| **HIV/AIDS** |  |  |  |  |  |  |  |  |
| Recurrent as % |  |  |  |  |  |  |  |  |
| Total HIV/AIDS | 14.0 | 13.0 | 15.9 | 7.4 | 4.0 | 3.1 | 2.3 | 2.4 |
| Development as % |  |  |  |  |  |  |  |  |
| Total HIV/AIDS | 86.0 | 87.0 | 84.1 | 92.6 | 96.0 | 96.9 | 97.7 | 97.6 |
| Recurrent as % |  |  |  |  |  |  |  |  |
| Total Recurrent | 0.0 | 0.0 | 0.0 | 0.0 | 0.0 | 0.0 | 0.0 | 0.0 |
| Development as % |  |  |  |  |  |  |  |  |
| Total Development | 1.9 | 2.2 | 0.5 | 1.0 | 1.7 | 2.2 | 3.1 | 3.7 |
| Total as % |  |  |  |  |  |  |  |  |
| Total Expenditure | 0.2 | 0.2 | 0.2 | 0.3 | 0.6 | 0.7 | 0.9 | 1.2 |
| Total as % of GDP | 0.1 | 0.1 | 0.1 | 0.1 | 0.2 | 0.2 | 0.3 | 0.4 |
| **Human Development Sector** |  |  |  |  |  |  |  |  |
| Recurrent as % |  |  |  |  |  |  |  |  |
| Total Social Sector | 85.8 | 81.7 | 78.5 | 75.6 | 70.0 | 79.0 | 76.5 | 72.6 |
| Development as % |  |  |  |  |  |  |  |  |
| Total Social Sector | 14.2 | 18.3 | 21.5 | 24.4 | 30.0 | 21.0 | 23.5 | 27.4 |
| Recurrent as % |  |  |  |  |  |  |  |  |
| Total Recurrent | 21.1 | 23.6 | 26.4 | 25.5 | 27.6 | 30.4 | 26.1 | 29.0 |
| Development as % |  |  |  |  |  |  |  |  |
| Total Development | 33.1 | 58.1 | 20.3 | 22.8 | 25.6 | 18.0 | 19.4 | 24.6 |
| Total as % |  |  |  |  |  |  |  |  |
| Total Expenditure | 22.2 | 26.5 | 24.8 | 24.8 | 27.0 | 26.5 | 24.2 | 27.6 |
| Total as % of GDP | 6.3 | 7.2 | 7.9 | 8.3 | 9.6 | 8.9 | 7.5 | 8.8 |

*Source:* Education: annual budget appropriations and detailed costing analysis prepared for the New Education Plan 2005–2014; Health: Ministry of Health Analysis of Health Expenditures—various years. HIV/AIDS: annual budget appropriations—various years and data collected from development partners.

**Table 5A.3. Real Social Sector Expenditures 1997–2004**
*(year 1996 = 100) (unit: kina million)*

|  | 1997 | 1998 | 1999 | 2000 | 2001 | 2002 | 2003 | 2004 |
|---|---|---|---|---|---|---|---|---|
| **Education** | | | | | | | | |
| Recurrent | 208.6 | 236.0 | 257.9 | 225.4 | 227.1 | 275.6 | 192.3 | 211.4 |
| Development | 25.6 | 35.1 | 44.8 | 60.1 | 92.3 | 0.8 | 23.1 | 47.8 |
| Total | 234.2 | 271.2 | 302.7 | 285.5 | 319.3 | 276.4 | 215.4 | 259.1 |
| **Health** | | | | | | | | |
| Recurrent | 159.6 | 154.0 | 144.1 | 156.7 | 162.4 | 126.5 | 127.6 | 144.6 |
| Development | 31.9 | 49.0 | 62.5 | 57.9 | 63.7 | 92.6 | 59.7 | 66.9 |
| Total | 191.5 | 202.9 | 206.6 | 214.6 | 226.1 | 219.2 | 187.3 | 211.5 |
| **HIV/AIDS** | | | | | | | | |
| Recurrent | 0.6 | 0.5 | 0.5 | 0.4 | 0.5 | 0.4 | 0.4 | 0.5 |
| Development | 3.6 | 3.4 | 2.7 | 5.5 | 11.3 | 13.3 | 15.5 | 20.0 |
| Total | 4.1 | 3.9 | 3.2 | 6.0 | 11.8 | 13.7 | 15.8 | 20.5 |
| **Total Human Development Sector** | | | | | | | | |
| Recurrent | 368.8 | 390.5 | 402.6 | 382.5 | 389.9 | 402.5 | 320.3 | 356.5 |
| Development | 61.1 | 87.5 | 110.0 | 123.6 | 167.3 | 106.7 | 98.2 | 134.7 |
| Total | 429.9 | 478.0 | 512.6 | 506.1 | 557.2 | 509.3 | 418.5 | 491.2 |
| **Government Expenditure** | | | | | | | | |
| Recurrent | 1,747.4 | 1,652.1 | 1,522.2 | 1,499.4 | 1,414.3 | 1,325.9 | 1,225.8 | 1,230.1 |
| Development | 184.6 | 150.7 | 542.1 | 541.1 | 652.8 | 594.6 | 505.9 | 547.4 |
| Total Government Expenditure | 1,932.0 | 1,802.7 | 2,064.3 | 2,040.5 | 2,067.1 | 1,920.5 | 1,731.6 | 1,777.5 |
| GDP | 6,612.6 | 6,361.3 | 6,844.8 | 6,762.7 | 6,607.1 | 6,554.3 | 6,737.8 | 6,926.5 |

*Source:* Education; annual budget appropriations and detailed costing analysis prepared for the New Education Plan 2005–2014; Health: Ministry of Health Analysis of Health Expenditures—various years. HIV/AIDS: annual budget appropriations—various years and data collected from development partners.

## Notes

1. The population is increasing by 2.7 percent per year.
2. World Bank (2004), Papua New Guinea: Poverty Assessment (2004).
3. The work of the National Economic and Fiscal Commission during the past three years has extensively documented the shortcomings of the present devolution arrangements arising from deficiencies in the OLPLLG and has fostered an informed dialogue about these issues.
4. The national government has made extensive use of the "exceptional economic circumstances" provision of the OLPLLG to justify lower grant levels to provinces than are provided for under the Organic Law.
5. Discretionary expenditure is here defined as nondebt and nonstaff remuneration expenditures. In the medium term, of course, both staffing and debt can

be reduced; discretionary expenditure is a measure of the resources available for the nonstaff operational costs of the government.

6. World Bank (2002) overview, p. 2.

7. Systematic data on expenditures on postsecondary education and training expenditures over this period are not available.

8. Given that debt servicing rose significantly over this period as the share of resources devoted to the human development sector relative to all government expenditures, excluding debt servicing, would have grown more dramatically in proportionate terms.

# CHAPTER 6

# Next Steps: An Approach to Revised Strategic Directions for Human Development

## Introduction

In this review of strategy options for health, HIV/AIDS, and education, we have argued that these sectors are at an important crossroad and are facing a range of critical challenges. Health outcomes have stalled over the last quarter-century and have even been in decline over the last decade. An HIV/AIDS epidemic is now raging and is particularly well established in the rural areas of the country and becoming a fully generalized epidemic. This has occurred despite significant increases in public expenditures on health and HIV/AIDS over the past decade, largely financed by PNG's development partners. While efforts to move toward UBE have met with some success because of the major education reform that increased overall access and significantly improved efficiency, some 19 percent of children do not yet attend school, and many who start school do not complete the basic cycle. Similar issues confront the secondary school system, but the government has found it difficult to resist the very strong private demand for secondary education at the expense of the basic education cycle. The postsecondary and technical and vocational school systems, while accounting for considerable resources, do not provide appropriate training to meet the demands of the labor market and are characterized by serious fragmentation and a lack of coordinated oversight.

Given this "crisis" of outcomes, each of our sectoral chapters—on health, HIV/AIDS, and education—proposes a core strategy for that sector consistent with our situational assessment of each sector as the starting point. These individual sector strategies take account of a number of core "cross-cutting" issues that are outlined in Chapter 5. Specifically, the chapter emphasizes the need for (i) a coherent national policy in each of the sectors that is enforceable at subnational levels of government; (ii) the reform of decentralization and devolution arrangements to reduce the level of fragmentation and isolation in the policy making, financing, and implementation of sectoral programs; (iii) a reversal of the long-term decline in the integrity of core government systems (particularly the personnel management, payroll, and budget institutions and systems—including procurement systems); and (iv) the introduction of sectoral budgets (however they may be financed) to reflect the policy and strategy needs of each sector.

In the situational assessments, we have argued that, given the limited capacity of the public sector to deliver services, a central aim of any revised strategy should be to reduce direct government involvement in service delivery by finding alternate, more viable options for doing so. However, the strategy must also take into account the need for accountability and transparency, the limited integrity of government systems as presently constituted, and the need to provide services that will improve high-priority outcomes, particularly for the poor. Further, each sectoral chapter and Chapter 5 has emphasized the need for a "whole-of-government" approach to policy development, program design, and accountability for implementing, monitoring, and evaluating programs.

## Proposed Sectoral Strategy—Formulation Process by Government

To this end, we argue that each sector should develop a strategy covering six elements:

1. *Take the "situational assessment" as the starting point* and focus on the key desired outcomes (e.g., the sectoral MDGs) using the most cost-effective options, with emphasis on the poor. This will require (i) identifying technical options for achieving the agreed outcomes and the ways in which the options might be packaged for delivery; (ii) prioritizing these packages in terms of public expenditure, using public finance criteria; and (iii) establishing appropriate indicators for monitoring

sector outcomes and ensuring consistent evaluation that progress is being made toward meeting agreed targets.

2. *Identify ways* to (i) confine the role of the public sector to delivering those public services that it can deliver effectively; (ii) encourage the private sector to deliver private goods and services (in other words, those with limited "if any" benefits to society as a whole as a consequence of their private consumption); and (iii) strengthen the collaboration between the public and private sectors in service-delivery management, including churches, which manage about 50 percent of health and education services delivered in the country, albeit largely financed by government.

3. *Prepare an expenditure and implementation plan* for the whole of the publicly funded part of each sector (covering all programs financed by either the government or its development partners) based on the high-priority activities identified in the preceding steps and consistent with the indicative available resources (see below).

4. *Create fiscal space to make high-priority sectoral expenditures*. This can be achieved in three ways: (i) by generating savings in the sector, (ii) by making more efficient use of existing resources, and (iii) by allocating additional resources to the sector.

5. *Prepare a financing plan*. To finance the strategy, it will be necessary to identify and secure the required resources. A medium-term financing plan will need to be prepared, in which the national government, provincial governments, and the major development partners all indicate what resources they can make available to the sector over the next specified number of years. This will then enable the line departments working with the central agencies to make realistic plans tied to a specific amount of resources, which it is now almost impossible for them to do as the resource flows over time are not clear. This would, in effect, be a necessary complement to and elaboration of the current process used in the health sector to develop the health MTEF. Present ongoing reforms to the budget process are a significant move in the right direction, but they need to cover all public finances and expenditures at both the national and provincial levels—including that financed by developement partners.

6. *Restore and guarantee the integrity of government processes*. Consistent with the analysis and core recommendation of the PERR, this report has identified the lack of integrity of the governance in PNG as a critical challenge that confronts each of the human development sectors. Therefore, there is a pressing need to restore the integrity of

(i) the personnel management and payroll system, including reducing the size of the public service workforce to fit into the budget; and (ii) budget institutions and systems, including procurement. If the government fails to make progress on these issues, this will make it extremely difficult for its development partners to increasingly deliver their aid through government systems, an objective which the Joint Donors believe is critical as part of the effort to increasingly shift accountability for outcomes to government, enhance government ownership, and develop national capacities to design, implement, monitor, and evaluate progress.

The Joint Donors recognize that the NDOH, the NDOE, and the NACS have developed plans and strategies that contain many of these suggested elements. Furthermore, the DNPRD has developed the MTDS as a guide to national development priorities, and it emphasizes the importance of trying to achieve the MDGs. The MTDS and other government policies also emphasize the importance of developing detailed sectoral strategies consistent with the resource constraints as embodied in the MTEF. The proposals in this report are entirely consistent with the objectives of the MTDS, with its emphasis on the importance of working within resource constraints; however, none of the six core elements of the proposed strategy is fully completed or in place in any sector as yet.

We argue in this report that each of the six elements is necessary to develop and implement the strategies for health, HIV/AIDS, and education; however, none of them is sufficient in itself. Sectoral outcomes can only improve if expenditure priorities are adjusted accordingly. This means that fiscal space must be created to enable the changes in expenditure priorities and that the funds thus allocated are used in an efficient and transparent manner. Therefore, it is critical that the government and its development partners achieve a consensus on the six elements of the sectoral strategies. They should be implemented using a dual-track approach that will simultaneously:

- Address the issues that fall within the scope of national and provincial sectoral authorities to increase the ability of the sectoral systems to provide high-quality services.
- Assist the central agencies (the Treasury, the DNPRD, the DPM, the Auditor General's Office, and the Department of Intergovernmental Relations) to strengthen their capacity to support the national line departments and the provinces.

While the Joint Donors argue that it is critical for the government and its development partners to reach a consensus on the substance of the six elements outlined above, it is equally important for the government to own and manage the process of reaching that consensus. Without agreement on each of the six elements and on a process for the government and its development partners to work jointly, it will be hard to move forward in a systematic manner. Furthermore, carrying out each of the elements of the proposed strategy will require inputs from different agencies. This emphasizes that it will be essential to take a cooperative "whole-of-government" approach that involves the central agencies, the core line departments, and the provinces at every stage of the process.

## The Importance of the MTDS and MTEF

The most relevant starting point for initiating a sector strategy is PNG's Medium-Term Development Strategy (MTDS), which has set the broad sectoral and subsectoral priorities in these and other sectors for 2005 to 2010. The MTDS highlights the need for each key sector to develop its own detailed sectoral strategy and programs within a medium-term expenditure framework. The Medium-term Economic Framework (2002–2007), which is primarily the responsibility of the Treasury, will be essential to the framing of this process. To be fully developed, the MTEF should be updated at least annually as part of the budget preparation process and cover the consolidated budget, including all development assistance. It should also prepare forward projections for both the recurrent budget and the development budget consistent with the agreed debt strategy, albeit with an explicit recognition of the difficulty of making projections of either expenditures or revenues in PNG.

At present, the MTEF focuses mainly on the domestic budget and revenues and does not include donor assistance as part of the overall resource envelope. This is a significant omission. PNG's development partners finance almost 30 percent of all spending in the education and health sectors and over 90 percent of spending in the case of HIV/AIDS. Nevertheless, the recent move by the Treasury to use the MTDS as a guide in preparing sectoral budget priorities by issuing departments with indicative (domestic) budget ceilings within which to develop their budget proposals is an important first step toward linking the MTDS and the MTEF.

Developing a more comprehensive MTEF will require the cooperation of the Treasury and the DNPRD. In particular, the DNPRD has a strategic role in working with PNG's development partners to develop estimates of the current and likely future assistance to be available in the medium term. Second, the DNPRD and the Treasury need to develop indicative sectoral ceilings covering both recurrent and development expenditures, taking into account the broad developmental priorities set in the MTDS. Third, in this framework, the DNPRD will have an important role to play in negotiating with PNG's development partners to ensure that their future assistance is given in support of the established developmental priorities.

It is fundamental to a sound public expenditure planning process that:

(a) Agencies that are developing plans—primarily national line departments and provinces—should be given a hard budget constraint within which to develop their medium-term sectoral plans. All sources of revenue from national and provincial sources and from development partners should be included in the budget constraint.

(b) There is a mechanism that encourages priority-setting and budget scrutiny, by the line departments, the provinces, and the central agencies (those agencies responsible for finance, planning, and personnel policies), which can be enhanced by ensuring appropriate incentives for agencies are in place to seek budget savings and efficiency gains.

(c) There is a close professional working relationship between the central agencies and the line departments in this process, and that the budgeting process is policy-based and does not degenerate into an arbitrary bargaining process.

There needs to be an agreement among all relevant parties that both capital and recurrent resources will be allocated to meet the objectives of specific agreed policies within the hard budget constraint, regardless of how they are financed. The starting point must be to determine how to implement a specific policy in the most cost-effective manner as a basis for deciding whether to include the policy or activity within the budget. In other words, the budget process should focus on the implications (outcomes) of doing more or less in support of the costed policy and not on arbitrary "across-the-board" cuts (or additions) to specific inputs (such as staff, textbooks, and pharmaceuticals).

## Implementing the MTEF and the Sectoral Strategy Plans

Within this suggested MTEF framework, which provides indicative medium-term hard budget constraints, it is the prime responsibility of line departments (NDOH, NACS, and NDOE) to develop strategies and programs that:

- Clearly focus on the agreed priority outcomes and the most cost-effective strategies to make progress toward those goals, especially in terms of targeting the poor.
- Take account of the limited implementation capacity of the government sector. This will require finding other mechanisms for delivering services to achieve the desired outcomes. Doing this will involve (i) reviewing the technical options that will achieve the desired outcomes; (ii) grouping (packaging) these options into activities that can be implemented; (iii) identifying how and in what circumstances the private sector might be able to deliver some of the options; and (iv) using public finance criteria to identify which services can justifiably receive public subsidies (funds). Another aim for those services that are justified should be to reduce the extent to which the government provides and manages services directly, and to hand many of these over to the private and NGO and church sectors, so that the remaining government services can be improved and made more efficient. (An example of this approach is illustrated in Annex 2 to Chapter 2 on health.)
- Actively involve provincial and LLGs as appropriate in developing programs that are the responsibility of provinces to implement and, at least partially, to finance.

While the primary responsibility for developing strategies and plans, particularly the technical options, to achieve agreed outcomes resides with the line departments, provinces, and LLGs also have considerable responsibility for this. In the past, the DOH and the NDOE (and the NACS to a much lesser extent) have put great emphasis on the development of provincial health and education plans by provinces to act as a guide to the provinces when implementing national plans. Unfortunately, these plans have never been developed within the MTEF framework with province-specific ceilings and envelope, nor have financing plans been developed. This has often resulted in financially unrealistic plans that could not be financed, which has in turn resulted in considerable frustration at the provincial level and in strained relationships between line departments, provinces, and the central agencies. It has also resulted in development partners funding their programs outside of the government budget.

To overcome these problems, there is a clear need for the central agencies to work cooperatively, strategically, and proactively with the line departments and provinces in these strategic planning efforts. Without this, it will be all but impossible to break the current cycle of unrealistic provincial planning, which also results in disillusionment among hard-working sectoral planning officials at both the national and provincial level.

### Developing and Executing Implementation Plans

This report has also emphasized the importance of developing a realistic implementation plan for strategy and expenditure plans for each sector. As discussed throughout the report, the lack of implementation capacity in each sector—at both the national and provincial level—has been an important element in the failure so far to design and implement strategies to achieve the desired outcomes. The introduction of decentralization, as discussed, has increased the fragmentation of responsibility for designing and implementing programs. The tensions and frustrations arising from (a) poorly structured fiscal relations between the national government and provinces, and (b) the inability of the national (sectoral) line departments, with the proactive support of the central agencies, to work together in a manner designed to compensate for these structural problems have also contributed to sectoral line agencies (national and provincial) feeling increasingly isolated from each other and unable to effectively communicate with each other.

Therefore, developing a solid implementation plan requires cooperation between the central agencies, the line departments, and the provinces. The line departments and the provinces need to be able to restructure their budgets and staffing. What will also be crucial is a strong and reliable central information system to which provinces and agencies report information on budgets, staffing, and outcomes on a timely basis. This, notwithstanding considerable investments in this area, is not the case at present.

A range of specific suggestions has been made throughout this report, including establishing a Teacher Position Allocation Committee to make collective decisions on the allocation and deployment of teachers across the country in line with national policy, and the involvement of the central agencies of government in managing and accounting of interim trust accounts for donor funds supporting health programs at the provincial and national government levels.

## Creating Fiscal Space and a Compact to Implement Expenditure Reforms

Our situational assessments for each of the sectors (and as discussed above) have identified areas where increased fiscal space can be achieved through:

(a) *Sectoral savings.* We have identified savings that could be made in each sector, not least by eliminating "ghost" staff from the public payroll. Considerable savings could be realized by this measure alone. Improving the management and procurement of inputs (particularly of pharmaceuticals, textbooks, school materials, office and housing rentals, civil works, and casual staff) would also yield important savings, as well as minimize opportunities for theft.

(b) *Increased efficiency of departmental expenditures.* Expenditures should be reduced on lower-priority sectoral activities that make little or no substantive contribution to desired sectoral outcomes. Focusing public expenditures on those goods and services that the public sector is best equipped to provide and enabling the private sector to deliver those services that can be delivered more effectively by the private sector (for example, delivering materials to schools and caring for those with AIDS) would also allow existing resources to be used more efficiently and effectively.

(c) *Increased sectoral allocations.* Once savings have been realized and efficiency has been increased, it will become increasingly feasible and justifiable to increase the budget allocations for high-priority sectors. Increased sectoral allocations will also become more feasible if PNG's revenue position improves because of mineral, oil and gas projects, as discussed in Chapter 5.

A central theme of this report is the critical need to focus public resources on achieving key outcomes and to use these resources efficiently and cost-effectively; however, the line departments and the provinces cannot do this without the active cooperation of the central agencies. In the current adversarial relationship between central agencies and the line departments (and provinces), there is little incentive for the line departments to propose any initiatives to alter the status quo, as any implicit admission by them of overstaffing or inefficient use of resources would simply result in the Treasury cutting their budgets and trying to reduce staff numbers. Thus, there are powerful incentives for public servants and agencies to maintain the status quo and not try to effect savings and efficiency gains.

There is a need for a compact or agreement between the line departments, the provinces, and the central agencies (particularly with the Treasury on budgets and the DPM/TSC on staffing) that would create incentives for making fiscal space (savings) within the line departments and provinces. Given the size of the workforce in the education and health sectors, increasing the efficiency of staff deployment and eliminating "ghosts" from the payroll would generate massive savings. Such savings could be shared among the parties to the compact; however, it will be essential to provide the flexibility to redeploy staff from low-priority activities to high-priority activities or to be made redundant if absolutely necessary. Thus, the DPM and the TSC would need to work closely and cooperatively with both the Treasury and the line departments (and provinces) on staff redeployment.

To give effect to this, we propose that sectoral task forces should be established comprising representatives of the central agencies, the line departments, and the provinces. Given that initiatives already exist in the health sector to establish a health MTEF, a draft strategic plan for 2006–2008, and an embryonic SWAP, it might be appropriate to establish a pilot task force in the health sector immediately. This would be a pragmatic way to move forward, and PNG's development partners would surely embrace and support such an initiative.

The case for allocating additional resources to the key human development sectors (from the government and from its development partners) would be considerably strengthened if such progress were to be made.

## Developing a Financing Plan for Each Sector

It is important to make a clear distinction between developing an *expenditure* plan designed to implement and achieve the agreed objectives and a *financing* plan. In PNG, there are four main sources of revenue to finance public expenditure plans for health, HIV/AIDS, and education: (i) national government revenues (including commercial and domestic borrowing) and revenues allocated to provinces for specific sectoral purposes; (ii) provinces' own revenues, largely provided by the national government but made available to the provinces for discretionary spending on the functions for which they are responsible; (iii) funds from development partners in the form of grants, credits, and loans; and

(iv) fees and costs collected from clients receiving services (including parental payment of school fees).

Developing a financing plan for each sector is complicated in PNG because of the decentralized nature of fiscal relations between national and subnational governments. While the line departments can develop an expenditure plan with detailed costings, it is critical for the Treasury, DNPRD, and the Department of Intergovernmental Relations to work closely with the line agencies and the provinces to assist in developing financing plans.

The national government has lacked the resources to finance the provinces to the constitutionally mandated level during much of the period of decentralization (particularly since 1996), which has been a source of tension between the national and provincial authorities. Addressing and overcoming these issues is the subject of the current work plan of the NEFC, but this is an initiative that will take time to come to fruition. In the short term, the national and provincial authorities will need to reach pragmatic agreements on how to address financing plan issues. An initial step would be to clearly outline funds that are available for each sector in a systematic manner as part of the budget process. At present, there is not a consolidated statement of either expenditure of funds available or expenditure by sector at a whole-of-government level in the budget.

A second problem with developing a financing plan for each sector is that national government resources for health and education are not allocated very equitably across provinces. This is partly because current financial arrangements ensure that historically, established staffing patterns are sustained, and because any additional resources, including those made available by development partners, have not been used to explicitly redress any imbalances.

Third, provinces' own revenues are very unequally distributed as discussed in Chapter 5, and it is by no means evident that those provinces that should be expanding their services on equity grounds have the capacity to finance their responsibilities under the current decentralization arrangements. This last point is further compounded by the fact that provincial authorities do not, by and large, allocate their considerable discretionary funds to health, education, or HIV/AIDS, even though these sectors (together with rural transport infrastructure) are the key sectoral responsibilities under the constitution of provincial governments.

This problem clearly emerges in the new NEP. As discussed in Chapter 4, the plan assumes that provinces and LLGs will have the resources to finance the program of new infrastructure and of vitally needed maintenance and refurbishment of schools. The poor record of subnational governments in maintaining infrastructure and the lack of financial capacity of many of the poorer provinces to build new high schools suggests that this aspect of the plan is not credible and will simply not happen.

Clearly, taking a "whole-of-government" approach is the best way to develop a compact between national and provincial government to finance these programs. The DOH has expended considerable effort to develop a compact with provinces, with the active support of PNG's development partners aimed at ensuring that provinces allocate at least 6 percent of their own funds to the health sector. This is a first step that enshrines the principle that provinces should be at least partly financing programs. There are, however, two key problems with this arrangement. First, it is unenforceable without the involvement of the Treasury and other central agencies. What is needed is for the Treasury to exercise its power (via the power of the minister responsible for Treasury having to approve budgets) to refuse to approve a province's budget if it reneges on this agreement. It may also be a good idea to make grants to provinces conditional on their adherence to such agreement. Second, the figure of 6 percent is arbitrary. It will be necessary to take a "whole-of-government" approach to determine the appropriate allocation of the provinces' own resources, as decisions taken about one sector affect the capacity of provinces to fund other sectors—and, as discussed, provinces have significantly different capacities to finance such programs independently.

Given the large amount of development-partner financing of these sectors, the Treasury and the line departments need to cooperate with their development partners to develop a pipeline of support for the sectors consistent with the agreed expenditure plan. The final section of this report discusses how this might be done.

## Restoring the Integrity of Government Processes

Restoring the integrity of government processes has been a central theme of both the PERR and this report. The preceding discussion has emphasized the need for line departments to have the flexibility to restructure the deployment of staff and to reallocate their own budgets—subject to appropriate review by the central agencies. Budget accounts are important instruments for evaluating the performance of sectoral management and for ensuring financial accountability and propriety in the use of funds. The government has made an important start in reforming these systems in response to the PERR by initiating its public-sector reform program. It is critical to list and prioritize the necessary actions to sustain this momentum. Approaching the human development sectors in the manner outlined in this report could reap very large developmental dividends. On the other hand, failing to address these issues would make it extremely difficult for PNG's development partners to increasingly deliver their aid through the government's budget, an objective that the Joint Donors believe is critical because the shift in accountabilities and the emphasis on accountability for outcomes.

## The Role of Development Partners in Support of Government Sectoral Plans

Development partners play a critical role in the human development sector by providing policy advice and by financing about 30 percent of health expenditures, over 90 percent of HIV/AIDs expenditures, and about 20 percent of education expenditures—high proportions by international standards. Further, development partners finance a significant share of critical recurrent expenditures, much of which, given public finance principles, should be financed by the government. So far, this chapter has emphasized the critical importance of government committing to (i) a soundly based sector strategy-formulation process in each sector, (ii) grounding sectoral policies and plans in the MTDS and a hard budget constraint embodied in a rolling MTEF, (iii) developing and executing realistic implementation plans for strategy and expenditure plans for each sector, (iv) working to create fiscal space and to implement expenditure reforms, (v) developing financing plans for each sector, and (vi) restoring the integrity of government processes. With this in mind, what should the role of development partners be?

It is critical that development partners do not add to the problems associated with: (i) developing national policy coherency in each sector; (ii) undermining efforts to focus on priority sector outcomes; (iii) fragmentation of accountability and sector-financing arrangements by establishing multiple projects with differing (and even foreign) financing and management accountability frameworks; (iv) competing inappropriately for scarce management time; and (iv) operating outside the budget framework and the hard budget constraint established by the rolling MTEF.

Achieving these goals is not easy and will require a long-term commitment from key stakeholders and development partners. This will require consistency in policy advice and a strategic focus on outcomes and stakeholder inclusiveness in designing and implementing strategies, strengthening efforts to work through government systems to restore their integrity and to build systems capacity, identifying options to ensure sustainability of sector financing, and collaborating on economic and sector work with government to underpin sectoral policy dialogue.

## A Sectoral Compact Between the Government and Its Development Partners

The discussion so far has been about how the government can establish clear, coherent sectoral strategies, focused on agreed priority outcomes within a hard budget constraint as embodied in a rolling MTEF process, and the principles by which development partners should cooperate with government to assist this process. In this report, we have tabled a set of recommendations for devising (i) sectoral strategies that focus the capacity of government to the interventions that it is most capable of ensuring that services are delivered efficiently and equitably and outcomes achieved; (ii) reforms to create fiscal space to fund high-priority sectoral programs accurately; (iii) a feasible and enforceable financing plan that includes the provinces; and (iv) consensual compacts (agreements) between the line departments, the provinces, and the central agencies of government on sector strategies, outcomes to be achieved, and restoring the integrity of core government systems.

The final element of a more coherent, outcome-focused approach is how the government and its development partners can best support such an effort. We recommend that an appropriate way forward should be structured along the following lines:

(1)  An agreement on a strategy and a long-term vision for the outcomes to be achieved for each of the sectors that is developed nationally, but is clearly owned by the provinces, line departments, and the central agencies (in other words, by the "whole government").

(2)  A set of program and policy reforms (such as an essential health care package, preventing the transmission of HIV as the primary-sector objective for HIV/AIDS, and universal completion of the basic cycle of education) and a set of organizational policy reforms aimed at implementing the programmatic reforms according to agreed benchmarks and monitoring indicators.

(3) A rolling public expenditure and implementation plan covering three to five years consistent with the medium-term resource envelope determined by the government. This should be updated annually consistent with 1 and 2 above.

(4) The planned total expenditures for the current year (both recurrent and development), an associated financing plan (including both government and donor financing), and a procurement plan for each provincial plan and for the central sectoral department.

(5) An annual operational plan setting out the detailed reform program designed to be implemented that year (derived from 2 above) and monitoring indicators and benchmarks for each element of the operational plan (including provincial plans) that can be achieved within the available resources and known capacity constraints.

Elements 1–3 above represent the medium-term strategy and implementation plan. Elements 4 and 5 are annual plans (activity plans) developed by provinces and national departments to implement the agreed program. They should be used as the basis for disbursing resources from PNG's development partners in support of the agreed program. To the extent possible, these resources should be disbursed through the government's own budget. In the interim, special arrangements may need to be made (with the agreement of the development partners) to ensure that development partner funds are soundly managed while core government systems are being reformed. The objective is to include development assistance in the government's budget, accounting, and accountability systems. The purest form of this would be for all funding from any source, including development partners, to appear in the budget as financing items rather than as expenditure items financed by the development partners.

We suggest that the government and its development partners conduct a midterm review of elements 1–3 after two years and elements 4 and 5 in conjunction with the semiannual budget review exercise to enable them to make any necessary adjustments in policies, reforms, implementation plans, expenditures, and financing. This would allow for strategies and programs to remain flexible and to be adjusted over time in response to feedback and outcomes. As part of these agreements, there would be a clear set of baselines and a monitoring and evaluation framework.

This kind of approach has been found in other countries to increase the effectiveness of expenditures and provide sector managers with a very useful management and planning tool.

This process also reinforces the importance of focusing on the entire resource envelope and management process and not just the recurrent budgeting process or the development budget. Agencies at the national and provincial level need to make and implement regular activity plans to implement agreed policies, to ensure the timely funding of these activities, to manage the flow of financing, and to ensure that accounting and auditing mechanisms and procurement processes are in place.

## Knowledge Gaps

In a number of areas of this report, there are important questions that cannot be fully or adequately answered based on existing knowledge. The area where improved knowledge would probably most help policy making is in better understanding the demand for services—health, HIV, and education—by clients and families. It is critical that we know more about the health-seeking behavior of parents and mothers of sick children, and of the clients themselves. Improved knowledge about how different groups at risk of HIV infection behave and seek services is also critical. In education, some 19 percent of children do not enter school, and about 50 percent of those who do attend drop out before completing the basic cycle. Population-based surveys in each of these areas would add valuable information for planners.

Another area critical to planning for HIV is better understanding of the distribution of the disease throughout the country, together with information on the characteristics of those currently with the disease. Population-based HIV surveys are now standard practice in most parts of the world seriously threatened by the HIV epidemic. Of course, improved surveillance and documentation of the characteristics of those tested would, as discussed in Chapter 3, also make an important contribution in this area.

There is quite limited labor-market information in PNG since the collapse of the annual Labor Market Survey. Improved knowledge of trends in the labor market through surveys (including tracer or reverse tracer studies) of graduates of different types of education and training facilities would add extremely valuable insights into education and training planning.

It is now 10 years since there was a survey that could directly measure poverty levels in PNG, and without a special effort to do so it will be a long time before another survey is able to do so. The decision by government and many development partners not to include a modest income and expenditure module (or a HIV module) in the Demographic

Household Survey is a missed opportunity. Given the importance of poverty and HIV to the MDG agenda, it is important that we are able to benchmark current status and monitor trends.

As we move forward, these knowledge gaps can be jointly addressed by government and development partners as an important part of next steps.

## A Final Word

We hope that this report, with its situational assessments and proposed strategies for health, HIV/AIDS, and education will enable all parties to enter into a productive partnership and will form the basis of a policy dialogue that will decisively improve sectoral outcomes in PNG. This is an ambitious but feasible objective if consensus can be built on the way forward.

# References

ADB. 1999a. Impact evaluation study of the technical and vocational education projects in Malaysia, Pakistan, Papua New Guinea, and Sri Lanka. December. Impact Evaluation Study (IES): Reg. 99035. Manila.

ADB. 1999b. Project preparatory technical assistance final report on the Skills Development Project in Papua New Guinea. April.

Aitken, Richard et al. 2002. *Papua New Guinea human resource development study: Realigning and enriching the skills of a workforce that cannot be enlarged.* Mimeo.

Australian International Development Bureau (AIDAB)/ADB/GOPNG. 1995. Resources study. Mimeo, Port Moresby.

AIDAB/PNG. 1993. Working paper on manpower development and training. PNG Education and Training Sector Study. PNG-Australia Development Cooperation Program. March–May.

AusAID. 1999a. National Trade Testing & Certification System Support Project. Project review. April.

AusAID. 1999b. *The economy of Papua New Guinea.*

AusAID. 2000. Strategy for AusAID support to the Papua New Guinea education sector 2000–2010. Final report. Vol. 1: Report and annexes. March.

AusAID. 2002. Papua New Guinea. Program profiles 2001–2002.

AusAID. 2003a. PNG education sector affordability studies: Appendix A to Paper 4, education financial statistics. September.

AusAID. 2003b. PNG education sector affordability studies: Paper 1, financing elementary primary and secondary education. September.

AusAID. 2003c. PNG education sector affordability studies: Paper 2, financing of tertiary education. September.

AusAID. 2003d. PNG education sector affordability studies: Paper 3, financing vocational, technical, and distance education. September.

AusAID. 2003e. PNG education sector affordability studies: Paper 4, overview of financing the education sector. September.

AusAID. 2004. *Review of AusAID support to basic education*. Final report.

AusAID/PNG. 2004. *Technical vocational education and training rationale, policy, and action plans. Education capacity-building project*. Final draft. October.

Bank of Papua New Guinea. 2004 and various years. *Quarterly Economic Bulletin*.

Basu, I., S. Jana, M. Rotherdam-Borus, D. Swendeman, S-J, Lee, P. and Newman. 2004. HIV prevention among sex workers in India. *Journal of Acquired Immune Deficiency Syndromes* 36 (3): 845–852.

Bradley, C. 2001. *Family and sexual violence: An integrated strategy*. Report to the Family Violence Action Committee of the Consultative Implementation and Monitoring Committee, Discussion Paper No. 84, Institute of National Affairs, Port Moresby.

Brouwer, E., B. Harris, and S. Tanaka, eds. 1998. *Gender analysis in Papua New Guinea*. Washington, DC: The World Bank.

Campbell, C. and S. Mdaizume. 2001. Grassroots participation, peer education and HIV prevention by sex workers in South Africa." *American Journal of Public Health* 91:1978–1986.

Center for International Economics. 2002. *Potential economic impact of an HIV/AIDS epidemic in Papua New Guinea*. AusAID.

Cibulskis, R. and G. Hiawalyer. 2002. Information systems for health sector monitoring in Papua New Guinea. *Bulletin of the World Health Organization*. 80 (9).

Decock, A-M. 1997. *Talking health. The wisdom of the village. Adults/youth*. National Department of Health, Papua New Guinea.

Dunkle. K., R. Jewkes, H. Brown, G. Gray, J. McIntyre, and S. Harlow. 2004. Gender-based violence, relationship power, and risk of HIV infection in women attending antenatal clinics in South Africa. *The Lancet* 363:1415–1421.

Gerland, P., 2004. *Do social interactions affect individual HIV/AIDS attitudes and prevention strategies in rural Malawi?* Paper presented at the Annual Meeting of the Population Association of America in Boston, Mass., April 1–3.

GOPNG. 1998. National budget papers.

GOPNG. 1999. National budget papers.

GOPNG. 2003a. Public Expenditure Review and Rationalisation (PERR)— Overview of discussion papers. September.

GOPNG. 2003b. Public Expenditure Review and Rationalisation (PERR)— Discussion Paper No 1—Road map to fiscal sustainability. September.

GOPNG. 2003c. Public Expenditure Review and Rationalisation (PERR)— Discussion Paper No 2—Civil Service size and payroll, September 2003.

GOPNG. 2003d. Public Expenditure Review and Rationalisation (PERR)— Discussion Paper No 6—Improving education expenditure, September.

GOPNG. 2003e. The Medium-Term Development Strategy 2003–2007. December.

GOPNG. 2004. National budget papers.

GOPNG. 2005. National budget papers.

GOPNG and UN. 2004. Papua New Guinea—Millennium Development Goals Progress Report 2004. Government of Papua New Guinea and the United Nations.

Guy, R., U. Kombra, and W. Bai. 2000. *Enhancing their futures: An action plan to reposition \skills education in Papua New Guinea*. National Research Institute.

Guy, R., P. Paraide, and L. Kippel. 2001. *Mi Lusim Skul. Participation and retention in primary and secondary schools in Papua New Guinea*. National Research Institute.

Hammar, L. 1998. Sex industries and sexual networking in Papua New Guinea: public health risks and implications. *Pacific Health Dialog* 5(1):47–53.

Help Resources/UNICEF. 2005. *A situational analysis of child sexual abuse and the commercial sexual exploitation of children in Papua New Guinea*. Draft report. January.

Hughes, J. 1991. Impurity and danger: The need for new barriers and bridges in the prevention of sexually-transmitted disease in the Tari Basin, Papua New Guinea. *Health Transition Review* 1(2):131–141.

Jenkins, C. 1993. Culture and sexuality: Papua New Guinea and the rest of the world. *Venereology* 6(3):55.

Jenkins C. 1994a. *Final report: Behavioral risk assessment for HIV/AIDS among workers in the transport industry*. Papua New Guinea. PNG Institute of Medical Research, Goroka. Arlington, Va.: Family Health International.

Jenkins, C. 1994b. *Situational assessment of commercial sex workers in urban Papua New Guinea*. Mimeo Port Moresby. Submitted to GPA, September.

Jenkins, C. 1994c. *Social marketing for AIDS prevention in Papua New Guinea*. Discussion paper, GPA, WHO, September.

Jenkins, C. 1995a. *A study of the acceptability of the female condom*. A report prepared for UNFPA and Chartex, May.

Jenkins, C. 1995b. Final report on youth, urbanization and sexuality. Submitted to WHO, GPA, October 29.

Jenkins, C. 1995c. Technical report on HIV prevention among sex workers along the Highlands Highway. Submitted to WHO, PNG.

Jenkins, C. 1996. The homosexual context of heterosexual practice in Papua New Guinea. In Aggleton, P., ed. *Bisexualities and AIDS: International perspectives.* London: Taylor and Francis Inc., 191–206.

Jenkins, C. 1997. *Youth, sexuality, and STD/HIV risk in the Pacific: Results of studies in four island nations.* Paper presented at the 4th International Congress on AIDS in Asia and the Pacific, Manila, October, Abst.# A (O) 084, p. 44.

Jenkins, C. 1998. *Love magic and HIV risk in Papua New Guinea.* Paper presented at 12th World AIDS Conference Record, Abst. # 96/14318:246.

Jenkins, C. 2000. *Female sex worker HIV prevention projects: Lessons learnt from Papua New Guinea, India and Bangladesh.* UNAIDS Case Study, UNAIDS, Geneva. 2000. http://www.unaids.org/html/pub/publications/irc-pub05/ jc438-femsexwork_en_pdf.pdf.

Jenkins C. 2005a. Sex workers and police in Port Moresby (1994–1998): Research and intervention. In Luker, V., S. Dinnen, and A. Patience, eds. *Law, order and HIV/AIDS in Papua New Guinea.* Forthcoming.

Jenkins, C. 2005b. *Sexual cultures, STIs and HIV in contemporary Papua New Guinea.* Paper submitted to *Culture, Health and Sexuality,* (Mimeo).

Jenkins, C. and M. Alpers. 1996. Urbanization, youth and sexuality: Insights for an AIDS campaign for youth in Papua New Guinea. *Papua New Guinea Medical Journal* 39(3):248–251.

Jenkins, C. and M. Passey. 1998. Papua New Guinea. In Brown, T., R. Chan, D. Mugrditchian, B. Mulhall, D. Plummer, R. Sarda, and W. Sittitrai, eds. *Sexually transmitted diseases in Asia and the Pacific,* Armidale, New South Wales, Australia: Venereology Publishing. pp. 230–254.

Jenkins, C., and K. Pataki-Schweizer. 1993. Knowledge of AIDS in Papua New Guinea. *Papua New Guinea Medical Journal* 36(3):192–204.

Jenkins, C., and D. Robalino. 2003. *HIV/AIDS in the Middle East and North Africa. The costs of inaction.* Washington, DC: The World Bank.

Johanson, R. K., and A. V. Adams. 2004. *Skills development in Sub-Saharan Africa.* Washington, DC:World Bank.

Kovacs, J. Hagen. 2005. Sex behavior study. *IMR Nius* 12(Jan–Mar):4, 2005.

Lemeki, M., M. Passey, and P. Setel. 1996. Ethnographic results of a community STD study in the Eastern Highlands Province. *Papua New Guinea Medical Journal* 39:239–242.

Lepani, K, 2002. *"Everything has come up to the open space": talking about sex in an epidemic.* Paper presented at the Gender, Sexuality and Culture Seminar Series, Australian National University, June 13.

Levantis, T. 2000. *Papua New Guinea: Employment, wages and economic development.* Asia Pacific Press, Australian National University, Canberra.

Luker, V. 2003. *Civil society, social capital and the churches: HIV/AIDS in Papua New Guinea.* State, Society and Governance in Melanesia Project. Working Paper 2004/05. Presented at the Governance and Civil Society Seminar, in Symposium Governance in Pacific States: Reassessing roles and remedies, University of the South Pacific, Sept. 30–Oct. 2.

Luluaki, J. 2003. Sexual crimes against and sexual exploitation of children and the law in Papua New Guinea. *International Journal of Law, Policy and the Family.* 17:275–307.

Maman, S., J. Mbwambo, N. Hogan, G. Kilonzo, J. Campbell, E. Weiss, and M. Sweat. 2002. HIV-positive women report more lifetime partner violence: Findings from a voluntary counseling and testing clinic in Dar es Salaam, Tanzania. *American Journal of Public Health* 92(8):1331–1337.

McMurray, C. 2001. *Employment opportunities for Papua New Guinea youth.* Report prepared for the ILO/Japan Tripartite Regional Meeting on Youth Employment in Asia and Pacific, Bangkok, 27 March, 2002.

Martin, S., B. Kilgallen, A. Tsui, K. Maitra, K. Singh, and L. Kupper. 1999. Sexual behaviors and reproductive health outcomes: Associations with wife abuse in India. *Journal of American Medical Association* 282(20):1967–72.

Mgone, C., M. Passey, J. Anang, W. Peter, T. Lupiwa, D. Russell, D. Babona, and M. Alpers, 2002b. Human immunodeficiency virus and other sexually transmitted infections among female sex workers in two major cities in Papua New Guinea. *Sexually Transmitted Diseases* 29(5):265–270.

Mgone, C., T. Lupiwa, and W. Yeka. 2002a. High prevalence of *Niesseria gonorrhoeae* and multiple sexually transmitted diseases among rural women in the Eastern Highlands Province of Papua New Guinea, detected by polymerase chain reaction. *Sexually Transmitted Diseases* 29(12):775–779.

NAC and NDOH, 2005. The report of the 2004 National Consensus Workshop of Papua New Guinea. World Health Organization and the National HIV/AIDS Support Project. National AIDS Council and the National Department of Health.

NSRRT and C. Jenkins. 1994. National Study of Sexual and Reproductive Knowledge and Behavior in Papua New Guinea. Goroka: Papua New Guinea Institute of Medical Research. National Sex and Reproduction Research Team.

National HIV/AIDS Social Marketing Campaign. 2003. Quantitative Research Report Postphase II (Wave 3) Survey, June.

NHASP. 2003. Milestone 57. Situational analysis for strategic planning at district level, Morobe Province. Pilot Social Mapping Project. National HIV/AIDS Support Project, December.

Over, M. 1997. *The effects of societal variables on urban rates of HIV infection in developing countries: An exploratory analysis.* Mimeo. European Commission.

Passey, M., C. Mgone, S. Lupiwa. 1998. Community-based study of sexually transmitted diseases in rural women in the highlands of Papua New Guinea: Prevalence and risk factors. *Sexually Transmitted Infections* 74:120–127.

PNG CHE. 2001. Handbook on the Administration of the Tertiary Education Study Assistance Scheme (TESAS). March.

PNG DFP. 1986. National Manpower Assessment 1982–1992.

PNG Ministry of Health. 2001. Report on the Future of Nurse and Community Health Worker Education.

PNG NDOE. 1996. National Education Plan. 1995–2004.

PNG NDOE. 1997. *Education Statistics 1996.* NDOE.

PNG NDOE. 1998. *Department of Education Corporate Plan.*

PNG NDOE. 1999a. National Education Plan. 1995–2004. Update 1.

PNG NDOE. 1999b. *Technical Vocational Education Corporate Plan 1999–2003.* May.

PNG NDOE. 2002. *The state of education in Papua New Guinea.* March.

PNG NDOE. 2003a. *Education Statistics 2002.* NDOE.

PNG NDOE. 2003b. *The state of education in Papua New Guinea.* March.

PNG NDOE. 2005a. *Achieving a better future: A national plan for education 2005–2014.* NDOE, Port Moresby.

PNG NDOE. 2005b. *Education Statistics 2003.* NDOE.

PNG NDOE. 2005c. *Prosperity through self-reliance. 2004 Annual Report.* NDOE.

PNG NDOE. 2003. National Education Plan Steering Committee. *Report on Deliberations.* Recommendations for the National Education Board. December.

PNG NDOE/UNESCO. 2002. *Education for all: Papua New Guinea National Action Plan, 2004–2015.* NDOE.

PNGIMR, 1998. *Eastern Highlands youth survey: Follow-up study of Goroka youth peer education project.* Unpublished data.

PNG MHERST. 2004. *Charting pathways for entrepreneurialism in higher education, 2005–2015.* Higher Education Symposium, 2004. Selected background papers.

PNG Ministerial Review Committee. 1997. *Report and recommendations on the operations of the National Training Council.* Ministry of Industrial Relations. June.

PNG National Technical and Vocational Training Committee. 1997. *According to their talents: A draft national policy for improving and co-ordinating competency training in Papua New Guinea.* Ministry of Educatio, Port Moresby.

PNG NATTB. DOLIR. 2005. *Toward a skilled Papua New Guinean workforce 2005–2007.* NATTB, Port Moresby.

PNG NTC. 2005. National Human Resource Development Policy and Strategy. 2005.

PNG OHE. 2003. *Labour market analysis.* Discussion paper.

PNG OHE. 2004. Compendium of Higher Education. *Trends in higher education, research science and technology: Implications for the the NHEP III. 2005–2015.* Draft for the Commission for Higher Education. September.

PNG OHE. 2005. National Selection Report. Draft. April.

PNG. NEFC. 2003. Review of Intergovernmental Financing Arrangements— Interim Report and Proposals for a New Framework.

PNG: World Bank/AusAid. 1998. Education sector review. Final report for technical and vocational education subsector. April.

Population Council and UNFPA. 2002. *HIV/AIDS prevention guidance for reproductive health professionals in developing-country setting.* New York.

Ramdas, K. 2004. Interview on the real meaning of the "A" in the Ugandan "ABC" model, on "Now with Bill Moyers." Public Broadcasting Service, April 23.

Schofield, K. 2002. *Skills formation in PNG: Some personal observations about the present and future.* Internal discussion paper. September.

Speizer, I., R. Magnani, and C. Colvin. 2003. The effectiveness of adolescent reproductive health interventions in developing countries: A review of the evidence. *Journal of Adolescent Health* 33:324–348.

Steen, R., B. Vuylsteke, T. DeCoito, S. Ralipeli, G. Fehler, J. Conley, L. Bruckers, G. Dallabetta, and R. Ballard. 2000. Evidence of declining STD prevalence in a South African mining community following a core-group intervention. *Sexually Transmitted Diseases* 27(1):1–8.

Suligoi, B., R. Danaya, L. Sarmati. I. Owen, S. Boros, E. Pozio, M. Andreoni, and G. Rezza. 2005. Infection with human immunodeficiency virus, herpes simplex virus type 2, and human herpes virus 8 in remote villages of southwestern Papua New Guinea. *American Journal of Tropical Medicine and Hygiene* 72(1):33–36.

Sullivan, N. 2004. *Sullivan Report on Tuna.* Mimeo. Port Moresby.

UNICEF, 2005. *Families and children affected by HIV/AIDS and other vulnerable children in Papua New Guinea: A national situation analysis.* Draft report. January 31.

USAID Policy Project, 2005. Ending inequity: Strengthening the HIV/AIDS response for women. Draft.

USAID/Synergy, 2004. *Women's experience with HIV serodisclosure in Africa: Implications for VCT and PMTCT.* Meeting report, Washington, DC: USAID, March.

Van der Staten, A., R. King, O. Gronstread, E. Vittinghoff, A. Serufilira, and S. Allen. 1998. Sexual coercion, physical violence, and HIV infection among women in steady relationships in Kigali, Rwanda. *AIDS and Behavior* 2:61–73.

Varkey, L., A. Mishra, A. Das, E. Ottolenghi, D. Huntington, S. Adamchak, M. Khan, and F. Homan. 2004. *Involving men in maternity care in India.* New Delhi, India: Population Council, Frontiers in Reproductive Health Program.

Wardlow, H. 2004. Anger, economy, and female agency: Problematizing "prostitution" and "sex work" among the Huli of Papua New Guinea. *Signs: Journal of Women in Culture and Society* 29:1017–1040.

Welbourn, A. 1999. *Gender, sex and HIV: How to address issues that no one wants to hear about.* In Preiswerk, Y., ed. Tant qu'on a la Santé, Berne, Switzerland: Institut Universitaire d'Etudes du Developement (IUED).

World Bank. 1994. *Higher education: The lessons of experience.*

World Bank. 1999. Resource Allocation and Reallocation Study.

World Bank. 2004a. Papua New Guinea. Poverty assessment. June.

World Bank. 2004b. Papua New Guinea. Public Expenditure and Service Delivery (PESD). June.

World Health Organization. 1997. *Violence against women: Rape and sexual assault.* World Health Organization, July. https://www.who.int/gender/violence/v6.pdf. Accessed June 24, 2005.

WHO, NAC, and NDOH. 2000. *Consensus report on STI, HIV and AIDS epidemiology in Papua New Guinea 2000.* World Health Organization/National AIDS Council/National Department of Health.

Ziderman, A. 2003. *Financing vocational training in Sub-Saharan Africa.* Washington, DC:World Bank.

# Index